On **SECOND** Thought

On **SECOND** Thought

OUTSMARTING YOUR MIND'S Hard-Wired Habits

**WRAY
HERBERT**

CROWN PUBLISHERS
NEW YORK

Library of Congress Cataloging-in-Publication Data
Herbert, Wray.
On second thought : outsmarting your mind's hard-wired
habits / Wray Herbert.—1st ed.
p.   cm.
Includes index.
1. Thought and thinking. I. Title.
BF441.H46   2010
153.4—dc22   2010003073

ISBN 978-0-307-46163-6

Printed in the United States of America

2 4 6 8 10 9 7 5 3 1

First Edition

TO SUSIE

CONTENTS

On **SECOND** Thought

Introduction

‖‖

O N FEBRUARY 12, 1995, a party of three seasoned backcountry skiers set out for a day on the pristine slopes of Utah's Wasatch Mountain Range. Steve Carruthers, thirty-seven years old, was the most experienced of the group, though they were all skilled skiers and mountaineers. Carruthers had skied these hills many times and was intimately familiar with the terrain. Their plan was to trek over the divide from Big Cottonwood Canyon to Porter Fork, the next canyon to the north.

Two hours out, they met another skiing party. A storm had dropped almost two feet of new snow on the range the day before, and the two groups stood together for about five minutes, chatting about the best routes through the mountains. A couple of skiers in the other party were a bit spooked by the foggy conditions, but they all decided that they would be okay if they chose a prudent route across the lower slopes. Carruthers' party broke trail through the sparse woods of Gobbler's Knob.

Within the hour, Carruthers was dead. As the skiers headed across a shallow, treed expanse, they triggered an avalanche. More than a hundred metric tons of snow roared down the mountainside at fifty miles an hour, blanketing the slope and pinning Carruthers against an aspen. The other party heard the avalanche and rushed to the rescue, but by the time they dug Carruthers out, he was unconscious. He never regained awareness.

The other two skiers in Carruthers' group survived, but they faced some serious criticism back home. What were they thinking? This pass was well known as avalanche terrain, and February was considered high hazard season. The chatter in the tight-knit skiing community was that Carruthers had been reckless, that despite his experience he had ignored obvious signs of danger and tempted fate.

None of this rang true to Ian McCammon. McCammon had known Carruthers for years, and the two had been climbing buddies at one time. Sure, Carruthers may have been a risk taker when he was younger, but he had matured. Just recently, while the two men were riding a local ski lift together, Carruthers had talked adoringly about his lovely wife, Nancy, and his four-year-old daughter, Lucia. His days of derring-do were over, he had told McCammon. It was time to settle down.

So what happened on that fateful afternoon? What skewed this experienced backcountry skier's judgment that he would put himself and his party in harm's way? Did he perish in an avoidable accident? Saddened and perplexed by his friend's death, McCammon determined to figure out what went wrong.

McCammon is an experienced backcountry skier in his own right, and a wilderness instructor, but he is also a scientist. He has a Ph.D. in mechanical engineering, and as a researcher at the University of Utah, he once worked on robotics and aerospace systems for

NASA and the Defense Department. He already knew snow science pretty well, so he began reading everything he could on the science of risk and decision making. He ended up studying the details of more than seven hundred deadly avalanches that took place between 1972 and 2003, to see if he could find any commonalities that might explain his friend's untimely death.

With the rigor of an engineer, he systematically categorized all the avalanches according to several factors well known to backcountry skiers as risks: recent snowfall or windstorm, terrain features like cliffs and gullies, thawing and other signs of instability, and so forth. He computed an "exposure score" to rate the risk that preceded every accident.

Then he gathered as much information as he could on the ill-fated skiers themselves, all 1,355 of them: the makeup and dynamics of the skiing party, the expertise of the group leader as well as the others, plus anything that was known about the hours and minutes leading up to the fatal moment. Then he crunched all the data together.

His published results were intriguing. He found many patterns in the accidents, including several poor choices that should not have been made by experienced skiers. He concluded that these foolish decisions could be explained by six common thinking lapses, and he wrote up the work in a paper titled "Evidence of Heuristic Traps in Recreational Avalanche Accidents." The paper has become a staple of modern backcountry training and has no doubt saved many lives.

Heuristics are cognitive rules of thumb, hard-wired mental shortcuts that everyone uses every day in routine decision making and judgment. The study of heuristics is one of the most robust areas of scientific research today, producing hundreds of academic articles a year, yet the concept is little known outside the labs and offices of academia. This book is an attempt to remedy that.

Heuristics are normally helpful—indeed, they are crucial to getting through the myriad of decisions we face every day without overthinking every choice. But they're imperfect and often irrational. They can be traps, as they were in the frozen mountain pass where Carruthers perished. Much has been written in the past couple of years about the wonders of the rapid, automatic human mind and gut-level decision making. And indeed the unconscious mind is a wonder. But it is also perilous. The shortcuts that allow us to navigate each day with ease are the same ones that can potentially trip us up in our ordinary judgments and choices, in everything from health to finance to romance.

Most of us are not backcountry skiers, and we will probably never face the exact choices that Carruthers and his friends faced at Gobbler's Knob. But just because the traps are not life threatening does not mean they aren't life changing. Here are a few of the heuristics that shaped the backcountry skiers' poor choices—and may be shaping yours in ways you don't even recognize.

Consider the "familiarity heuristic." This is one of the cognitive shortcuts that McCammon identified as a contributing factor in many of the avalanche incidents he studied. The familiarity heuristic is one of the most robust heuristics known, and indeed one of the original heuristics identified and studied by pioneers in cognitive science. It is a potent mental tool that we draw on every day for hundreds of decisions, and basically what it says is this: if something comes quickly to mind, trust it. It must be available in your memory for a reason, so go with it. The basic rule of thumb is that familiar equals better equals safer.

That's a very useful rule for, say, grocery shopping. There are potentially thousands and thousands of choices that must be made every time you enter your local supermarket. But what if you actually had to make every one of those judgments, comparing every kind of yogurt and every couscous brand before making a selection? You'd be paralyzed. So instead you spot the brand of yogurt or couscous you've bought dozens of times before; you grab it, you pay for it, and you're out of there. No need to study every item on the shelf. It's also a useful rule for ER physicians, airline pilots, and soccer players—people who have to make rapid-fire decisions and are trained to quickly identify familiar patterns and react.

Heuristics are amazing time savers, which makes them essential to our busy lives. Many, like the familiarity heuristic, are an amalgam of habit and experience. We don't want to deliberate every minor choice we make every day, and we don't need to. But there are always risks when we stop deliberating. McCammon's avalanche victims, for example, were almost all experienced backcountry skiers, and indeed almost half had had some formal training in avalanche awareness. This expertise didn't guarantee that they would make the smartest choices. Paradoxically, their expertise may have hurt them. They were so familiar with the terrain that it seemed safe—simply because it always had been safe before. It was familiar, and thus unthreatening. The skiers let down their guard because they all remembered successful outings that looked pretty much the same as the treacherous one. In fact, McCammon found in his research that there were significantly more avalanche accidents when the skiers knew the specific locale, compared to ski parties exploring novel terrain.

Most of the avalanches in our modern lives have nothing to do with snow. The familiarity heuristic (including the related fluency heuristic, discussed in Chapter 4) has been widely studied in the area of consumer choice and personal finance—and not just how we buy groceries. Princeton psychologists have shown that people are more apt to buy shares in new companies if the names of the companies are easy to read and say, which actually affects the performance of the stock in the short run. University of Michigan psychologists have shown that language (and even the typeface in which something is printed) can affect all sorts of perceptions: whether a roller coaster seems too risky or a job seems too demanding to take on. Even very subtle manipulations of cognitive familiarity are shaping your choices, big and small, every day.

So familiarity and comfort can be traps. But the fact is, Carruthers' decision making really started to go wrong long before he even started waxing his skis. It started back in the warmth of the living room, when he or one of his buddies said, "Hey, let's take a run out to Gobbler's Knob tomorrow." At that point, they triggered another powerful cognitive tool, known as the "default heuristic" or "consistency heuristic." At that point, with their adventure still an abstract notion, they no doubt discussed the conditions, the pros and cons, and made a deliberate assessment of the risks of going out. But once they made that initial decision, the cold calculation stopped. They made a mental commitment, and that thought took on power.

We have a powerful bias for sticking with what we already have, not switching course. Unless there is some compelling reason not to, we let our minds default to what's given or what has already been decided. We rely on stay-the-course impulses all the time, often with good results. Constant switching can be perilous, in everything from financial matters to romantic judgments, so we have become averse to hopping around.

But this powerful urge for steadiness can also lock us into a bad choice. Just imagine Carruthers' ski party standing out there on the slope, chatting with the members of the other ski party. At this point, they could have made the decision to turn around and go home. Perhaps the snowpack seemed too unstable, or a certain gully looked worrisome. The skiers were no doubt taking in all this information, but they were not deliberating the pros and cons with their full mental powers because they had really already made their choice. The heuristic mind doesn't like to second-guess itself once it has momentum, and these skiers already had two hours of trekking invested in this decision. It would have taken a lot of mental effort to process all the logical arguments for turning around and going home.

So they didn't. They stuck to their plan because they were cognitively biased toward going ahead rather than switching gears. They were stubborn, but not in the way we commonly use the word to mean an obstinate attitude. Their brains were being stubborn, in the most fundamental way, right down in the neurons. We default hundreds of times a day, simply because it's effortful to switch plans. We stay in relationships that are going nowhere simply because it's easier than getting out. We buy the same brand of car our father did and hesitate to rearrange our stock portfolio. And we uncritically defer to others who make decisions for us—policy makers, who make rules and laws based on the assumption that we will act consistently rather than question. Similarly, it's safer to need an organ transplant in Paris than in New York City. You'll find out why in Chapter 20, but the short answer is that it's the default heuristic at work.

There were other heuristics reinforcing the ill-fated skiers' commitment. They probably got some additional mental nudging from what McCammon calls the "acceptance heuristic." Also known as the "mimicry heuristic," it is basically the strong tendency to make choices that we believe will get us noticed—and more important, approved—by others. It's deep-wired, likely derived from our ancient need for belonging and safety. It can be seen in the satisfaction we get from clubs and other social rituals, like precision military formations and choral singing. It's a crucial element in group cohesion, but we often apply it in social situations where it's inappropriate—or even harmful, as it was in many of the accidents that McCammon studied. His analysis showed a much higher rate of risky decision making in groups of six or more skiers, where there was a larger "audience" to please.

Then the snow itself can make skiers do senseless things. Every skier knows the phrase "powder fever," which means the unreasonable desire to put down the first tracks in freshly fallen snow. Powder fever begins with the first flakes of a long-awaited snowstorm and peaks as soon as conditions permit the first treks out. The virgin powder won't last long; everyone knows that. So for a few hours it's like gold, valuable simply because of its scarcity.

Psychologists think this "scarcity heuristic" derives from our fundamental need for personal freedom. We have a visceral reaction to any restriction on our prerogatives as individuals, and one way this manifests itself is in distorted notions about scarcity and value. Humans have made gold valuable because there is not all that much of it to go around, not because it's a particularly useful metal. So it is with new powder, and so it is with anything else we might perceive as rare, from land to free time. Scarcity can even skew our choices of lovers and partners, if we're not careful.

These are just a few of the heuristics you will learn about in the chapters ahead. This book is not intended to be exhaustive. Some psychologists estimate that there are hundreds of powerful heuristics at work in the human brain, some working in tandem with others, sometimes reinforcing and sometimes undermining one another. As readers will see in the chapters ahead, aspects of the arithmetic heuristic overlap with the futuristic heuristic; the cooties heuristic sometimes resembles certain visceral heuristics; and so forth. The intertwining of these powerful impulses in the mind is in fact very messy, and these tidy chapters are meant as guideposts through the messiness.

So where do these potent heuristics come from? And why, if they can be so troublesome, are they seemingly universal? Presumably these cognitive shortcuts are deep-wired into our basic neurology, although their locations in the brain are as yet unknown. What is known is that eons ago, when humans were evolving on the savannas of eastern Africa, the brain was going through all sorts of changes to help the species adapt to a shifting environment. Because that world was so full of risks, the primitive brain wired itself for action, including the ability to make very rapid choices and judgments. Many of these powerful, evolved tendencies remain in the modern mind as heuristics. They remain as potent as ever, though many are no longer adaptive to our current way of life—and lead to faulty thinking.

Here's an example of a powerful heuristic with evolutionary roots. I have a young friend who recently applied to medical school. He really wanted to go to a particular school in Chicago, for a variety of reasons, both academic and personal. But knowing that this school was one of the most competitive med schools in the country, he applied to six schools. They were all excellent schools, but he had a clear favorite.

He got accepted to his number one pick. But, surprisingly, he was rejected by all of the others. How did he feel? Well, logically, he should feel deliriously happy. He just got into one of the top-notch med schools in the nation; more important, it was the very one he wanted most. The rejections should be totally irrelevant to him at this point. But he wasn't deliriously happy. He was disappointed and hurt. Even though he knew the rejections were meaningless, even though his reasonable mind wanted to focus on his success and celebrate, he couldn't shake the feelings of disappointment and resentment.

Psychologists talk about our negativity bias, which is another perilous form of heuristic thinking. Over eons of human evolution, we as a species learned to focus on the negative, because if we didn't, we died. It was essential to stay alert to the dangers and threats in our world—predators, poisons, competitors in the tribe. This tendency became deeply ingrained in our psyche, where it remains. But negativity isn't always effective in our lives today—at least not in the life-saving manner it once was. Indeed, the opposite is often true. We often get hung up on meaningless negative events and details of life, and that distracts us from the real business of life, including being happy.

So some heuristics are the legacy from our ancient past. Others are products of our culture, which get passed on, learned and relearned from generation to generation. Others are rooted in our earliest experiences—the fears and needs of infancy—but shape our thinking as adults. Consider the visceral heuristic that links the physical sensation of cold and the emotion called loneliness. Infants come into the world with very primitive needs and desires. They seek comfort and safety. These needs become a basic, internal "idea," a kind of heuristic foundation onto which others are added with time and experience.

Psychologists call this "cognitive scaffolding." We layer more complex social behavior and thought on top of the more primitive systems the body already has in place for survival. So, for example, the infant who seeks comfort from the cold, clinging to its mother's body for warmth, gradually comes to associate cold with being alone, exposed, lacking support—in short, with loneliness. Eventually the concepts of cold and loneliness are so tightly entwined that the body and mind no longer distinguish the two kinds of experience.

You'll read more about visceral heuristics and scaffolding in Chapter 1. Many of these basic bodily heuristics are so powerful that they get embodied in the metaphors of our poetry and passed on in maxims, slogans, and fables. Recall the consistency heuristic that put the backcountry skiers in harm's way. Strip away the academic jargon and it might be phrased: "Don't change horses in midstream." This powerful bias probably emerged because it was cognitively easier and less risky to stay the course, but today it's universal and pervasive in our lives.

So are heuristics a good thing or a bad thing? There is an energetic debate going on right now within the halls of academe on just this question. One camp argues that heuristics are the best tools in our cognitive toolbox for many complex life decisions, precisely because they are so fleet and efficient. According to this view, it is simply impossible to calculate the best answers all the time, to use what's called "balance sheet reasoning" with columns of plusses and minuses totaling up. The opposing camp views heuristics as traps and biases, outdated and maladaptive rules that cause bad choices more often than not in the modern world.

This book will not resolve that academic dispute. Instead it stakes out a middle ground that other academic psychologists call "ecological rationality," which simply translates this way: Heuristics are neither good nor bad all the time. What's good or bad is the fit. Sometimes life demands heuristic thinking, and other times it can be perilous. The trick of modern living is in knowing what kind of thinking best matches the challenge at hand. It's all about getting the balance right, and this book is a guide to achieving that balance.

Heuristics are one of the major ideas to come out of cognitive psychology in the past decades, and the idea goes hand in hand with another: the dual-processor brain. This is not the split brain you learned about in high school, with its left and right hemispheres dedicated to different tasks. The exact anatomy of the dual-processor brain is still being worked out, and won't be discussed much in this book. What's important to know is that the human mind has two very different operating systems. One is logical, slow, deliberate, effortful, and cautious. The other—much older and more primitive—is fast and impressionistic, sometimes irrational. That's the heuristic mind.

We constantly switch back and forth between rational thought and rash judgment. Sometimes we have no control over our thinking. If we are overtired, mentally depleted, our brain switches automatically to its less effortful mode; it's just too difficult to crunch a lot of information and sort it intelligently if we—literally—lack the fuel for thinking. We also default to our heuristic brain if we are under stress or time pressure, or if we are trying to do too many things at one time. Indeed, multitasking is the perfect example of our brain toggling between rash and rational—and our tendency to make mistakes as we multitask is a good illustration of our limits in doing so.

Here is a metaphor that captures both the virtues and the

imperfection of heuristic thinking: packing the car trunk for a summer beach vacation. You know how much stuff you need for the beach: folding metal chairs, umbrellas, balls, and plastic buckets. And it's not like packing a rectangular box full of rectangular objects, like books. Beach things are irregular and the trunk itself is curved and oddly configured. So how do you pack it the best way? What's the optimal strategy? Most people will rely on heuristic thinking.

The word *heuristic* comes from philosophy by way of computer science. It's based on the Greek verb that means "to find." Computer scientists realized early on that some problems are too complex even for high-powered computers. These problems might have perfect solutions, but the computers would have to crunch away for weeks or months or years to figure them out. Consequently, computer scientists used shortcut algorithms that produce good-enough solutions in a reasonable time. As with those computer programs, our natural heuristics offer us a trade-off: we accept some imperfection in our decisions for the practicality of getting the job done.

So there are many, many ways to pack that car trunk, and some people will spend a lot of time trying to arrive at the optimal method. They'll spread everything on the lawn, then start methodically arranging the contents, large items first, filling in the nooks with smaller pieces. The solution will never be perfect: those folding chairs will always be an annoyance to these people.

Psychologists call these people "optimizers." The world is divided into optimizers and the rest of us—whom psychologists call "satisficers." *Satisficing* is just a Scottish colloquialism for *satisfying*, but it has that added sense of "good enough," as in satisfying enough to suffice. Satisficers (and I count myself here) can't be bothered with optimal solutions; they're way too difficult and time-consuming. You can't simply toss the beach stuff in capriciously, because it won't fit that way. But you don't fuss either, because once you slam that trunk closed and start driving, you won't even see it.

Obviously there are times when optimizing is essential. If you are designing a skyscraper and need to know precisely how much weight a beam will carry, you can't settle for a good-enough answer. But for many of life's problems, satisficing does fine. The trick is in knowing when to be deliberate and calculating and when to choose speed over perfection. It's all in the fit.

Think about the simple act of driving a car. I live in a big city, and I have lived here for a long time, so I know my way around. As a result, I don't have to plot out my routes to most familiar places, and I don't need maps. I simply start up the engine; then I arrive at my destination. I have little or no recollection of making any deliberate choices in between. I didn't have to think about turning right here, negotiating a traffic circle, using my indicator light, shifting gears, braking. I may even have switched radio stations and carried on a conversation during the drive. It was all automatic and unconscious.

That's good. More than good—absolutely necessary. What a drag life would be if you had to think about every minor step in driving your car to the grocery store. But what if a four-year-old child darts out into traffic, right in front of the car? If I'm lucky, I switch instantaneously back to the here and now. I am fully alert, and my focused, attentive mind trumps all those heuristic processes that add up to what we call cruise control. This is the brain toggling, but it's more of a jolt than a toggle. It's an emergency brain switch, and people who have experienced such incidents report having a flood of memories, many totally irrelevant. That's because when we're on automatic, we disengage not only our attention but our memory and just cruise. The sudden reengagement of those conscious processes floods the brain with detail—the stuff of focused decisions.

Now think of another kind of driving that's a completely different cognitive experience: snow driving. I learned to drive in northeastern Pennsylvania, where driving implicitly acknowledges the dual-processor brain. Learning to handle a car is a two-step ordeal in that region. In the late spring or summer, when the weather is fair, you learn to drive the usual way, steering and braking and working the clutch and gears and so forth. Then, when winter sets in, you learn snow driving. The state gives you a license for learning the regular stuff, but being a skillful snow driver carries infinitely more weight in the community: being unable to handle yourself and your car in nasty weather is a moral failure.

I learned the fundamentals of snow driving in the parking lot of the Acme supermarket on a cold Sunday. My father took me there after three or four inches of snow had fallen, when the macadam surface was slick, and told me to drive recklessly: accelerate and brake hard, make sharp turns, left then right. It was all to get the feel for a car on snow, sliding and correcting, sliding again. "What you've got to learn," he said, "is to turn into the skid."

I did learn it, but it's not intuitive. When your back wheels hit a slick patch and skid—to the right, let's say—most people's gut reaction is to correct by turning hard left, away from the skid. It's wired into our neurons, and we do it automatically, without thinking— heuristically. But it's wrong. Doing that just makes the skid worse. As my father said, you need to turn into the skid, which means turning right when it feels wrong.

Turning into the skid means trumping our heuristic impulses. Inept snow driving can land you in the body shop, or worse. But many of our everyday decisions and choices and judgments have profound and lasting consequences. This book is about defusing our misguided heuristic impulses, and in that sense it's a how-to book. The best way to rein in bad thinking is to recognize it, because once we recognize faulty thinking, we are capable of talking ourselves into better thinking. We have the power to engage the more deliberate and effortful part of our brain, and that process starts with understanding the heuristic brain in action. Let's begin.

‖‖

One

THE BODY IN THE WORLD

The **VISCERAL** Heuristic

||||||||||||||||||||||||||||||||||||||||||||||||||||||||||||||||||||||||||||||||||||||||||||||||||||||||||||||||||||||||||||||||||||||||||||||||||||||||

COLD SHOULDERS AND CLEAN HANDS

THERE WAS A time when the world was full of women named Daisy and Iris and Lily and Rose. Naming daughters after nature's blooms was considered a high compliment, a celebration of feminine beauty and vitality. Flowery names aren't in fashion so much these days, but the tradition of linking blossoms and womanhood runs long and deep. Just think back on the romantic imagery of Shakespeare, Burns, or Keats.

The tradition may go back even further than that, as it turns out, way back before poetry and language, and indeed may be part of our basic neurology. Some psychologists are now suggesting that the association between blooming flowers and womanhood may have ancient evolutionary roots, indeed that our liking for sprays of heather and violets may be the vestige of a once powerful survival skill: the ability to spot a good sexual partner. What's more, this primordial connection may as a component of the visceral heuristic explain all sorts of modern human—men's and women's—preferences that are completely unrelated to sexuality or mating.

Here's the basic idea. When our ancient ancestors were first becoming human, the key to the species' survival was sexual fitness. That is, primitive humans had to find strategies to produce hardy offspring, who then did the same, and on and on. One of these primitive strategies was an ability to select, from all the possible mates, the most healthy and fertile. Put another way, early humans became hypersensitive to any signs of ripeness in the world, and this hypersensitivity became deeply engrained in our perception and thinking and emotion, where it remains today.

The problem with these primitive skills, though, is that they are blunt instruments. They don't discriminate well, so a cognitive shortcut that was intended for mate selection is also applied to other living things—apples, for example, or greyhounds or marigolds. So today we retain a stubborn bias that makes us favor any living thing at its peak, and to disfavor anything that's unripe or in decline.

At least that's the theory, which Yale University psychologists Julie Huang and John Bargh have been studying in a variety of ways. They designed a series of experiments to see if, by piquing the fundamental human desire to mate, they could increase people's sensitivity to a variety of cues to immaturity, growth, peak ripeness, and decay—and in that way shape all sorts of social preferences.

Here's an example of their innovative work. The psychologists had a group of volunteers, all young adults, read a passage from the book *See Jane Date,* by Melissa Senate. This book is a classic of "chick lit," focusing on the lives of unmarried but nubile young women, and it was intended to jump-start the readers' mating instinct. Another comparable group of volunteers read a bland passage describing the interior of a building.

Then they had both groups look at four photographs of the actress Jane Withers, each from a different stage of her long acting career. Some may remember Jane Withers as "Josephine the Plumber" in the TV ads for the cleanser Comet, in the 1960s, but she actually began acting in the 1930s as an adorable toddler, and also played roles as a teen and as a leading lady. The photos showed all of these stages of her life.

The volunteers were then asked to rate the four images in terms of the actress's appeal. The idea was that those with mating on their mind would find the actress much more appealing in her sexual prime and devalue her when she was either older or sexually immature. And that was true. Those who had not been primed for sex showed no strong preferences for sexual peak years over youth or later years; it was just Jane Withers at various stages of her career. Those who had been primed for sex were much more interested in the starlet at her prime.

So this supports the evolutionary link between the "ripeness bias" and tastes in human beauty. But does the bias go beyond human attractiveness? Huang and Bargh speculated that it does, and they modified the experiment a bit to get an answer. They again primed some of the volunteers with the passage from *See Jane Date,* but this time they had them look at photographs of bananas. Some of the bananas were green, some yellow-green, some completely yellow, and some mottled with brown spots. All the volunteers then rated the attractiveness of the fruit.

I know what you're thinking. Yes, most of us prefer yellow bananas to either green or brown bananas. They generally taste better and have better texture. But as with the Jane Withers experiment, what the psychologists were measuring was the group *difference* between volunteers who had been primed for mating and those who had not. And they did find a big difference in their preference for perfectly ripe bananas and for bananas before or after their peak. That is, those with sex on their minds were more finicky about the color of their bananas.

So it really does seem that people are hard-wired for ripeness. But for those who remain skeptical, the psychologists decided to check this notion one more way. There were no automobiles on the savannas three million years ago, not even carts. So if the theory is sound, these same fundamental preferences for peak age over newness and senescence should apply only to living things, not artifacts. The psychologists ran one more experiment, basically the same as the other two, but in this one they had the volunteers rate photos of flowers and cars. They predicted that they would have maturity-related preferences when it came to flowers but not when it came to cars.

An automobile's peak, for this study, was when the car rolled off the assembly line, spanking new. Other photos showed the car under construction or beginning to rust with age. The flowers went from bud to full flowering to wilting. And the scientists saw just what they expected. That is, being primed for mating did shape people's preference for blooming flowers, but it had no effect on their preferences for the life stages of a car. We may not like to see our trusty old Mustang rust out, but apparently that sentiment doesn't resonate in our loins—or our psyche.

These findings may go way beyond our preferences for floral imagery and women's names, the authors conclude. Picking potential mates for their sexual "ripeness" may have been adaptive eons ago, when the future of the species was on the line, but is it the best dating strategy for modern times? Aren't there other traits to consider in a date or partner, ones not wired into our psyche? Or think of a completely unrelated social domain, such as the workplace. If these age-related biases really do run so deep and are so easily activated, might they have an effect on, say, our judgments of career ability? In that sense, ageism may have deeper roots than we know.

The work on sexual ripeness is just one example of the visceral heuristic and what psychologists call "cognitive scaffolding." Think of yourself—your thoughts, emotions, judgments, goals—as a building under construction. It's one of those projects that's never completed, but over the course of your lifetime you build it higher and higher, adding layers of experience and understanding.

At the very bottom is the foundation, and this is made up of the most fundamental perceptions and needs. They never change; they are the rock upon which all else is built. These foundational ideas, manifestations of the visceral heuristic, derive from our bodies' primary interaction with the world, including other bodies. Some, like sexual ripeness, have evolved over eons as survival mechanisms. Others emerge in infancy as the new mind is taking in whatever information it can gather about this strange place called the world. Whatever their source, they become the templates that shape much of our abstract thinking and our behavior.

Here's a really straightforward example of scaffolding. As a rule, we move forward, not in reverse, whether we're strolling or jogging or skipping; it's just our anatomy. So over eons the concept of "forward" has come to be tightly intertwined with the psychological concepts of "progress" and "advancement," which are universally equated with good. We admire advanced thinking; people who are "backward" are unsophisticated losers. Similarly, we are more apt to look upward than downward, just because there is more up there than down on the ground. So the concept of "up" (and height and ascendency) also has good associations. We aspire to move up in the world, not down; heaven is up, hell down.

Other visceral heuristics have to do with primitive physical needs and desires, for comfort and safety. These basic, internal concepts explain the power of metaphors. Consider this brooding metaphor, from the Sylvia Plath poem "Winter Landscape, with Rocks," written when the poet was twenty-four years old:

> *Last summer's reeds are all engraved in ice*
> *as is your image in my eye; dry frost*

glazes the window of my hurt; what solace
can be struck from rock to make heart's waste
grow green again? Who'd walk in this bleak place?

It would be another seven years before the young artist's depression would drive her to suicide, but the pain of her isolation was already apparent in the cold, wintry metaphors of this poem. But why cold and wintry? What made this troubled young woman think of ice and frost when she wanted to depict the emotional bleakness of her life, her desperate sense of disconnection? Why not searing heat and punishing sunshine? What does loneliness have to do with the temperature?

If this seems like a silly question, it's because we all make this automatic connection in our minds all the time. It's so universal that we don't even stop to wonder why. Just think of the clichés: the cold shoulder, a chilly reception, an icy stare. The idea of being alone—including social disconnection and rejection—appears to be inextricably tied in our minds to the subzero end of the thermometer.

Psychologists are curious about this metaphor, and others. Some believe that metaphors are much more than literary inventions, indeed that they are constellations of ancient and recent experience that we use to help us comprehend the complexity of our emotional lives. According to this view, some metaphors are universally resonant because they are etched in our brain tissue.

But how did they get there? Two psychologists at the University of Toronto decided to explore this question systematically. Chen-Bo Zhong and Geoffrey Leonardelli wanted to see if our use of metaphor in thinking and judgment might be influenced by our most basic perceptions of the world—the information that enters the brain through the senses. Our ancient ancestors probably linked warmth and togetherness as tools of survival, as do infants still; bodily warmth often means comfort and safety. Might the opposite also be true? Might cold and isolation be similarly linked in the mind?

Here's how the psychologists tested this provocative idea. They divided volunteers into two groups and had half of them recall a personal experience in which they had been socially excluded—rejection from a club, for example, or getting cut from the varsity basketball squad. This was meant to prime their unconscious feelings of isolation and loneliness. The others recalled a happier experience, one in which they had been embraced by the same type of group. All the volunteers tried to recall as vividly as possible the details of the experience—where they were standing, who brought the news—but they also tried as hard as they could to summon up the long-lost feelings and visceral sensations. The researchers wanted them to reexperience the sting in all its unpleasantness.

Immediately after, they had all the volunteers estimate the temperature in the room, on the pretense that the building's maintenance staff wanted that information. The estimates ranged widely, from about 54 degrees F to a whopping 104 degrees F. That's surprising in itself, but here's the more interesting part: those who had been primed to feel isolated and rejected gave consistently lower estimates of the temperature, by almost five degrees. In other words, the conjured-up sting of being ostracized actually made people experience the world as colder.

Add a layer of clothing. Five degrees is not a subtle difference in perception; it's dramatic. So dramatic that the psychologists needed to verify the results to make sure they weren't a fluke. In fact, they decided not to rely on the volunteers' memories. Instead, the researchers actually triggered feelings of exclusion. They had the subjects play a computer-simulated ball-tossing game, but the game was actually rigged. Some of the volunteers tossed the ball around in a normal friendly way, but others were left out, just as an unpopular kid might be left out by other kids at the playground.

Afterward, all the volunteers rated the desirability of certain drinks and foods: hot coffee, crackers, an ice-cold Coke, an apple, hot soup. The volunteers hadn't a clue to the purpose of the experiment. They simply acted on their preferences, and the results again were striking. The "unpopular" volunteers who had been ostracized on the virtual playground were much more likely than the others to want either hot soup or coffee. Their preference for warmth, for "comfort food," presumably resulted from actually feeling the cold in the cold shoulder.

It appears that physical sensations and psychological experience are tightly intertwined, and that intertwining may influence our social relationships in powerful ways. This intertwining may also illuminate the relationship between our very real moods and our perceptions of the world around us. Experiencing cold may actually act as a catalyst in mood disorders, the psychologists suggest, exacerbating feelings of isolation and loneliness, in a cyclical way: isolation makes us feel left out in the cold, which makes us even lonelier, which makes the mercury plummet even more, and on and on. So it's literally a cold, cruel world for some, which makes one wonder about Sylvia Plath's suicide. The poet killed herself in London in February 1963, in the middle of England's coldest winter in hundreds of years. She died by sticking her head in an oven.

If warmth was a basic human need back in prehistoric times, so too was cleanliness. We may think of our ancient ancestors as pretty scruffy folks, but in fact their survival depended on avoiding various kinds of contamination. Contamination often caused illness, so early humans had to be hypervigilant. Cleanliness was a survival tool, but over time, as we modernized, it became a metaphor for what's good, and eventually was adopted as an ideal of almost every religion. The Virgin Mary is immaculate. Cleanliness is next to godliness. Many religions require that believers wash before they pray. The idea of "purity" is as much a spiritual concept as a physical one.

Psychologists have also demonstrated this visceral heuristic in action. In a series of studies published in the journal *Science,* psychologists explored more secular expressions of this urge for daily cleaning rituals and moral purity. In one experiment, for example, the psychologists primed volunteers' minds by asking them to recall either an ethical or unethical act from their past. The recollections were all kept strictly confidential in order to encourage the volunteers to be as vivid and specific as possible.

Then they had them complete a list of words by filling in the blanks: for example, W_ _ H or S_ _ P or SH_ _ER. The word puzzles were deliberately selected to offer the volunteers many word options. So, for example, they could come up with *wish, soup,* and *shiner,* or *with* and *ship* and *shiver.* Or, alternatively, they could come up with *wash, soap,* and *shower.* The idea is that when you do a whole slew of these exercises, they add up to a statistical view of where your mind is at that moment. And here's what the data showed: Those who recalled a good deed made up random words; there was no pattern in their thinking. But those who had recalled things like stealing a library book, lying to a friend, or cheating on a spouse were much more apt to come up with words related to cleansing. In other words, acknowledgment of unethical behavior triggers thoughts of cleaning and cleanliness.

This visceral heuristic is closely connected to the cooties heuristic, which will be discussed later in relation to superstitions and beliefs. But here the scientists were focused on the idea of ethical dirt—what we call slimy behavior. In another study, the scientists focused not on the volunteers' own ethical (or unethical) past but instead on a stranger's. The researchers had all the volunteers read a short story about a lawyer at a prestigious law firm who discovers a document that is crucial to a colleague's successful prosecution of an important case. In one version of the story, the lawyer gives the document to his colleague, saving the case. But in another version, the lawyer tells nobody about the document he discovered; in fact, he shreds the papers, sabotaging the case. After reading one version or the other, all the volunteers were given a choice of several seemingly meaningless rewards for participating in the experiment: crackers, shampoo, batteries, soap, and so forth. And yes, those with the scoundrel lawyer on their minds were much more apt to reach for the personal hygiene products.

This is incredible when you stop to think of what it means. A complete stranger's slimy actions rubbed off on a mere observer, making him feel dirty. But the findings held up when the scientists ran a completely different version of this same study. In fact, in one experiment fully two-thirds of the volunteers thinking about immoral behavior picked a hand wipe over a pencil, compared to just a third of those primed for ethical thoughts. The researchers call this the "Macbeth effect," named in honor of Shakespeare's Lady Macbeth, who tried desperately to wash her hands clean of her complicity in murder. It appears that her effort to literally cleanse her conscience may not have been completely irrational. Indeed, it may have worked on a basic heuristic level.

It may work too well, in fact, and backfire in modern life. In a different study, psychologist Simone Schnall of the University of Plymouth explored whether ritual acts of cleaning can actually affect the severity of our moral judgments—not only toward ourselves but toward others as well. She basically reversed the experiments just described: she used word games to prime thoughts of cleanliness and washing and immaculate order in volunteers' minds, then tested the volunteers' ethics.

She did this by having volunteers (both clean-minded and others who were not primed for cleanliness) confront a series of moral dilemmas, some more ambiguous than others. If you found a wallet, would you keep the money inside? That's an easy one, but how about these: Would you ever consider putting false information on a resume? What if you were in a plane crash in a remote mountain location and a survivor was dying—would you hurry his death and eat his flesh to avoid starvation?

The findings? Those who had been "cleansed" were much less strict in their moral standards than were those who were unclean. They were more apt to fudge their resumes just a bit, or pocket a bit of someone else's cash. Of course, you could construe this differently, depending on your own moral compass. That is, it appears that the clean-minded let themselves off the hook more easily for theft and cheating—and even murder.

Schnall replicated these unsettling findings with a much more literal cleansing. She did the same study, except that the volunteers were required to watch a disgusting video beforehand. This was meant to "dirty" their minds. Then she had half these volunteers actually go to a wash basin and scrub their hands before confronting the moral dilemmas. Those who had actually taken the soap and hot water and scrubbed their palms and knuckles were much more lenient than were those whose hands were unwashed. Think Lady Macbeth.

Or think of a trial by jury, which is probably more relevant to most of our lives. And think of yourself as a juror, judging not yourself but one of your fellow men for an ambiguous crime. What does it mean that we are so easily manipulated by these heuristic-driven intuitions? Do our own feelings of cleanliness and purity make us unreliable judges of guilt and moral turpitude? Is a crime more reprehensible if it is disgusting? Is the accused guiltier if he is slovenly? More innocent if he is well scrubbed and nattily dressed? What does this mean for jury selection? For victims' rights?

These are all questions without answers, because this line of scientific inquiry is still new. But clearly the implications go far beyond naming our daughters Violet or Heather. The visceral heuristic long ago ceased to be merely about the body and basic needs such as warmth and cleanliness, and today influences everything from personal attraction to moral judgment.

WOMEN ARE MUCH choosier than men when it comes to romance. This is well known, but the reason for this gender difference is unclear. New research from Northwestern University suggests that this pickiness—or lack of it—may derive from the body
in motion. In a novel study of speed dating, the researchers reversed
the usual arrangement and had the women approach the sitting men.
When they did this, women became less discriminating—in short,
more like men. The scientists think that the very act of approaching
someone makes the potential date more appealing. Think about that:
a simple social convention is shaping desire. The bodily heuristics are
among the most fundamental cognitive biases operating in the mind.
They grow out of our interactions with a complex world. This is true
of all the heuristics discussed in this first section of the book. The visionary heuristic, the subject of the next chapter, is so named because
it likely derives from the way our eyes process size, shape, height,
and slope. But like all heuristics, it has a sphere of influence that en-
compasses core psychological traits including fear, confidence, and
self-esteem. It even offers some insight into the great Yankee slugger
Mickey Mantle.

The **VISIONARY** Heuristic

||||||||||||||||||||||||||||||||||||||||||||||||||||||||||||||||||||||||||||||||||||||||||||||||||||||||||||||||||||||||||||||||||||

HILLS AND HOME RUNS

THE FRENCH FRIAR and explorer Louis Hennepin, the first European to describe the wonder of Niagara Falls, suffered from a pathological fear of heights. There is no clinical record of Father Hennepin's disorder, nor did he write about his phobia. We know this from his lousy guesstimating of the height of the future honeymoon destination. In a 1677 journal entry, he put the height at a "prodigious high" of 600 feet. In fact, North America's largest waterfall is only 167 feet high.

That's way off, not even close, and according to psychologist Jeanine Stefanucci, Hennepin's error is a reliable indicator of acrophobia. Stefanucci, who works at Virginia's College of William and Mary, is one of a group of psychologists who have been studying the intricate connection between fear and our most basic perceptions of the physical world: heights, slope, size, and so forth. We "see" the world through the lens of our emotions, and our vision in turn shapes our fears, motivation, and self-esteem. Call it the visionary heuristic.

But let me back up a bit and describe my own experience as a lab rat in one of these intriguing experiments. In 2008, I visited the laboratory of psychologist Dennis Proffitt at the University of Virginia and took part in a perception experiment. Psychology labs are for the most part pretty dull places—no Bunsen burners or beakers, just desks and computer screens. Many of Proffitt's experiments are actually done outside, on UVA's rolling campus, since it's the normal navigation of the world that interests him. He wants to know how we get from here to there, and what psychological obstacles can hinder our travels.

For the particular experiment I was in, we just went outside onto the second-story balcony of the psychology building. It was twenty-six feet to the lawn below, but I only learned the precise height later on; part of the experimental task was to estimate the height, like Hennepin only on a much smaller scale. I was in a group of volunteers, and we stood on the balcony looking down at a disc that had been placed on the ground below. One of the tricks in measuring basic perception is getting rid of the mental baggage we all carry around that might influence and distort our sense of the world. So, for example, instead of asking me to give a verbal estimate of the distance in feet and inches, the experimenter (a grad student) had me use him as a kind of human tape measure. I looked from the balcony to the ground, then the experimenter walked away, toward the end of the balcony, then I looked down again, then back at him, and so forth. When his horizontal distance from me matched my estimate of the distance to the ground, I was told to say, "Stop."

It may seem like a trivial detail, but it's not. Estimating height this way clears away (to an extent) the contaminating effects of memory and conscious, deliberate calculation. If I had been asked to estimate the height in feet, I might have been influenced by my memory of my ten-foot ceilings at home or my own height; I would "interpret" the height rather than just sense it. The idea here was to zero in as tightly as possible on what my eyes and my heuristic mind were telling me. The experimenter also had me estimate the size of the disc on the ground below, to get yet another indirect measure of how I sensed the height of the balcony. Again, he didn't ask for inches; he slowly extended a tape measure and stopped when I told him to.

I was participating in an informal version of the height experiment. When Proffitt and his students do the study systematically (as they have done hundreds of times), they run each volunteer through it alone, then have him or her complete a battery of other psychological tests, including one for acrophobia. The experimenter didn't know anything about me—my life experiences, my fears. One thing he didn't know is the fact that I had a serious fall from a balcony years ago, in which I was badly injured. Lots of broken bones; long rehab. I have since had what I'd label a moderate fear of heights, high balconies especially; I don't tremble or perspire, but I don't especially like looking over railings at any height, and tend to avoid them. I never lean on them.

So it wasn't surprising that in our little informal experiment, I overestimated the height of the balcony by a couple of feet. I truly thought that my estimate was accurate when I told the experimenter to stop walking, but I was way off. When Proffitt runs this experiment with people who are very fearful of heights and compares them to those who are not fearful, the acrophobics "see" the ground about five feet farther away than do nonfearful volunteers. So it makes sense that my misperception puts me in the middle, between absolutely precise perception and badly distorted phobic perception.

But here's the interesting part: almost everybody overestimates the height, even those not plagued by a clinical fear of heights. That's because on the most fundamental level, we're all afraid of falling; it's a basic heuristic-driven survival mechanism, ingrained over eons of evolution. It's a cognitive strategy for safety and self-preservation. Our ancestors' survival was much more precarious than ours on a daily basis, and they learned to perceive the world as opportunities and costs. Getting dangerously close to the edge of a cliff might be an opportunity—if there was an unpicked blueberry shrub there, for example—but it also carried risk of falling.

In that sense, Proffitt explains, our perceptual "errors" may serve a beneficial purpose. Indeed, they may be one of the brain's fundamental mechanisms for negotiating a dangerous world. He and his colleagues have run a whole battery of experiments to demonstrate this idea, most involving University of Virginia students, recruited from those walking around the Charlottesville campus.

Proffitt documented the same distorted perception regarding the slopes of hills. In one experiment, he had participants stand on the top of a thirty-degree rise. That's a very steep slope, almost impossible to descend without falling. He discovered that people consistently saw the hill as steeper when they were at the top of it than when they were at the bottom. Why? Probably that same ingrained fear of falling, Proffitt speculates, the same fear that made me overestimate the balcony height. The top of a thirty-degree hill is a dangerous place, he notes. People likely see steep descents as even steeper because part of the mind is imagining a skull-cracking injury—or death.

The link between perception and fear of falling is theoretical, of course. So Stefanucci ran a series of experiments to explicitly test the idea, actually creating fearful arousal in volunteers to see if it influenced their height estimates. For example, in one experiment she showed a group of volunteers (none of whom suffered from acrophobia) a series of thirty PowerPoint images, none related to height but all known to trigger a powerful fear response. Others viewed thirty neutral photographs. Then she immediately walked them out onto a balcony and basically ran the same experiment I took part in.

Stefanucci revealed that those who had been manipulated into a state of fearfulness distorted height much more than the others, over-estimating the drop to the ground. Then she ran another experiment to see if fear influenced perception of horizontal distance—looking down an ordinary hallway—and it did not. The distortion was specific to height. Father Hennepin might as well have been on a roller coaster—front car, no hands—plunging downward at high speed, because that's how his body "saw" the beauty of Niagara Falls.

This may be more than mere metaphor, in fact. The feeling of plunging or diving—that is, the mental simulation of movement—may be part of a cognitive style that's characteristic of all phobias. Psychologists have a wonderful, awful name for such fearful thinking: "looming maladaptive style." It basically means that fear makes people see even mundane things as things in motion—moving at them at untoward speed, and threatening them, when in fact they are not. In short, people with phobias experience a different world than the rest of us, a world with a lot of things looming at them.

The interesting thing is that we all have a touch of this dysfunctional thinking, left over from our primordial past. And fear of falling is just a part of it. Proffitt has also turned up evidence for what we might call "fear of climbing"—the same kind of distorted perception when people were standing at the bottom of a hill looking up. In one series of experiments, he had students stand at the bottom of various hills and estimate the angle of the slope. They were very bad at this, though not as bad as when they stood on top. For example, state law in Virginia prohibits any roads with a grade greater than nine degrees; the students consistently estimated steep roads to be twenty-five degrees or more. The scientists used the same kind of experimental techniques to guarantee that this was pure perception—that is, volunteers did not have to rely on their knowledge of what a degree represents. These distortions were so common that Proffitt believes they also represent a universal bias.

Fear of falling is an easy-to-grasp concept. But why fear of climbing? Well, think of it this way. Our ancient ancestors had to conserve energy. It was perilous and arduous out there on the savanna, and on the most basic level humans learned not to waste their most valuable resource: oomph. They did this in part by constantly "choosing" how hard to work. This wasn't a conscious calculation, of course; they didn't estimate each hill's slope in degrees and weigh it against their stamina at that moment in time. Such calculations are impossible; we would be paralyzed if we had to deliberate every movement. But in effect that's what they were doing day in and day out on an unconscious heuristic level.

Proffitt demonstrated this heuristic thinking in several experiments. Volunteers consistently overestimate the slant of hills (and indirectly the work required to climb) even when they are feeling fit and rested. But even more interesting, these distortions get more exaggerated when volunteers are weighed down, actually or psychologically. For example, Proffitt deliberately fatigued some participants by having them jog—not enough to completely exhaust them, but enough to get them tired out. When he did this, their distortions of the hills' grade became even more unrealistic. Similarly, he made others wear a heavy backpack, with the same result. This is interesting because the volunteers were factoring in not actual fatigue but anticipated fatigue. He also compared fit and unfit students, and those who were unfit saw the hills as impossibly steep for climbing. He got similar results when he studied people who were elderly and frail. In every case, the participants' fatigue (real or anticipated) made them overestimate the slope of the hill in front of them.

These collected findings may have important public health implications. Most exercise is in one form or another a variation on climbing hills; that's how Physics 101 defines work. So if we're deep-wired to conserve energy, and specifically to avoid all but essential forms of work, that means there is a significant psychological disincentive to move at all, much less to hop on the Stairmaster and climb for half an hour.

Proffitt believes that these deep-wired perceptual distortions are so fundamental that they are a basic component of all fear. Psychologists have typically described the fear reaction as having four basic parts: emotion, physiology (the sweat, tension, beating heart, and so forth), thoughts of harm, and actions (pulling away, holding tight to the railing, and so forth). These experiments suggest that basic perception might be a new mode of fear expression, a fifth component of this most basic of human conditions.

So if fear and perception are so intimately intertwined, would it follow that allaying fear might also have an effect on what we see—or think we see? The psychologists did a simple experiment to find out. As with the earlier studies on steepness of hills, they recruited students who just happened to be walking around campus. But in this experiment, they deliberately recruited some who were alone and others who were walking with a friend. They wanted to see if social support, the comfort of companionship, might influence perception. And it did, clearly. Those who were accompanied by a friend perceived hills as much less steep than did those who came to the task alone. Every serious exerciser has heard the advice: train with a partner. These findings add some science to that folk wisdom. It's not just having someone to chat with; the tasks really appear more doable in our minds when we're not alone.

The psychologists did another version of the experiment to look at the question a slightly different way. They recruited only students who were walking alone, but asked some of them to think of a supportive friendship; they wanted to prime unconscious feelings of security and support. Others were told to think of someone neutral—a store clerk, say—or someone they actively disliked. And again, those who were feeling secure in the knowledge of a close friendship had a less distorted view of the hill's pitch. In other words, they saw the hill as less threatening.

So this adds a social dimension to the whole fear and perception interplay. And in fact, many of our most common fears today, in modern times, are not of bodily injury or running out of fuel but rather of social injuries—harm to our group standing, our confidence, our self-esteem. In effect, our ancient fears of falling and running out of gas translate today into pervasive anxiety about failure. That is, we retain our fundamental impulse for safety, but apply it in the world of emotions.

Consider this wonderful quote from the late great Yankee slugger Mickey Mantle. When asked about his uncanny ability to blast home runs, the Hall of Famer famously replied: "I never really could explain it. I just saw the ball as big as a grapefruit." It's not surprising that Mantle couldn't explain his experience in the batter's box. What he was describing was one of the fundamental mysteries of human perception. His comment goes to the heart of heuristic thinking, in particular the way the human mind comingles vision and emotions like confidence and fear of failure.

Proffitt was inspired by Mickey Mantle's uncanny hitting ability—and intrigued by his comment. He figured there might be a link between old fears of falling and more subtle psychological threats today. Superstars often embody in exaggerated form the abilities and traits of us mortals, so they can point scientists toward valuable questions about normal behavior. With Mantle's grapefruit-sized baseball in mind, Proffitt wondered if other, lesser athletes had similar experiences—that is, if they "saw" things in distorted ways depending on their ability. He wanted to investigate the psychological forces that affect something as fundamental as vision.

So he went to a local softball game out in the Virginia suburbs. What better place to find athletes with a wide range of skill, from major-league wannabes to benchwarmers? He watched the game and kept careful records of how well all the players hit the ball that night. And then, after the final out, he went down to the field where the players were mingling and asked them if they would participate in a small psychological study. Many did.

It was a simple experiment. He had the volunteers estimate the size of a softball. Again, he didn't ask them inches or centimeters, because he didn't want them to overthink it; he wanted to tap into how the brain actually "sees" the ball. So he had them look at several discs of different sizes and choose the one that best matched the size of a regulation softball. Then he took these perceptions and compared them with the players' batting averages from the evening. When he ran all the data through the computer, the findings were clear and interesting: the bigger the softball players perceived the ball to be, the higher their batting average that evening. Like Mickey Mantle, the most talented Charlottesville softball sluggers (or at least the hottest hitters that evening) saw the ball as bigger than it actually is.

This was obviously a small and somewhat informal study. Yet according to Proffitt, it demonstrated an important principle—that human perception is much more complex than simple vision. It includes vision—what's actually recorded on the retina—but the brain mixes that imagery with all sorts of mental and emotional baggage. For poor hitters, the ball is perceived as tiny and distant because it is "out of reach"—beyond their ability to connect with it, emotionally and actually. Their lack of self-confidence in their hitting ability made the ball appear impossibly small.

The softball study left a lot of questions unanswered, and Jessica Witt, one of Proffitt's colleagues, decided to take a swing at them. She designed a series of studies to expand on these preliminary findings a different way, through the eyes of golfers. Most people can play softball respectably, or at least fake it for an evening, but golf is an incredibly difficult game, both physically and mentally. Many weekend hackers (myself included) spend a lot of money on pricey clubs and

equipment, only to give up the game in frustration. It's that challenging. The "short game" is especially difficult—chipping the ball to the
flagpole and putting the ball into the hole.

The long game doesn't really involve the hole, because it's too
distant, out of sight and mind. When you're on the tee of most holes,
you're really aiming for the fairway. When you get to the short game,
you are actually seeing the hole, so perception shifts. That's why Witt
decided to focus on the hole. Just as Mickey Mantle saw the baseball
as the size of a grapefruit, many professional golfers report highly
distorted perceptions of the hole depending on how they're putting.
It can be as big as a bucket or basketball hoop, or as tiny as a dime or
an aspirin, according to reports from the sports pages. To study these
variations in perception, Witt headed to the Providence Golf Club in
Richmond, Virginia.

She recruited forty-six golfers, almost all men, right after they
had completed a round of golf. She showed them nine circles of
different diameters and asked them to choose the one that best rep-
resented the actual size of a real golf hole. She also gathered information on their golf scores that day, the number of putts they took
on the eighteenth hole, and the number of strokes they took on the
entire eighteenth hole.

She also collected one more piece of data—the golfers' handicaps.
Handicap is an indicator of how skilled a golfer is in general, based
on many rounds of previous golf. A low handicap, say two, is excellent; the higher the handicap, the less skilled the golfer. Witt wanted
to know the golfers' handicaps because she wanted to compare the
perceptions of accomplished golfers with those of golfers who were
simply having a good day. In other words, she wanted to know if
distorted perception (or accurate perception) was related to general
ability or if it was related to a temporary state of mind.

Her findings reinforced those from Proffitt's softball study: golfers who played well on the day of the study consistently saw the hole

as bigger than it actually is—and bigger than the less successful golfers saw it. But handicap was unrelated to perception. In other words, both accomplished golfers and hackers saw the hole looming large if they were playing well on that particular day.

And not just playing well but putting well. Size perceptions were related to how well the golfers putted on the eighteenth green but unrelated to how well they played the hole overall—including tee and fairway shots. That makes sense, since the hole size is not all that important when you're hundreds of yards down the fairway. The hole becomes the focus of attention when you step onto the green and pull out your putter. Witt did a variation of this study in her laboratory, using one of those practice putting mats, and got the same results.

Happily, all of these calculations—of danger, work, and likelihood of success—take place instantaneously outside our awareness. Imagine trying to get through a day if you had to consider risks and benefits of every footstep, and calculate in the value of your companions, and so forth. It would simply be impossible. As Proffitt says, "A principal function of perception is to defend people from having to think." Or as another famous Yankee, Yogi Berra, once quipped: "You can't think and hit at the same time."

HITTING ANY KIND of ball skillfully is a challenge. The visionary heuristic is illuminating because it shows how our basic perception is tightly interwoven with emotions and self-concept. Looked at another way, however, it's surprising we can hit a ball at all—or catch one. In addition to being a slugger, Mickey Mantle was also a very talented center fielder, which meant that when the batter hit a long shot toward the deep outfield, he had to do several highly complex calculations to judge the arc and speed of the ball as well as his own vector and speed in order to be at precisely the right spot to make the catch. How did he do it? Well, he didn't literally do any calculations, of course. No human could make those calculations that quickly, time and again. He relied on the momentum heuristic—intuitive physics, the topic of the following chapter. This ancient skill goes way beyond athletics, influencing our attitudes and emotions in uncanny ways.

The **MOMENTUM** Heuristic

||||||||||||||||||||||||||||||||||||||||||||||||||||||||||||||||||||||||||||||||||||||||||||||||||||||||||||||||||||||||||||||||||||||||||||||||||||||||||||||

INTUITIVE PHYSICS

I N THE OLD Road Runner cartoons, the luckless Wile E. Coyote lived by the laws of cartoon physics, defying Newton as he hurled himself through the American Southwest in pursuit of his nemesis. In one classic scenario, he would run off a cliff, where he would stand for a few seconds suspended in midair. Only when he looked down and realized his mistake would the force of gravity kick in, plunging him to the desert floor below.

Why did Wile E. Coyote's misfortunes make us laugh time and again? Sure, the exploding Acme products were good for a chuckle, but it was really the outlandish misuse of physics that made the Road Runner one of Looney Tunes' most popular features in the 1950s. Though physics may not seem like a natural for humor, in fact defying Newton's laws is funny. And it's funny because we all have a heuristic sense of what's physically possible and what is not.

The momentum heuristic explains why we can interact with the physical world so effortlessly, whether it's ducking a dodge ball or driving a car in heavy traffic. We move through our world and rarely collide, and amazingly we don't need any calculations for these complex actions. We simply "know" in our neurons. But as with all heuristics, the momentum heuristic is imperfect; the same basic sense that helps us navigate the environment can be misapplied to our social world. Our brain takes ideas like momentum and trajectory and applies them to events and social situations that have nothing to do with physical movement. We "see" these physical forces where they may not exist—leading to inaccurate judgments and choices.

Let's look at some experiments. Psychologist Neal Roese of the University of Illinois is one of a cadre of psychologists who have been examining people's perceptions of motion to see how they affect social judgment. In one experiment, for example, he and his colleagues turned to a not-so-loony subject: serious highway collisions. Roese had volunteers watch two computer simulations of head-on collisions, each one prepared for use in an actual courtroom trial. In one case, a car attempts to pass a tractor-trailer on a two-lane highway, crashing head-on into a second tractor-trailer. In the other case, a tractor-trailer swerves to avoid a slow-moving car that has just pulled into traffic; the truck crashes into a bus coming in the opposite direction.

For the purposes of the study, some of the volunteers were spared the worst of the mayhem, viewing simulations that stopped short of the actual crash. In addition to watching the videos, Roese had the volunteers read descriptions of the accidents and view diagrams, much as if a lawyer were presenting traditional courtroom testimony. All were then asked to estimate the likelihood of an accident occurring, as a juror would do. The most interesting finding was that even when they had just seen an incomplete simulation of the accident, stopping just short of impact, volunteers "knew" that a crash was inevitable. Apparently when people perceive a dynamic event—with motion, momentum, trajectory—their intuitive physics click in and they become hyperconfident about the outcome.

Roese calls this new psychological phenomenon the "propensity effect," which is just one manifestation of the momentum heuristic. This gut-level feeling is probably most familiar to sports fans. For example, baseball fans see a ball hit toward the outfield bleachers and "know" that you can kiss that one goodbye. Indeed, fans say the actual home run is a letdown after the momentary excitement of "knowing."

These findings have important legal implications because computer simulations are increasingly used in courtrooms as a form of persuasive evidence. But the implications are much broader than that. Apparently, when it comes to motion, the mind plays tricks, distorting what we think we know about where things are heading—not only physical objects but life events as well. Our innate sense of the physical world—and impersonal forces such as speed and momentum—may carry over directly to our understanding of the psychological world.

Look to the world of sports: fans and players both will swear to the validity of momentum in athletic contests, both individual momentum and team momentum. Players, for reasons not fully understood, will suddenly go "on a roll," or they'll get a "hot hand." Or they'll just as suddenly lose their momentum, and the contest will shift in an opponent's favor.

Is this merely magical thinking, or is there something to the idea that psychological momentum affects performance? Psychologists have begun to study the link between what they call "intuitive physics," the propensity effect, and seemingly unrelated attitudes and beliefs, with some interesting results. Indeed, some have begun work on a unifying theory of psychological momentum that begins with the basic laws of Newtonian physics.

Newtonian physics says that momentum equals velocity times

ﾂﾂ

mass. It's simple. But what does this mean in the realm of human motivation and performance? Well, according to these theorists, psychological velocity is provided by some important event. In sports that is usually a big play that turns the tide: a key interception in a football game or a steal and slam dunk in hoops.

Mass, according to this theory, is provided by the social context. How important is the game? Is a team emotionally invested in the outcome of this game more than others? I live in Washington Redskins country, where the biggest game of the year is always the home game against the Dallas Cowboys. It's a major topic of conversation not only on Sunday but for the entire "Dallas Week" leading up to the game. According to psychologists, the unusual focus and attention qualify as mass. When combined with the velocity from a big play, it can produce psychological momentum, the sensation of an invisible force at work in the realm of emotions.

Our expectations—and even our regrets—can be shaped by the momentum heuristic. In one study, Ohio University psychologists Keith Markman and Corey Guenther recruited a group of knowledgeable basketball fans and had them view a film clip from an actual basketball game, a 1998 contest between Duke University and the University of North Carolina. The Redskins-Cowboys rivalry pales next to this college rivalry between the Duke Blue Devils and the Carolina Tarheels, and in 1998 the Devils were ranked number one in the country and the Tarheels number two.

In the ten-minute film clip used for the experiment, the Blue Devils ran off fifteen unanswered points, although they trailed the Tarheels during the entire segment. Duke ended up losing the game to North Carolina, 97–73, but the study volunteers didn't know this (and interviews revealed that none of them recalled this game). The psychologists stopped the film every minute and asked the fans these two questions: Who has the momentum now? Which team do you believe will win the game? After viewing the film clip, they were asked what specific event during the game was most important in shifting the momentum of the game.

When they analyzed the data, the psychologists found some confirmation for their notion of psychological momentum. Most of the fans perceived that Duke had momentum during the game, and most predicted that Duke would go on to win. When asked, the volunteers named either a technical foul against one Carolina player or a key rebound and three-pointer by a Duke player as the turning point that gave Duke the momentum.

Markman and Guenther wanted to further explore the analogy between physics and psychology, including the idea of mass. Remember that mass, in the psychological sense, is the emotional importance of an event. In a second experiment, they had volunteers read a description of a hypothetical basketball game involving a team called East Midland, a very competitive squad. Some volunteers read a scenario in which East Midland played Millersville, another team in their division. Others read a scenario in which East Midland played West Midland, a crosstown team with whom they have had an intense ninty-year rivalry. In both scenarios, East Midland wins a hard-fought game and is going on to play Conner for a playoff spot.

Which East Midland team has the greater momentum going into the game against Conner? This is the question the psychologists asked the volunteers. And they found what their theory predicts: fans believe that a win against a long-time rival would give East Midland more momentum than a more neutral win, even though both are just as important in the standings. This lends support to the idea that "mass," in the form of emotional importance, contributes to psychological momentum.

I have not been a competitive athlete since high school, and I don't watch sporting events as much as I once did. But I confess to using phrases like "hot hand" and "on a roll"—and believing them. It feels like a physical force. And this goes beyond sports. People perceive momentum in the stock market, in political campaigns, in progress on social issues such as gay marriage. It's even apparent in people's perceptions of their own personal performance in relationships, school, and careers.

Consider Jane. Jane is a made-up character with a lot on her plate. Her apartment is a mess because she has been so busy lately. She's finally got an open Sunday without obligations, and she sets an ambitious agenda for herself: clean her entire apartment and write a twenty-page paper on the poetry of Emily Dickinson. The researchers asked volunteers to read a scenario in which Jane starts cleaning at one in the afternoon, hoping to finish both tasks by nine o'clock. But some read a scenario in which she plodded along steadily, while others read about her getting on a cleaning roll and zipping through the mopping, dusting, and scouring almost effortlessly. Then they asked the volunteers to imagine her writing the paper.

The psychologists wanted to see if residual momentum from one event can carry over to another, completely different event. And that is exactly what they found. Those who "watched" Jane sail through her household cleaning thought Jane was more likely to "have the wind at her back" when she started writing, and that she was much more likely to meet her self-imposed nine o'clock deadline.

Unless Jane's mother phoned.

The psychologists decided to complicate matters for Jane, to see if they could experimentally make her lose her momentum. They wanted to see if it is harder for someone with momentum to get back on track than it is for someone just plodding along. So in a final study, we rejoin Jane while she is actually writing the Emily Dickinson paper. She is halfway through, with just two hours left to deadline. Again, some of the volunteers read about Jane being "on a roll" and "focused," while others simply read that she was writing the paper.

Jane is annoyed when her mother rings. She knows there is no such thing as a brief conversation with her, and that she will likely be on the phone for forty-five minutes. But she's a good daughter and she picks up the phone anyway. How difficult will it be for her to get back in the groove after this unexpected interruption?

Volunteers believed it would be very difficult for Jane to regain her momentum. As with an automobile that is cruising along a highway and is then forced to stop, it takes effort to regain lost momentum, to get back up to speed. Or at least that is how many people conceive of it.

So let's assume for a minute that Jane is indeed thrown off by her mother's ill-timed phone call, that she loses her sense of momentum and gives up on the Emily Dickinson assignment. No, let's make it even worse than that: let's say she never finishes the paper and ends up failing the course. How will she make sense of that later on? Well, if she's like too many of us, she will convince herself that her failure was inevitable. Here's how.

If momentum and propensity are all about the future and where we (or others) are heading, the flip side of momentum is hindsight. We are constantly looking back at events and actions to explain how we ended up where we did. Unfortunately, the lens we use for looking back in time is often badly distorted. Psychologists call this lens the "hindsight bias." We know it as the familiar I-knew-it-all-along syndrome.

Hindsight bias means that we are much more likely to see an outcome as inevitable once it has occurred than we were before it took place. That may seem obvious, but it's not simply that we learn from experiencing the events. It seems that our memories of past events are eclipsed by new, more powerful memories of what actually happened in their wake, so we are psychologically incapable of being honest with ourselves about what we really knew earlier.

This cognitive bias is double-edged. It can keep us from ruminating endlessly about what might have been, what we could have done differently, and so forth—and thus allow us to look forward and move on. On the other hand, believing bad outcomes are inevitable makes it difficult to learn from mistakes, and indeed can keep people from taking personal responsibility for their actions.

So how do we get rid of this delusional thinking? How do we more honestly examine the connection between actions and consequences? Well, it's not easy, as it turns out. It would seem that the way to undo the I-knew-it-all-along effect would be to come up with alternative explanations. Considering Jane again, she could, instead of deciding that her failure was a foregone conclusion, say something like: "If I had just ignored my mother's call, I would have completed the paper and the course." That if-then explanation should deflate the sense of inevitability.

But it doesn't—at least not automatically. Indeed, the opposite seems to be true in many cases. Psychologists call these alternative explanations "counterfactuals," which is just a jargony way of describing events that didn't happen but might have, would have, could have. Neal Roese—the psychologist who ran the auto crash experiments—has also run several experiments to untangle the relationship between hindsight bias and counterfactual thinking.

Most of the studies involved imagined scenarios, like missing a plane or failing an exam. In every case, the study volunteers concluded that the untoward event was completely predictable—that is, they demonstrated the hindsight bias. Then Roese asked them to counter that biased thinking with what-if thoughts: "If I had studied more, I might have passed." "If I had been more organized, I would have made my flight," and so forth.

These cognitive antidotes failed. The induced thoughts were meant to undo the delusional thinking, but in most cases they did the opposite—they reinforced the sense that the outcome was inevitable.

Imagined scenarios are tricky, however, and Roese wanted to test this idea in the real world. So he and one of his students, Sameep Maniar, decided to study the minds of football fans at nearby Northwestern University. Spectator sports provide an excellent psychology lab because the passionate involvement in the games can intensely focus both emotion and thinking—at least for a brief period of time. Any normal distortions in human reasoning are exaggerated.

Roese and Maniar picked three Northwestern football games during the 1995–96 season for study. Northwestern is part of the Big Ten Conference, and these were all conference games, and all played at Northwestern's Dyche Stadium: against Wisconsin in October, and then against Penn State and Iowa in November.

An unexpected twist made the studies even more intriguing than anticipated. Although Northwestern plays in the prestigious Big Ten Conference, the school is not a football powerhouse. In fact, the Wildcats are not very good compared to their conference rivals. But 1995–96 was a Cinderella season for the Wildcats. Against all expectations, the squad defeated all three of these rival teams; indeed, they crushed all three teams and went on to win an invitation to the 1996 Rose Bowl.

So it was a unique opportunity to study the hindsight bias. The psychologists asked Wildcats fans before each of these games to predict the likelihood of a Northwestern victory, and also to predict the point spread: Would they lose by more than ten points, or less than ten? Or would they win by more than ten, or less than ten? They also had them predict the likelihood that they would gain 350 yards in any of the games—an indicator of total dominance.

Then they watched the games. Afterward, the researchers corralled the same group of fans as they were shuttling back to campus and asked them to recall their expectations before the games were actually played. And as predicted, they found that the Wildcat boosters exaggerated their powers of prediction: even though theirs was an unrated team with low expectations for victory, the fans recalled otherwise, believing that they had known "all along" that upsets were in the making.

Then the psychologists tried to undo this delusional thinking. They had some of the fans imagine how the game might have turned out differently: "We might have lost if not for that penalty on the kickoff" or "If not for that fumble, we could have really dominated." The idea is that imagining an alternative outcome—an alternative to reality—might weaken the illusion of inevitability. But as with the lab studies of missed planes and failed exams, imagining a different past only served to reinforce and inflate the fans' belief that they "knew it all along." Their thoughts seem to go something like this: "Things could have gone otherwise, sure, but they *didn't*. It must be fate."

So what do we make of these cognitive peculiarities? Let's move outside the Wildcats stadium and beyond sports altogether. A sense of inevitability and predictability in life can certainly be tonic. It's calming to know that you don't have complete control over every outcome, and it's probably unhealthy to obsess about what might have been. Obsession can be paralyzing.

On the other hand, a little regret may not be a bad thing. Much counterfactual thinking is just that, regretting a mistake that we might have avoided, imagining how we could have made things turn out better. Such what-if thoughts happen on their own all the time, and it may be that hindsight delusions and regret are two sides of the same cognitive coin, partners in the mind. Indeed, it may be the interplay of these heuristic forces that lets us make sense of the world.

Robert Frost's 1920 poem "The Road Not Taken" captures this psychological dynamic more lyrically. The traveler in the poem faces two diverging paths in the woods and must make a choice. It's a difficult life choice, and after some internal debate he chooses. The final stanza captures the interplay of one's powerful sense of momentum and doubts about life's inevitability. He pictures himself in the future, looking back at his choice:

I shall be telling this with a sigh
Somewhere ages and ages hence:
Two roads diverged in a wood, and I—
I took the one less traveled by,
And that has made all the difference.

S O WE LAUGH at Wile E. Coyote for the same fundamental reason that we regret life choices. Our mind evolved in a dangerous
world of moving objects, and we adapted those physics lessons for
our modern sensibilities—and for a complex social world. Navigat-
ing this world is much more than avoiding falls and collisions. As the
next chapter on the fluency heuristic will show, our social world is
full of textual cues, ranging from the writing on a cereal box to stock
quotes to politicians' soaring rhetoric. Some of these cues are familiar, others strange, and how we react to them can shape everything
from our politics to how much risk we are willing to take in life.

4

The **FLUENCY** Heuristic

||||||||||||||||||||||||||||||||||||||||||||||||||||||||||||||||||||||||||||||||||||||||||||||||||||||||||||||||||||||||||||||||||||

THE POWER OF PENMANSHIP

I**T'S FUNDAMENTAL HUMAN** nature that people prefer what they already know. Familiarity influences how we process and comprehend just about every facet of the world—a face, a conversation, an op-ed piece, a stock prospectus, a ski slope.

To understand just how fundamental this bias is, consider this question: "How many animals of each kind did Moses take on the ark?"

It's a trick question, and if you took just a few seconds to deliberate, you probably figured that out. But most people, if they have to respond quickly to this question, say, "Two." That is, they don't really hear the actual question because they are on automatic pilot and the question has familiar elements. With a little mental work—very little, really—they would see the distortion and say: "Moses didn't take any animals onto an ark. Noah did." But it's easy to gloss over information, and we often don't even take a few seconds to analyze what's going on around us.

Cognitive psychologists call this common misperception the "Moses illusion." It's important to understanding how we navigate each day, because it's all about how we process and understand what we read, what people say—literally every utterance and text we encounter. Language is chock-full of distortions that can trip us up in many ways if we don't pay attention. But what determines whether we pay close attention or not?

Scientists have been using the Moses illusion to assess the potency of the fluency heuristic. The fluency heuristic is one of our most fundamental cognitive strategies, and its essence is that we are swayed by the ease and palatability of everything we encounter in our world. We not only process certain information more quickly and effortlessly, we like it more and trust it more.

Think about that trick question for another minute. What if, instead, I had asked you: "How many animals of each kind did Bill Clinton take on the ark?" You wouldn't have been fooled for a second—not a millisecond—because your brain would instantaneously see that Bill Clinton is not an acceptable substitute for Noah. There is no cognitive overlap. But Moses and Noah overlap: they are both ancient Biblical figures, men with beards who appear in stories having something to do with water. So it takes a little more work to sort out the distortion.

A growing number of psychologists speculate that the accessibility of language—its fluency—determines whether or not we slow our minds down enough to spot illogical thinking. Among them are Hyunjin Song and Norbert Schwarz of the University of Michigan, who have run a number of intriguing experiments to test this idea. In one, they simply asked a group of volunteers the trick question about Moses. For the purposes of the experiment the question was written on paper, and the psychologists used a simple but ingenious manipulation to make the text either cognitively accessible or challenging. Some got instructions printed in crisp black typeface, a plain font designed for easy reading, not unlike the one you are reading right now. Others got the question printed in light gray cursive script; it's unfamiliar and much harder to read.

The results are easily summarized. Those who read the question in the difficult-to-read typeface were much less likely to be tricked by the Moses illusion, and those who read the clear printing were much more likely to respond quickly (and erroneously) with "two." This may seem counterintuitive at first, but this is what the psychologists think is happening: The unfamiliar gray typeface was hard to process—it lacked fluency—so the brain was forced to slow down, to switch over to its more plodding, deliberate style. Once the brain slowed down to decipher the font, it also took time to notice the flaw in logic. To put this in terms of our dual-processor brain, the slow analytic brain trumped the rapid-fire brain, resulting in a sounder judgment.

But the fluency heuristic does not always work to our advantage, and here's where it gets interesting. Song and Schwarz ran the experiment again, exactly the same way, except they changed the question to this: "Which country is famous for cuckoo clocks, chocolate, banks, and pocket knives?" The correct (and easy) answer is "Switzerland," of course, and nine out of ten people who read the question in the clear black typeface got it right. Their automatic brain did the job. But of those who read the question in the difficult-to-read gray script, only about half got it right. That's a big difference, and really quite remarkable for such a familiar stereotype. But when the difficulty of the presentation made the slower, more deliberate brain click in, it overthought the question, making it more difficult than it had to be.

So the Switzerland test is an example of the fluency heuristic working well—automatically, without a lot of mental effort. But we have to be careful with this powerful bias because it can often lead to poor choices. Think about spending money, and all the financial decisions you must make every day. Is that mocha latte really worth $4? Will you finally write a $200 check to your chosen candidate? How about that $100,000 college education for your kid? Not a day goes by that we don't ask ourselves the question "So, what's it worth?"

Such questions have no absolute and universal answers, of course. That's what makes deciding so hard. Judgments of worth and value are a complex meld of attitudes and feelings about both money and thousands of commodities that defy comparison to one another. How can you say if hiring a plumber is worth more than buying a radio or a pet cat? Or if any of those things is worth the money in your wallet? Yet we make these market choices every day, confidently exchanging one thing for another.

Psychologists—especially a subgroup called behavioral economists—are very interested in how we value stuff. If these are not rational decisions, what are they? How does the brain sort through the impossible confusion of life's marketplace and arrive at a choice? Two scientists have taken the lead in investigating this problem, and they may have some clues to the subtle and surprising nature of these everyday decisions.

Princeton psychologist Daniel Oppenheimer and his New York University colleague Adam Alter believe that many of the economic decisions we make have little to do with objective value. Market choices have much more to do with the brain's basic internal perception of the world and the way those perceptions shape our feelings of comfort and ease. In this view, even currency has no clear and absolute value within one national economy. Regardless of those numbers on bills and coins, money derives its true value at least in part from the individual mind. In a series of experiments, these two psychologists have been studying the marketplace cues that trigger psychological comfort or discomfort, and thus shape us as economic beings. They've found that our economic behavior is driven by the same fluency heuristic at work in the Moses illusion.

The basic idea is that it's human nature to get anxious and wary when the world is strange or challenging. We're more at ease around the familiar and comprehensible. Think back to the avalanche fatalities described in the introduction. Most of them happened in places familiar to the victims. That's a version of the fluency bias, which is probably deep-wired from the days when the world was much more threatening. But the cues that signal us to be on guard in the modern social world—including the financial world—may not be obvious. Indeed, they may be almost undetectable at times. It's these nuanced signals that the psychologists have been exploring in the lab.

Here's an example of their work. Oppenheimer and Alter asked a group of volunteers to estimate how much of various commodities they could buy with a dollar. They were ordinary things like paper clips and gumballs and paper napkins. Some of the volunteers were given a regular old dollar bill, with George Washington on it, while others were given less familiar currency of the same value: a Susan B. Anthony $1 coin, for example. Invariably, the volunteers believed that the familiar old dollar bill was worth more—that it had more buying power—than the unusual currency.

That's not logical, of course. But it was not a fluke. They got the same result when they gave some people a rare $2 bill and others two singles. It's not as though people *never* see a $2 bill, and it does have Thomas Jefferson on it, after all. But just the slight unfamiliarity of the denomination was enough to make people devalue it. Why would this be? Oppenheimer and Alter believe this irrational behavior is rooted in our most fundamental mental processes: The world is full of stimuli of various kinds, some more familiar than others, and the brain is tuned to process the familiar ones rapidly, effortlessly, and intuitively. More difficult or alien cues require more mental work, more plodding deliberation; the brain switches to its more cautious and calculating style to be on the safe side. We intuitively know that familiar $1 bills are valuable items, but the dollar coin is an unknown commodity—and the difference shows just how hard it is for us to know the "value of a dollar."

This is humbling to know. But there's more. The psychologists wanted to see if the same cognitive bent shapes our perceptions and attitudes toward goods themselves, and they decided to use the typeface manipulation to find out. In this experiment, they gave everyone the same currency—the familiar dollar bill—but they made the commodities more or less accessible. Some of the "consumers" purchased the gumballs and paper clips from a form that was printed in a clear black font, while others had to select from a form printed in the difficult-to-read gray script—basically the same manipulation described before. The idea was to make the strangeness as subtle as possible, to reduce it to basic perception. Even at this most fundamental level, the differences shaped economic judgment: volunteers in the study consistently rated identical goods as less valuable when they came in an unfamiliar, cognitively challenging form. Many restaurants have recently switched to menus with very simple and clean design: sans serif fonts, uncluttered, with prices like 10 and 10.5 rather than the traditional dollars and cents. This research suggests that diners will respond positively to this stark simplicity.

These findings echo some earlier provocative studies of the stock market. In those studies, Oppenheimer and Alter looked at new stock offerings and found that companies with easy-to-read names were valued more highly by investors, at least in the short run. That is, companies with names like Barnings Incorporated consistently outperformed companies with names like Aegeadux Incorporated, simply because the names are more cognitively palatable.

So what do all these odd findings add up to? Well, the fluency bias is not a bad thing, even if it's a bit bizarre. In fact, such heuristics are essential to our everyday economic decision making. We'd be paralyzed if we tried to make every market choice logically, and the economic world would grind to a halt. But they should raise a cautionary flag as we head off to the mall of life every day.

And not just the mall. How about the workplace, the gym, or any other place where you need to motivate yourself? Can the complexity of the world actually inspire us to work or discourage us? Here's one way to think of it. Remember those old Rube Goldberg cartoons? Each of these comical inventions depicted a complex series of "instructions" for completing what should have been a fairly simple everyday task. His Self-Operating Napkin, for example, required a dozen sequential steps involving a parrot, a cigar lighter, a rocket, and a sickle, and of course various strings and springs and pendulums.

The cartoons were funny because they poked fun at some fundamental facts of human psychology. People will go to great lengths to avoid effortful tasks; it's human nature. Just think about sticking to that new exercise regimen or taking a course in statistics. Yet it also doesn't help to overexplain tasks, to make them more complicated than they need to be. Indeed, the opposite may be true: Rube Goldberg's convoluted how-to instructions may make us laugh, but they also leave us feeling exhausted. If that's what it takes to use a napkin, why bother?

Scientists study the complex interplay of motivation and cognitive effort—the ease with which we think about a task in our minds. Is it possible that the simplicity (or complexity) of how a task is described and processed—its fluid or difficult "feel"—actually affects our attitude toward the task itself, and ultimately our willingness to put our heads down and work?

This seems far-fetched at first glance, but the same two Michigan psychologists who did the Moses studies—Song and Schwarz—have made some tantalizing discoveries in their lab. They wanted to see if they could motivate a group of twenty-year-old college students to exercise regularly—not an easy task. They gave all the students written instructions for a regular exercise routine, but they used the typeface trick to make the how-to instructions either easy or difficult to comprehend. Some got instructions printed in the simple, clean Arial typeface, while others got their instructions printed in the Brush font, which looks like it's been written by hand with a Japanese paintbrush.

After the students had all read the instructions, the researchers asked them some questions about the exercise regimen: how long they thought it would take, whether it would flow naturally or drag on endlessly, whether it would be engaging or tedious, and so forth. They also queried them on whether they were likely to make exercise a routine part of their day in the future.

The findings were remarkable. Those who had read the exercise instructions in an unadorned, accessible typeface were much more open to the prospect of exercising: they believed that the regimen would take less time and that it would feel more effortless and easy. Most important, they were much more willing to make exercise part of their day—they planned on it. Apparently the students' brains mistook the ease of simply *reading* about exercise for ease of actually *doing* the sit-ups and bench presses, and this misunderstanding motivated them to actually think about a fairly significant life change. Those who struggled through the Japanese brushstrokes had no intention of heading to the gym. The reading alone tired them out.

These are not the kind of findings you accept based on just one experiment, and indeed Song and Schwarz revisited the question in several ways. One involved a completely unrelated activity: cooking. Not scrambling eggs, but learning a new cuisine—Japanese cooking, for the purposes of the experiment. Again they used easy- and hard-to-read typefaces, but in this case the instructions were a recipe for making a sushi roll. The volunteers read the recipe, then estimated how long it would take them to make the dish and whether they were inclined to do it. They were also asked how much skill a professional cook would need to prepare the sushi roll.

The results were basically the same as before, but in a completely unrelated realm of activity. Those who read the cooking instructions in the mentally challenging script saw the prospect of Japanese cooking as time-consuming and requiring a high level of culinary skill; they weren't apt to try it themselves. They in effect used the alien writing as a proxy for the actual task, and as a result ended up avoiding it. Those with the more digestible instructions were much more likely to sharpen their knives and head for the kitchen.

Our brains employ all sorts of tricks and shortcuts to get us through the day, but it's good to be wary of these automatic judgments. If unchecked, our tendency to confuse thoughts and actions can make dubious choices seem easier and more desirable than they ought to be, or they can discourage us from healthy habits and creative exploration. After all, most of the time, using a "self-operating" napkin is just as simple as it appears to be.

This use of strange typefaces is really just a convenient way to simulate the fluency heuristic in the lab, but it's not hard to imagine the real-world versions of this. Every single day we encounter information about the world that is presented to us in a thousand ways, some more accessible than others. Some of it rhymes, some is illustrated, some uses arcane vocabulary. Some of it is simply gobbledygook, and much of it is trying to persuade us to do something, one way or another.

Or warn us not to. The Michigan psychologists ran one more, similar study, only this one had to do with risk perception. It was also different from the typeface studies, because this one used pronunciation as the lab variable. That is, they wanted to see if the difficulty or ease of actually saying words affected attitudes and intentions.

So they took a group of volunteers to an amusement park. Not literally, but in a laboratory simulation they told volunteers to imagine a roller coaster and to estimate how risky the ride might be. For some, the roller coaster had a simple name, like the Chunta, while for others the ride had a nearly impossible-to-pronounce name, like the Vaiveahtoishi. The psychologists had them estimate both "good risk," that is, how exciting and adventurous it would be, and "bad risk," which for the purpose of the experiment was defined as likelihood that it would make them throw up.

Again, presentation mattered. Those assigned to the Vaiveahtoishi did think it would be more exciting, but they also found it threatening. They thought it was much more likely to make them queasy. In other words, the unfamiliarity of the word itself was enough to make them perceive their prospect as perilous.

We make risk decisions every single day, and often the downside to risk is much more frightening than throwing up on a thrill ride. Think back on the presidential election of 2008. Republican John McCain often gave halting and awkward speeches, and he was well aware that he was at a great disadvantage when it came to using the English language. That's why he tried again and again to dismiss Democrat Barack Obama's soaring speeches as "mere" eloquence.

But, as these studies show, eloquence is never mere. And the same holds true for disjointed use of the language. If something as superficial as the name of a roller coaster can scare people off, why wouldn't bumbling language make voters see a candidate's ideas as threatening? Conversely, Obama's accessible speeches probably made the substance of his ideas appear less threatening and more doable. McCain intuitively knew he had something real to fear in his opponent's lofty rhetoric.

THINK BACK TO those backcountry skiers out on Gobbler's Knob. It may feel odd to think of a snowy valley as "eloquent" or "fluid," but heuristically, that's exactly what led to these experienced skiers' poor judgment. They had trekked these Utah mountains so many times and knew the landscape so intimately that they never really slowed down to give it a close read. They were also heuristically linked to the other skiers—though they didn't know it. The fluency heuristic shapes the way individual minds interpret the world, but the fact is we are never truly independent agents in our highly social world. Many of the world's cues come not from a newspaper or a bank statement but from others just like us. We not only see and perceive their signals but respond on a very primitive level to those signs. More than we realize, we are tightly entwined with the minds of others, and our actions and attitudes are shaped by this interaction. This deep neuronal connection is called the mimicry heuristic, and it is the cognitive force that makes us social beings—and less-than-perfect decision makers.

5

The **MIMICRY** Heuristic

||||||||||||||||||||||||||||||||||||||||||||||||||||||||||||||||||||||||||||||||||||||||||||||||||||||||||||||||||||||||||||||

FEELING YOUR INNER APE

MOVING A COUCH into a third-story walk-up is one of those everyday miracles that isn't celebrated nearly enough. The couch is heavy and unwieldy, the staircase is steep and angular, and the banister is always in the way. There is no way you can manage this job by yourself, but the cousin who agreed to help out is surely more trouble than he's worth. Yet somehow you do it. Grunting, not speaking, often without eye contact, the two of you nudge and jostle and heave, and just when the threshold seems impossibly narrow . . . it's in!

But how? Men and their cousins have presumably been performing these feats of cooperation for centuries, eons probably, though perhaps with felled trees or mastodon haunches instead of couches. It's so fundamental to our nature that we don't even need to talk in order to coordinate; indeed, talking is often a hindrance. But how do we do it? How do we get two complex, independent nervous systems to work together on such a complicated task? The answer is the mimicry heuristic, which often works in subtle ways.

Northwestern University's Kyle Reed put together a team of psychologists and engineers to explore this phenomenon in a laboratory, to see how perception and touch combine in everyday acts of cooperation. He needed the engineers to devise a complex piece of equipment, one that basically simulates the act of cooperatively moving a couch up the stairs. Two laboratory "cousins" held the two ends of a crank; separated by a screen, they couldn't see each other or talk to each other, but together they had to manipulate the crank to play a rudimentary video game. Each also had a go at doing the task alone.

The findings, from hundreds of trials, were somewhat surprising. Each of the participants worked harder when paired with someone else, exerting more force on the crank than when they worked solo. But here's the counterintuitive part: the participants sensed that they were using the extra exertion to work against the partner, not with him. It was like being convinced your cousin is useless. Some volunteers actually complained afterward that the partner was more of a hindrance than a help.

But this perception was wrong. When the actual times were tallied, the participants consistently did better working together than either of them did working alone. The physical resistance that they felt the other exerting was real, but it was somehow contributing to their shared success. The researchers speculate that the two participants' physical contact, even though it was by way of a mechanical device, acted as an effective form of communication. They used this tugging and pulling to come up with a cooperative strategy that even they were unaware of.

This mundane activity illustrates an important point—that the mimicry heuristic acts constantly and out of awareness. We can all think of many more: a military battalion, Fred Astaire and Ginger Rogers, two lovers strolling hand in hand down a busy city sidewalk.

But the mimicry heuristic is not confined to acts of physical contact. That is probably how it originated, but today it influences all sorts of social interactions as well, for better or worse.

Consider this example from *Seinfeld.* Fans will recall the episode where the hapless George has a crush on Elaine's latest boyfriend, Tony. It's a nonsexual infatuation. George is attracted by Tony's confidence and daring, and wants desperately to be like him. At one point, George and Tony are at the diner, facing each other in a booth, and Tony has his baseball cap on backward. George is also wearing a cap, the conventional way, but as they chat, George gradually turns his own cap around. At the end of the scene, he is an exact mirror of his hero.

This bit of comedy captures the mimicry heuristic, the barely conscious aping that serves a vital part in human connection. It's not always as obvious as George's pathetic mirroring, but it is often literally a physical kind of imitation. I once had a colleague who, whenever I spoke to him, would inaudibly mouth my words, milliseconds later. There was no doubt that he was listening to me, because he always got my meaning, but while listening he would simultaneously move his lips. I am convinced he did not know he was doing this. And good thing too, because otherwise I would have felt that he was mocking me.

Well, it turns out that he was mocking me, though in a literal rather than malevolent way. My friend's tic may have been an aberration, but we all use (mostly undetectable) physical movement as a way to help us make sense of the world. Indeed, it turns out that perception is inextricably tied up with the brain cells that control movement. In order to understand me, he was "trying on" my actions for fit—or "reliving" them. We all do this kind of cognitive processing, though most of us do it internally, where it's not so distracting or annoying. Indeed, new research is demonstrating that the brain is hard-wired for aping, and that such mimicry is essential to our very existence as social beings.

But let me back up a bit. Psychologists used to think that perception and movement were two completely separate processes, lodged in different regions of the brain. The common wisdom was that we perceive the world with our eyes and ears and so forth, and send that information to the mind, which processes the data and in turn instructs the limbs and lips to act in certain ways. But apparently it's not so tidy. According to Rutgers University psychologists Günther Knoblich and Natalie Sebanz, the latest evidence suggests that it doesn't matter whether we're performing or observing. Each mental task activates the mind's mimicry heuristic.

This is why some undisciplined soccer fans twitch and squirm in their seats when they watch their favorite striker fake out an opponent. Or why even professional golfers try to use their hips to steer a putt toward the hole. Animal studies also provide biological evidence for this heuristic: the same nerve cells in monkeys' brains will fire whether the monkey grasps an object or watches someone else grasp it. Doing is a reflection of watching, and vice versa.

So the brain helps us—makes us—connect to the rest of humanity, but the neurons must also allow us to function as individual beings. To do that, according to Knoblich and Sebanz, we carry "common codes," or scripts, in our mind for specific kinds of movement, such as dancing or playing a video game. They are much like computer coding and, like computer coding, can be very precise. For example, the brains of highly trained dancers react more quickly and intensely to their dancing codes if they are watching the kind of dance they are trained in—ballet, say, or flamenco—than if they are watching something unfamiliar. And there is even more brain activity if the dancers are watching videos of themselves dancing rather than someone else. Knoblich and Sebanz speculate that this selective activation of the internal repertoire is what allows us to distinguish our own actions from those of others. Seeing ourselves in action has greater resonance in the neurons, even though we don't see ourselves all that often. There are also common codes for hearing: our brains respond to our own clapping or piano playing more than to someone else's, because our particular clapping or piano playing "style" is encoded in the mind.

Knoblich and Sebanz thought that the common code hypothesis might explain how we do things together, things such as playing duets, paddling a canoe, or moving a couch—all the things that make us social animals. They decided to do a scientific simulation of this dynamic. They devised a simple task in which participants, working together, had to push certain buttons in response to red and green lights. Then they tried to confuse just one of the participants with another stimulus. They found that both participants were thrown off by the distraction—and therefore more hesitant in their responses. It appears that people cannot help aping what others do, even when doing so hurts their own performance. I noticed this myself just recently, in the spinning class I take at my gym. With this kind of group exercise, you're *supposed* to mimic the leader, and I try my best to follow his pacing as closely as I can to get the full benefit. But if there is another spinner in the class who is pedaling at a noticeably slower or faster pace, I find it very difficult not to get out of sync with the instructor. I actually have to look away.

So there is a constant tension in the mind between the need to connect and the need to individuate—and studies of actual brain waves confirm this. When participants were asked to wait their turn but had to watch someone else, it took much more mental effort not to act than when they were waiting alone. The psychologists take all this evidence to mean that the mimicry heuristic is a crucial building block of all social understanding and social interaction. Indeed, it may be that over eons the demands of being social creatures have shaped our basic psychological processes, including perception, action, and cognition.

Many heuristics were first learned by the body but today are applied to a range of social activities. We looked at some of these visceral heuristics in Chapter 1. As with those primitive tendencies, the mimicry heuristic is sometimes a social lubricant, other times a trap. Here's an example: I attended an all-male college where the Greek system dominated residential and social life. Each year in the winter, most of the freshmen would rush a particular fraternity house, and rush week was little more than a ritualistic way of declaring: "Take me in, please. I'm just like you." The ones who were accepted would "pledge" themselves to the house. But many of the hopefuls were not accepted, and the rejects were often deeply disappointed.

The Greek system embodies much that is sad and unflattering about human nature, especially the cruelty of exclusion and the often desperate need to belong. Psychologists are very interested in these dynamics, because they apply beyond the frat house. Why is inclusion in groups and clubs so important to us, and what cognitive and emotional resources do we use to avoid rejection? Or, more important, to deal with the inevitability of rejection?

Psychologist Jessica Lakin of Drew University suspected that connecting is so essential to human functioning that we have deep-wired strategies for gaining entry to life's groups and clubs. But what are these strategies? One possibility, she theorized, is that people threatened with social isolation resort to automatic mimicry—a primitive, prelinguistic form of beseeching the in-group and pleading: "I really am just like you." Think back to George Costanza's insecure aping with his baseball cap. Lakin and her colleagues set out to prove this connection between physical mimicry and desire for belonging.

Lakin had a group of student volunteers play Cyberball, an arcade game loosely based on American football. The volunteers thought they were playing with and against other volunteers, but in fact a computer was controlling much of the play. The computer was programmed to "include" some players—that is, give them the ball about as often as everyone else got it—and to "exclude" others. The volunteers came away from the game feeling either accepted or rejected by their fellow students.

When the Cyberball game was over, the scientists devised another ruse, which they videotaped. They had the students sit alone in a room for a bit and videotaped their natural foot movements. Apparently some people naturally fidget more than others, and the scientists used this natural movement as a baseline for the study. After videotaping the volunteers, a young woman entered the room, ostensibly to take part in a shared task. But the task was fake; the woman was part of the experiment, and her real purpose in the room was to deliberately move her foot around, back and forth, up and down. She was a hired fidgeter.

The idea was to see if the volunteers increased their own foot movements once the woman entered the room and began her deliberate movements. They wanted to see if the students who were feeling rejected after Cyberball did more unconscious aping than those who felt included. And that's precisely what they found. People apparently "recover" from rejection by unconsciously attempting, through physical mimicry, to affiliate with someone new: "Hey, I may not be like them, but I'm just like you!"

But the "someone new" in this study was basically the first person to come along. She didn't do the actual rejecting. Lakin and her colleagues wanted to see if this unconscious mimicry is indeed indiscriminate, or if people use these rudimentary attempts at affiliation more strategically when (as in most of real life) they know who is rejecting them. So in a second experiment, only female volunteers played the Cyberball game, some against men and some against other women; some were rejected and others, not. Then they all took part in the foot movement study as before.

The psychologists predicted that the women would feel rejection more acutely if rejected by other women, their "in-group," and that these rejects would subsequently make a greater and more selective effort to win over another woman rather than a man. And again that's what they found. Even though the mimicry and supplication were completely outside of conscious awareness, they were strategically targeted at those in the in-group. Put bluntly, rejects didn't kiss up to just anyone simply because their feelings were bruised. They had a clear goal: to belong to the group that didn't want them.

It shouldn't be surprising that the need for belonging is so basic to our nature. The "clubs" of our primordial ancestors were basically survivalist groups, and rejects didn't last out on the savanna alone. But rejection is not often life threatening these days, and the desperation to be included appears not nearly so adaptive as it does unseemly.

The fraternities of my day had this especially perverse ritual called "post-rush." Sometimes a house would not get as many new pledges as it had hoped, so a couple of weeks later it would host beer parties and such to let the rejects try again. Here's where the real bathos played out. Already excluded once from membership in the club, the also-rans would do anything they could to show that their rejection had been a mistake and they really did belong: they would laugh unnaturally, drink inappropriately, and vigilantly scan the room for any clue to how a real fraternity man acts. Everything short of yelling outright, "Hey, I'll do anything! I'm just like you!" They're desperate to be accepted into a group that's already proved itself too exclusive for them. This brings to mind the dark humor of Groucho Marx, who quipped: "I refuse to join any club that would accept people like me as members."

Not all social mimicry is so sad. Indeed, this basic human impulse may play a crucial role in the cohesion of groups and societies. Think about this: There was a time when soldiers went into battle in columns and rows. They would line up and march in orderly formation toward the enemy, armed with spears or bayonets or some other weapon of close combat. The enemy would do the same thing, and one of these well-oiled formations would kill more soldiers than the other—and win the battle.

Advances in firearms long ago made the marching formation obsolete. It just doesn't work with machine guns and IEDs. Yet armies all over the world still train for this archaic kind of warfare, drilling soldiers in precision and synchrony that will almost certainly never be used on a battlefield.

Why is that? Or for that matter, why do high schools have marching bands? Why do churches have choirs? And perhaps most perplexing of all, why does synchronized swimming even exist? What is it about moving and chanting and singing in unison that appears to have universal appeal?

Anthropologists and cultural historians have offered up a variety of theories about synchrony over the years, mostly having to do with group coherence. One theory, for example, holds that various communities benefit from the actual physical synchrony, or "muscular bonding," which builds group cohesiveness. Another idea is that synchronous activities lead to "collective effervescence"—positive emotions that break down the boundaries between self and group.

But neither of these theories has been proven, and what's more, neither is complete. Muscle bonding may explain the coherence of the 14th Infantry Regiment, but those guys don't seem very effervescent—not in the way that, say, carnival revelers are. And gross motor coordination doesn't explain the almost motionless chanting of a roomful of Tibetan monks. Psychologists have been looking for a unifying theory for the appeal of synchrony.

One idea, put forth by psychologists Scott Wiltermuth and Chip Heath of Stanford University, is that all synchrony—movement, sound, and both together—is an ancient ritual that evolved for the economic benefit of the group. The primary goal of rhythmic dancing, marching, and chanting is to solve the problem of the free-loader—the community member who hurts the collective good by taking but not contributing. Here's how they demonstrated this idea in a series of laboratory experiments.

In the simplest version, the researchers simply took groups of Stanford students on walks around campus; some were instructed to walk in step—marching, basically—while others just strolled the way students usually stroll. Later, after the students thought the experiment was over, the psychologists gave them all what's called the "weak link test." In this test, each volunteer chooses to act either self-interestedly or cooperatively—giving or withholding resources—depending on what he anticipates others will do. The test basically measures the expectation that others will value the group over themselves.

The marchers acted more cooperatively than the strollers. They also said that they felt more "connected" than did the strollers. Notably, they did not report feeling any happier, suggesting that positive emotions were not necessary for achieving the boost in group cohesiveness.

The psychologists wanted to do a more fine-grained test of their idea. It's well known that a sense of common identity and shared fate boosts group cohesiveness, but the researchers wanted to see if synchrony contributes to group cohesiveness above and beyond this. They did a rather elaborate test to sort this out. They had students perform tasks—moving plastic cups—that required differing degrees of coordination with others. While doing this, they listened to "O Canada" through headphones; some sang along and some didn't. Remember that these were Stanford students, so the Canadian national anthem presumably had no emotional resonance for them; singing was merely a synchronous act.

So some of the students sang and moved the cups in rhythm, while others just sang in unison with the song and others merely read the lyrics silently. Still others sang and moved to different tempos—sort of like a really bad dancer moving at odds with the music. Then the researchers did the same weak link test on all of them. As before, those who had experienced synchrony were more cooperative and community-minded than those who had not. The bad dancers were bad citizens, but the physical movement otherwise made no difference; choral singers were selfless with or without the swaying, suggesting that muscle bonding is (like joy) unnecessary to get the desired group coherence. The swaying may be enjoyable, but the group singing was sufficient.

Wiltermuth and Heath did this "O Canada" experiment again, but instead of the weak link test they used what's called the "public goods game." This game uses tokens, and participants choose whether to contribute to a public kitty or their own private savings account. Self-interest has a higher payoff in the game for individuals, but the group benefits more if everyone acts unselfishly—so there's a conflict between self and community. They got the same results as before, but the interesting finding was this: the game has several rounds, and over time the choral singers increased their contribution to the group, keeping less money for themselves. They gave much more to the community fund in the last round than they did in the first, suggesting that the synchrony has persistent and growing effects.

The choral singers also said they felt more part of the team. They felt they had more in common with the others, and they trusted them somewhat more. Interestingly, they also made more money in the end, because they shared in the group bounty.

So synchrony rituals are powerful. So powerful they may have endowed certain groups with a competitive advantage over the eons, perhaps even causing some cultures to flourish while others perished. It's no wonder then that such powerful impulses remain entrenched in today's churches and armies—even in ritual for ritual's sake, such as synchronized swimming.

Is there a downside to this highly prized synchrony? Our tightly entwined nervous systems may benefit the community, but how about the individual? Some psychologists are now exploring the possibility that we pay a price for our cohesion. Think about it this way. I used to jog a fair bit, and when I did I loved having a regular running partner. It's not that I'm undisciplined, but my friend's company nudged me to run just a bit farther or faster than I might on my own. And some days the encouragement went the other way. It's as if we drew motivation and stamina from each other's presence.

This will come as no surprise to anyone who has ever enlisted a friend to go on a diet or joined a group to quit smoking or drinking. But is it possible that we might also be emotionally and physically depleted by others' efforts? In other words, can your self-discipline literally wear me out?

Psychologists are very interested in the power of vicarious thoughts and feelings because they have clear implications for everything from public health campaigns to personnel management. What if cohesion and camaraderie are actually taking an unseen toll on workers, dieters, and recovering addicts?

Yale University psychologist Joshua Ackerman and colleagues wondered if we might automatically and unconsciously simulate the behavior of others around us—and if such internal aping might lead to real mental exhaustion and breakdown of discipline. They devised a couple of clever experiments to test this theory of vicarious depletion.

In one study, they had a group of volunteers read a story about a waiter at a fancy restaurant. The waiter arrives at work hungry, but he is prohibited from eating any of the restaurant food. The story describes in mouthwatering detail the meals that the hungry waiter must serve: imagine cold poached salmon, roast chicken and fresh asparagus, chocolate mousse cake. Some simply read the story, but others were told to put themselves in the waiter's shoes, to imagine his thoughts and feelings.

Then all the volunteers played a version of *The Price Is Right.* They estimated the value of goods like watches and cars and major appliances and bid on them. The idea was to see if vicariously experiencing the waiter's self-discipline would deplete the volunteers' own self-discipline—and if that depletion would affect their behavior in a completely unrelated realm, namely, shopping. Would the torture of denying oneself all that delicious food make the volunteers into spendthrifts?

It did, dramatically. Those who suffered along with the fictional waiter spent a full $6,000 more than the others on imaginary luxury items. The psychologists did a separate test of mood just to rule out the possibility that they were not squandering their cash because of grumpiness. They weren't. It appears they exhausted their reserve of self-discipline in the restaurant and that the exhaustion carried over.

The psychologists wanted to double-check these findings using a more realistic and complex scenario. Some of the volunteers did the same hungry-waiter exercise, but others read about a well-fed waiter who worked in a mediocre fast-food joint. Afterward the psychologists had them complete a difficult and time-pressured word problem—one known to tax a host of executive skills including concentration, motivation, and information processing.

The results were interesting and not entirely expected. Again, those who actively empathized with the hungry waiter became cognitively depleted, leading to inferior performance on the problem-solving task. But those who merely witnessed the waiter's self-control were better problem solvers than those who witnessed the well-fed waiter. That is, seeing someone exert control sparked the idea of discipline and reinforced the goal, but actually experiencing the denial led to vicarious exhaustion.

This raises an intriguing possibility. It's well known that dysfunctional groups don't perform well, but these findings suggest that group coordination can also work too well. That is, if group members—workers, exercisers, addicts—are too tightly synchronized with one another, the exhaustion of one group member can spread to the entire group. Despite its name, self-control is a social enterprise, which means that our own successes and failures may be shaped by others more than we like to think.

||

I T'S A MYTH that lemmings dive off cliffs just because one lemming did. But humans do something similar, and just as dangerous. We've all witnessed this: A group of people are standing at a busy intersection, waiting to cross with the light, and one pedestrian decides to jaywalk. Without thinking—letting the mimicry heuristic take over—others follow the leader into the street, into traffic against the light. We can be too close to others, too connected. That's why the word *crowding* has such negative connotations. Despite our social impulses, we have a deep psychological need and yearning for space and distance, as the next chapter on the mapmaker heuristic will illuminate.

6

The **MAPMAKER** Heuristic

|||||||||||||||||||||||||||||||||||||||||||||||||||||||||||||||||||||||||||||||||||||||||||||||||||||||||||||||||||||||||||||||||||||||||||||||||||||||||||||||

GETTING AWAY FROM IT ALL

I AM THE SON of a map salesman. Every morning when I was growing up, my father would leave the house in his car, the trunk stuffed with maps and atlases and globes, and he would sell them to geography teachers and librarians throughout eastern Pennsylvania. I loved my dad's job, because it meant our home was also overflowing with my father's wares, and I would spend hour upon hour poring over the atlases, spinning the globes, or just staring at the various maps on my bedroom wall.

I still do this when I'm alone and have the time. And I've learned from my friends that I'm not the only one who finds maps seductive. It's not just the romance, imagining the cultures of Mozambique or Iceland or Bali. It's the maps themselves. I love local maps as much as global maps, and I now even love Google maps, with their street-level views of communities around the country.

What is it about a map that resonates so deeply in us? It's as if there's a universal explorer and mapmaker residing in our neurons—but why? Psychologists have some ideas about this deep, internal connection between physical space and distance on one hand, and thought and emotion on the other—or what we might call personal geography. We've all had the sensation of being "too close" to a situation, needing to "get away" and "put some distance" between ourselves and others. Our sense of emotional connectedness (or lack of it) is tightly entangled with our perception of geography and patterns in space.

Although the word *geography* summons up faraway foreign lands, in fact our personal geography begins at home. Indeed, it begins with the floor plan of your house or apartment. A perfect example of this is the ancient Chinese practice called feng shui. I tend to be a New Age skeptic, but feng shui has always had some intuitive appeal to me. It's basically the art of placement, and it's based on the belief that space, distance, and the arrangement of objects can affect our emotions and our sense of well-being. This makes sense to me on a gut level: I know that I feel a greater sense of psychological equilibrium in some spaces than I do in others. I just never knew why.

Scientists have been exploring the power of these perceptions in the laboratory, to see if indeed an ordered and open space affects people's emotions differently than a tighter, more closed-in environment. Put another way, do we automatically extract feelings from spaciousness and crowding?

Yale University psychologists Lawrence Williams and John Bargh have been running a research project that illuminates the mapmaker heuristic. All of their studies begin with what's called "priming"—the use of a cue to create an unconscious attitude or sensation. In one experiment, for example, they used a very simple but well-tested technique: they had respondents graph two points, just as you would on an ordinary piece of graph paper, but for some the points were very close together (for example, 2 and 4 and −3 and −1), while for others they were far away (12 and 10 and −8 and −10). This is rudimentary mapmaking, and it's known to bolster people's unconscious feeling of either congestion or wide-open spaces.

After priming the volunteers' internal mapmakers, they then tested them in various ways. For example, in one study they had the participants read an embarrassing excerpt from a book, then asked them if the passage was enjoyable or entertaining, whether they'd like to read more of the same, and so forth. They wanted to see if a sense of psychological distance and unfettered freedom might mute emotional discomfort—and it did. Those who had been primed for spaciousness were less discomfited by the embarrassing experience; they found it much more enjoyable than did those with a hemmed-in perception of the world.

This is an example of a hard-wired heuristic spilling over into the world of emotions. The brain takes a fundamental yearning—in this case for spaciousness and freedom—and overgeneralizes it to something completely unrelated: embarrassment. The psychologists ran another version of the same experiment, except that the book excerpt was extremely violent rather than embarrassing. They got the same basic results. Those who had been primed for closeness found the violent events much more aversive—just as we find an airplane crash in our own neighborhood much more upsetting than a crash three thousand miles away. Williams and Bargh believe this has to do with the brain's deep-wired connection between distance and safety, a habit of mind that likely evolved when our hominid forebears' survival was a much more precarious matter.

The psychologists wanted to explore more directly this link between psychological distance and real peril, and they did so in an unorthodox way. Again they primed the participants' minds, and then they had them estimate the number of calories in both healthy food and junk food. Their reasoning was that the calories in french fries and chocolate are perceived as a health threat—emotionally dangerous—whereas the calories in brown rice and yogurt are not, so that people primed for closeness would be more sensitive to the threat. And that's indeed what they found. Those who had been made to feel crowded and closed in thought there were more calories in junk food than did those feeling open and free. Their perceptions of healthy food were identical.

. That's pretty convincing evidence for a primal link between distance and emotional needs. But Williams and Bargh decided to run one more test, one that dealt head-on with the issue of personal security. They asked all the subjects about the strength of their emotional bonds to their parents, siblings, and hometown, and found that those primed for greater psychological distance expressed weaker ties even to these important emotional anchors. Or put another way, they had more emotional detachment from the world. Detachment and isolation are apparently the flip side of freedom.

. What's remarkable is that this all takes place unconsciously, out of awareness. The spatial distance between two arbitrary objects (in this case, merely two dots on a graph) is apparently powerful enough to activate an abstract sense of distance and emotional detachment in the brain, which in turn is powerful enough to shape our responses to the world.

This emotional detachment could very well explain the tonic effects of feng shui. But now think bigger—not the geography of your apartment but one of long distances. Distance shapes thinking in the sense that things that are visible but far away have no concrete detail; they are outlines or approximations, abstractions. Just as houses are mere shapes in the distance, so too are problems, challenges, arguments—they all become more hazy and rarified. Psychologists now think that emotional distance both influences and is influenced by actual distance: if something is distant, we feel it as more typical, more categorical than concrete and specific, perhaps more hypothetical. They call this "high-order thinking."

But why would our brains "see" and measure out emotional needs in inches and yards and miles? What does perspective—the kind we perceive with our eyes—have to do with perspective in our social world? New York University psychologists Kentaro Fujita and Marlone Henderson are among those who have been studying this psychological connection in the lab. They performed a couple of simple experiments in which they asked people to imagine a variety of ordinary, everyday events. For example, in one study they asked volunteers to imagine helping a friend move into a new apartment. But in some cases, they were told to imagine the event taking place nearby (just outside New York City, about three miles away), while others were told to imagine the same task taking place at a great distance (outside of Los Angeles, about three thousand miles away).

The researchers then asked the participants to imagine (and describe) a series of behaviors related to helping their friend move: locking a door, for example, and paying the rent. The findings were interesting. Those who imagined helping their friend nearby tended to think in rudimentary, mechanical terms. So locking a door became, in the volunteers' words, "putting a key in the lock," and paying the rent became simply "writing a check."

By contrast, those who had some distance from an event tended toward higher-level interpretations that emphasized a behavior's meaning. Thus locking the door was construed as "securing the house" and paying the rent was "maintaining a place to live." This striking difference was seen even with actions that had nothing to do with moving or living space. For example, those close to the imagined event described climbing a tree as "holding on to branches," while those at some remove thought in terms of "getting a good view." Similarly, the word *travel* for some may mean merely purchasing a ticket and boarding a plane, while for others it may conjure up something psychologically grander, more akin to "getting away from it all."

So distance gives us meaning. Or put another way, geographical mileage and psychological distance are just different dimensions of the same basic heuristic impulse. The brain appears to orient itself according to the world it perceives, and this mental orientation shapes thinking, problem solving, and so forth. In another interesting example from the NYU lab, the psychologists had some volunteers imagine they were on the NYU campus in Manhattan, while others imagined themselves in Florence, Italy. Then they gave them a series of problems to consider. For example, NYU students in Manhattan (or Florence) sleep between 6.3 and 7.1 hours a night, with an average of 6.7 hours. What is the likelihood that a student will sleep more than 6.2 hours?

Duh, 100 percent, right? You didn't read that wrong. They have the answer right in front of them. And indeed the students thinking about being in Italy did say this, in effect: "Duh, very likely." But here's the curious finding: the students thinking about the same problem close to home, in Manhattan, said it was less likely that the student would sleep more than 6.2 hours. That is, they expected the student to be an outlier, to fall outside the normal range. The psychologists ran this experiment with very different problems—rainfall, number of photocopies, visits to health clinics—and consistently found the same result. Those primed for long distance expected predictable pattern and typical behavior; they did not think about aberrations, as those close to home did.

Now let's add another dimension to these findings. If geographical distance and space are so powerful in shaping thinking and ideas, shouldn't time—often called the fourth dimension—also influence our thoughts and emotions? And shouldn't time also influence our perceptions of arguments? In other words, is it possible that near or distant messages and arguments are more or less persuasive?

Scientists have studied this in some fascinating ways. In one experiment in Israel, for example, student volunteers were told to imagine that they had found a DVD player for sale on the Internet. In some cases, the imaginary sale was right now, this week, while in others it was three months off. Then they read various arguments—sales pitches, really—for the DVD player: two-year warranty, student discount, high-quality digital sound, and so forth. In addition to those details, some volunteers also read that the DVD player was made of environment-friendly materials; others read that it came with a user-friendly manual.

The idea was that the environment-friendly materials made the player more desirable in an abstract and idealistic way, while the user-friendly manual made the product more practical, more feasible in a very concrete way. The researchers suspected that there would be interplay between time and these different features, so that those contemplating a future sale would focus on the ideal DVD player, while those buying now would focus on the practical matter of getting it home and hooked up as efficiently as possible.

And that's what the experiment showed. Apparently the brain automatically translates temporal distance into psychological distance into idealized, abstract thinking. Think about the 2008 presidential campaign, which took almost two years. None of the major candidates' stump speeches dealt with the difficult nitty-gritty of trying to get their proposed policies implemented—the obstructionist Congress, the lobbying pressures, the inevitable trade-offs. The speeches were all about ideals and values and change and belief— because that's what resonates most for voters looking way off into the future, past inauguration day. Actual policies were drawn in the broadest strokes, if at all, because people want to think about the future in ideals and abstractions, not details and difficulties. As the old political bromide says: we campaign on poetry, we govern in prose. Only after the inauguration did President Obama have to own up to the practicalities of actually making change happen. (I will be discussing time and thinking in a slightly different way in Chapter 12, on the futuristic heuristic.)

So time and distance mold the shape of persuasive arguments.

But does that include arguing with ourselves? What about the daily business of trying to persuade our better selves to do the right thing? In fact, there is some preliminary evidence that psychological distance can influence self-control. Here is just one example of this new line of inquiry.

In theory, greater distance from a situation should lead to more high-level, idealized thinking, and thus to greater self-control. Self-discipline requires seeing the big picture, the proverbial forest for the trees—not getting bogged down in painstaking calculation of effort and reward. The experiment focused on good health and healthy behavior, but the researchers framed the issue in two different ways for different volunteers. Some volunteers viewed a flow chart with four boxes connected by arrows, bottom to top. The bottom box contained the words "Maintain good physical health" and each subsequent box asked a "why" question: "Why do I maintain good physical health?" If the answer was "To do well in school," the next question was: "Why do you want to do well in school?" And so forth. The other volunteers did basically the same thing, except they answered "how" questions: "How do you maintain good health?" "By exercising." "How do you exercise?" And so on.

The idea was to get the volunteers thinking either in an abstract, theoretical way (why) or in a very practical way (how). Then the psychologists gave all the volunteers various tests of their willingness to delay gratification—a classic element of self-control. How much would they pay for a DVD player now versus later, or for a restaurant meal? They discovered that those who had been primed to think about why they wanted to be healthy—the ideal of good health—were more apt to delay rewards. That is, they showed more self-discipline.

The psychologists followed up this study with a more direct measure of self-control. They did the same priming of high- and low-level thinking, then had the volunteers squeeze a handgrip—the exercise tool commonly used to strengthen forearms—for as long as they could stand it. After controlling for differences in individual strength, they found that the abstract thinkers showed greater endurance and more tolerance for discomfort. In short, more self-control.

This is striking when you think of it all together. Just projecting into the distant future triggers the brain to think abstractly, and abstract thinking is sufficient to actually increase physical endurance.

But is there a downside to psychological distance and abstract, idealized thinking? A time when it's best to be up close and practical? Well, sure. Idealistic thinking focuses on the ideals at the expense of the practicalities. Think of the English settlers who in the seventeenth century left their homeland to found new colonies in Virginia and Massachusetts. These courageous colonists imagined creating idealized societies, far from the persecution and economic miseries they knew in England.

But these Utopian thinkers failed to think through the small stuff, such as mosquitoes, potable water, bellicose natives, and harsh winters, which many settlers in fact didn't survive. They weren't thinking about feasibility, but rather were motivated and guided by thoughts of a higher order. No surprise they forged their visions five thousand miles away.

Here's an example that almost everyone can relate to on some level: procrastination. Every one of us has a list of projects, a to-do list: updating that resume, cleaning out the attic, starting that exercise routine. But the sad reality is that most of us do not follow through on these commitments, and not because we're insincere. We just never get to day one. Tomorrow is always a better time to get going.

And tomorrow and tomorrow and tomorrow. Procrastination is a curse, and a costly one. Putting things off leads not only to lost productivity but also to all sorts of hand-wringing, regrets, and damaged self-esteem. For all these reasons, psychologists would love to figure out what's going on in the mind that makes it so hard to actually do what we intend to do. Are we fundamentally misguided in the way we think about plans and effort and work? Is there some perverse habit of mind that automatically dampens our sense of urgency? Are we programmed for postponement and delay?

Consider this work by an international team of psychologists. Led by Sean McCrea of the University of Konstanz in Germany, the researchers wanted to see if there might be a link between how we think of a task and our tendency to postpone it. In other words, are we more likely to see some tasks as psychologically "distant"—and thus to consign them to some vague future rather than tackle them now? McCrea and his colleagues suspected that this cognitive oddity might show up in the way we think about time and tasks. That is, vague, abstract tasks might be easier to mentally postpone into the future than concrete tasks.

Here's a glimpse of how they tested this. The psychologists handed out questionnaires to a group of students and asked them to respond by e-mail within three weeks. All the questions had to do with rather mundane tasks like opening a bank account and keeping a diary, but different students were given different instructions for answering the questions. Some were instructed to think and write about what each activity implied about personal traits: what kind of person has a bank account, for example. Others wrote simply about the nuts and bolts of doing each activity: speaking to a bank officer, filling out forms, making an initial deposit, and so forth. The idea again was to get some students thinking abstractly and others concretely.

Then the researchers waited. And in some cases waited and waited. They recorded all the response times to see if there was a difference between the two groups, and indeed there was—a big difference. Even though the students were all being paid upon completion, those in a what-does-it-all-mean mentality were much more likely to procrastinate—and in fact some never got around to the assignment at all. By contrast, those who were focused on the how, when, and where of doing the task e-mailed their responses much sooner, suggesting that they hopped right on the assignment rather than delaying it.

This makes sense in an odd sort of way. When you first think about the possibility of trying something new, you're focused on why: What's the purpose? Does it make sense for me to do this? It's still just a distant possibility, and these are the things that matter. Only as you get closer to actually taking on the task do you start to think of the more immediate how-to details. So conversely, thinking about the how-to of a job gives it immediacy—and urgency.

Even so, the scientists decided to double-check their initial findings with a different kind of laboratory technique. In this experiment, volunteers were told to complete sentence fragments, either in an abstract or a concrete way. For example, some might complete this fragment: "An example of a bird is _____." Others completed this kind of fragment: "A bird is an example of _____." The first requires a concrete example (an indigo bunting, for example, or scarlet tanager), while the second asks for an abstract category (warm-blooded vertebrates, say). So again the experiment primed one cognitive style or the other, and again the psychologists logged in the e-mail response times.

As expected, those primed for concrete thinking were much less apt to delay and postpone than were those primed for abstract thinking. They saw the task as more immediate and acted with more urgency. Those prompted to give vague and amorphous answers were inclined to procrastinate.

Lots of psychology experiments don't have a practical take-home message, but these do. You know that exercise routine you've been talking about starting up in January? Well, forget about how virtuous it is, or how healthy, or how it might boost your confidence. Instead, think about arriving home this afternoon and putting on your sneakers and tying them, one at a time; entering the front door of the gym and walking to the first treadmill you see; stepping aboard and starting to move your legs, right leg first.

I AM WRITING THIS during flu season, and this year we have not only the seasonal variety but the dreaded H1N1 swine flu as well. A new study shows that seeing someone sneeze in public is enough to trigger fears of serious health problems—not only sicknesses such as the flu but heart attacks and injuries resulting from accidents and crime. A sneeze will even boost support for health care reform. None of this makes any sense, of course. But it shows just how influential this whole class of bodily heuristics can be in our lives. The six chapters that make up this first section of the book all deal, in one fashion or another, with the body in the wide world. Sometimes the body is shivering, and sometimes it is climbing; other times it is contemplating travel and distance. The world is sometimes vast, other times in motion, other times full of risks and trials and promise. The point is that ancient humans learned to move through the world in a very rudimentary way, and these basic perceptual and navigation skills became embedded in our neurons; today they shape our emotions and actions in surprising and not always beneficial ways. The same evolving brain learned to make primitive calculations, to weigh odds and risks, to size up the world in quantities. Along the way, we have come to "feel" numbers, and today these numerical heuristics are at least as potent as the bodily brand. Let's start with the most basic of them all: the arithmetic heuristic.

Two

NUMBERS IN OUR NEURONS

The **ARITHMETIC** Heuristic

||||||||||||||||||||||||||||||||||||||||||||||||||||||||||||||||||||||||||||||||||||||||||||||||||||||||||||||||||||||||||||||||||||||||||||||||||||||||||||||||||||||||||||

"FOR JUST PENNIES A DAY"

A FUNNY SCENE FROM *Peggy Sue Got Married* has stuck with me since that movie came out way back in 1986. The middle-aged Peggy Sue, distraught about her failing marriage, has been improbably transported back to her high school days. But she is completely aware of everything in her future life, so when she finds herself sitting in algebra class once again, she can't even pretend she cares. She blows off the exam, and when the disgruntled math teacher demands that she explain, she says dismissively: "I happen to know that in the future I will not have the slightest use for algebra."

Many people would no doubt applaud Peggy Sue, as a few did in the theater more than two decades ago. There is a general sense that, beyond basic arithmetic, math is only useful for future math teachers, to torment another generation of high school students. Unhappily, such disdain for numbers has left a lot of Americans mathematically illiterate—or "innumerate," in the coinage of experts. New evidence suggests that inept everyday mathematicians make unwise judgments and regrettable decisions in everything from personal health to real estate. What's more, those of us who are bad with numbers appear more likely to make bad choices because we are under the sway of our own unchecked emotions.

Psychologist Ellen Peters works at Decision Research, a nonprofit company in Eugene, Oregon, that studies human judgment and choice. She is particularly interested in a phenomenon called "framing"—an idea in decision science that refers to the way information is presented, how life's questions are posed. So, for example, people rate a hamburger as tastier and less greasy if it is labeled 75 percent lean rather than 25 percent fat. They really do: this has been shown in the lab, and it's a good example of everyday innumeracy.

It's also a good example of the arithmetic heuristic in action. This is one of the most robust cognitive tools in our repertoire—and one of the most perilous. The arithmetic heuristic has mostly to do with the emotional content of numbers. Also known as the "affect heuristic," this mental shortcut causes our minds to assign emotional meaning to objective information—numbers, percentages, fractions, statistics. In fact, because numbers are so difficult for many of us to thoroughly process and understand, they are in a sense more susceptible to this emotional bias.

Peters and her colleagues decided to systematically examine the connection between innumeracy, framing, and emotion—emotion because choosing 75 percent lean over 25 percent fat is obviously not a purely logical choice. They did a set of experiments comparing mathematically savvy people with the mathematically challenged. Let's call them the nerds and the dimwits, just to save space. I put myself squarely in the dimwit camp, so I'm not shy about using the label.

In one experiment, Peters asked volunteers to judge whether a mentally ill patient, recently released from the hospital, posed a danger to others in the months ahead. Sometimes they were told that ten of a hundred patients "like Mr. Jones" tend to commit acts of violence, while at other times they were told that 10 percent do so. This was not meant to stigmatize the mentally ill, and may or may not be an accurate portrayal, but it was deliberately chosen to bring people's fears into play in their judgments. The result? The dimwits were far less fearful of the released patient if they were labeled with a percentage rather than a number.

It appears that simply expressing a particular statistic as a percentage seems to diminish its power—at least for people who struggle a bit with numbers. Indeed, many studies have shown that more abstract percentages consistently conjure up harmless images in the mind, whereas real numbers create frightening images: ten, count them, ten former mental patients on the loose. The nerds, on the other hand, since they are comfortable with changing fractions and percentages back and forth, were not fooled by the ruse.

Peters designed several more tests to get at this dynamic in more detail. Here's just one, known as the "jelly bean study." In a large bowl, there are one hundred jelly beans, nine red and the rest white. In a second, smaller bowl, there are ten jelly beans, one of which is colored red. Now, it doesn't take a nerd to see that the odds of picking a colored bean are better with the small bowl: one in ten. What's more, the bowls are clearly labeled 9 percent red and 10 percent red, to give the dim-witted every chance to make a smart choice. Yet they didn't when Peters ran the study. When told they could win money by blindly picking a colored jelly bean, they were far more likely to pick from the larger bowl despite the poorer odds of winning.

Psychologists have colorful names for the illogical way that dimwits treat percentages and ratios. Peters and her colleague Paul Slovic call it the "benign percentage," because inexplicably we don't find percentages as frightening as numbers. Cornell psychologists Valerie Reyna and Charles Brainerd use the phrase "denominator neglect" to describe the jelly bean phenomenon: many of us illogically prefer

$^9/_{100}$ odds to $^1/_{10}$ odds, meaning that we get overly focused on the top number, the numerator—which blinds us to the all-important denominator. But we neglect it at our own peril.

The colorful jargon is appropriate because, get this: when asked about their feelings, those who chose the poorer odds were much less precise about what motivated their choice, suggesting that the emotional "hit" from the vision of nine winners was just too irresistible to pass up. They ignored the many white jelly beans in the large bowl because those lacked emotional power; they focused instead on the nine brightly colored jelly beans. It simply felt "right" to reach into the bowl with more colored beans. The nerds were too focused on the numbers to get sidetracked by irrelevant emotional images. Or, alternatively (and this is going to be hard for many of us dimwits to compute), they may actually get their emotional kicks from manipulating the numbers.

It's important to clarify the meaning of "emotions" in the context of the arithmetic heuristic. We're not talking about the full range of human emotions—jealousy, pride, anger, and so forth. We're talking about much more fundamental feelings of good or bad, fitting or discomfiting; a situation sits right in our neurons or it doesn't. Here's another experiment that makes this point. Peters made up two wagers and asked people to say which one they thought was the better bet. If these numbers seem a bit arbitrary, it's because they are: In one wager, there was a 7-in-36 chance of winning $9 and a 29-in-36 chance of winning nothing. In the second, there was also a 7-in-36 chance of winning $9, but a 29-in-36 chance of losing a nickel. The point of this was to make the probabilities vague, not readily available even to the number lovers. Is winning $9 excellent or unremarkable? Are odds of 7 in 36 attractive? Interestingly, it was the nerds who made the worse decision in these somewhat murky circumstances. They chose the win-loss wager over the no-risk wager. Perhaps the possibility of losing a nickel, as trivial as that is, provided context for understanding a $9 win, making it more appealing. Whatever the mental and emotional dynamics involved, the take-home message is one we dimwits have always known: nerds can sometimes be too smart for their own good.

All of these findings reflect the arithmetic heuristic at work, and the findings have real-life implications beyond these provocative lab experiments. That's because we all deal with numbers and accounting every day—often without even recognizing that we're doing it. Here's an example of how the "feel" of various choices and opportunities can influence us. I work out in the gym just about every morning, but I can't say that I'm always eager to get started. I'm basically lazy, and exercise is hard. Many days I would much rather linger over a second mug of coffee and browse the newspapers. But I don't, because I have made a bargain with myself.

The bargain is simple: I pay a small price now for a big payoff later, in good health and well-being. I know there are no money-back guarantees, but it's a wager I'm willing to make. People strike similar deals all the time. We choose years of hard work and deprivation to go to college and graduate school, banking on later gratification, or we forgo this winter's tropical vacation to save for retirement.

Or we don't. Lots of people see these as bad deals and would rather take the money and run, live for today. Why is that? How can some of us see a particular trade-off as advantageous, while others of us see precisely the same deal as unattractive? These trade-offs are all about numbers in the broadest sense—of value, investments, risks, payoffs—and their intertwining with emotions. Psychologists aren't the only ones who are intrigued by this question. Policy makers see the huge social costs of impulsive decision making and would love to know how to remedy it.

One theory is that some people are simply not as good at forecasting the future. As we saw in Chapter 6, if something is way off in the distance, it's very difficult to keep its practicality front and center in the mind. So we discount it, literally. But is it possible to think about such trade-offs differently, in a way that might help us delay our immediate payoff for a better deal later on?

Here's where the arithmetic heuristic comes in. Stanford University psychologists Eran Magen, Carol Dweck, and James Gross are exploring the issue of personal discipline in the lab, using the same framing idea discussed before. Specifically, they wondered if the way a trade-off is framed in the mind might affect whether or not we choose an immediate but small payoff over a greater reward later on. For example, you probably think of a trade-off as two competing options: you can have $5 right now, or $6.20 in a month. By framing it this way, you focus on the difference between $5 and $6.20, which is $1.20. That's a lot less than the immediate $5, which has a great deal of emotional pull. So it's easy to understand why many people might go for the bird in hand.

But what if you conceptualized the trade-off in a very different way, focusing on the passing of time? Picture yourself on one of those moving walkways, going through life. Every so often, someone hands you an envelope, which contains your wages in cash. You could still take that $5 now, but that's not the end of the deal; time keeps moving, and a month later someone hands you another envelope. You open it expectantly and . . . nada, zero, zip. Think about the disappointment. The emotional power of zero is the arithmetic heuristic raising its head.

That's the real choice you have in life, and that empty envelope makes all the difference. The details of the trade-off haven't changed. The empty envelope was there all along, but it was hidden. That is, choosing between $5 and $6.20 suggests a choice frozen in time. But life is a continuum, and in reality there are two paydays, one of which must be a big zero. Projecting yourself forward to the day of the greater disappointment may be enough to make you opt for less disappointment today.

At least that's the theory, which the psychologists tested on the Internet. They had participants choose between immediate and delayed payments in a variety of scenarios. Sometimes the trade-off was stated as $5 now or $6.20 later. Other times it was $5 now and $0 later *or* $0 now and $6.20 later. Invariably, when the zero-dollar payday was spelled out, rather than hidden, the subjects were less impulsive in their choices. Put another way, they didn't like the feeling of opening that empty envelope, even off in the future, and it nudged them toward a more rational weighing of the options.

So what does this have to do with exercise and health? Say you blow off the gym and linger over coffee, or get another hour's sleep—whatever. That's like taking your $5 now. But it's harder to enjoy as much when you know that the walkway is still moving and somewhere down the line there is an empty envelope with your name on it. And who knows what an empty envelope might mean when it comes to personal health?

Marketers have known about the emotional power of numbers for a long time, even if they never heard of the arithmetic heuristic. Just think about that old marketing phrase "for just pennies a day." There are so many things you can purchase or accomplish for just pennies a day. You can get lots of interesting magazine subscriptions, or a good life insurance plan—no physical required. You can "adopt" a needy child in Africa. I just read recently that I can save the earth from global warming "for just pennies a day."

Whoever came up with that slogan showed extraordinary psychological insight. Indeed, science is only now beginning to demonstrate what these marketers sensed—that people are not entirely rational when it comes to processing numbers. What's more, the way we think about scales and rates and ratios can make us into either cautious or indiscriminate consumers.

In a way this is obvious. "Pennies a day" is a meaningless ratio, because we're not really reaching into our pockets each and every day for those copper coins. That's what the marketers want you to visualize, but most of us are not truly fooled by the ruse. We know automatically—without doing any arithmetic at all—that we're really talking about dollars a month and maybe hundreds of dollars over a year or years. It's all a matter of knowing the meaningful scale.

But what if the manipulation of numbers is more subtle or more complex? Are there marketing phrases and terms that do fool our imperfect minds? University of Michigan psychologist Katherine Burson and her co-workers believe so, and they've run a couple of interesting experiments to simulate the kinds of offers we might well encounter in our daily lives. Here's an example.

Imagine you're in the market for a cell phone plan. After shopping around, you've narrowed your choices to two. Plan A costs $32 a month, and for that you're guaranteed no more than 42 dropped calls out of 1,000. Plan B only costs $27 a month, but the number of dropped calls is 65. In other words, you get what you pay for, and consumers make their choice based on what's more important to them at the time—money or service.

But what if the same offer was phrased this way? Plan A costs $364 a year and drops 4.2 calls per 100. Plan B costs $324 and drops 6.5 calls per 100. It takes only the tiniest bit of arithmetic to see that nothing has changed. The offers are identical to what they were before, except that the scale has changed. But actually two scales have changed, and in different ways, so it's not a no-brainer like "pennies a day."

So how do consumers process these different offers? The psychologists gave these choices to a large group of volunteers, and the results were nuanced. Consumers preferred plan B when it was described as having a lower price per year, but they preferred plan A when it was described as having fewer dropped calls per thousand. Notice that it's the "per year" and "per thousand" that are important. Making the scale bigger also made the difference appear more exaggerated, so emotionally consumers feel as if they're getting much better service or a big savings in cost. Consumers actually changed their preferences with the larger scale—they became more discriminating—even though the real terms remained unchanged.

This is pretty remarkable—and unnerving. But there's more. In a second experiment, the researchers offered a slightly different choice for movie rental plans. In this scenario, plan A costs $10 a month for seven new movies per week. Plan B costs $12 a month for nine new movies a week. As before, either choice could make sense, depending on which meets your financial and movie-watching needs.

Then they once again changed the terms. This time the prices stayed the same, but instead of a weekly allotment of movies, consumers now got a yearly allotment. That is, for $10 a month they got 364 movies per year, and for $12 a month they got 468. How did the movie aficionados process these offers? Dramatically more consumers chose plan B when it was expressed in movies per year. It's the emotional impact of that number—468. That's a lot of movies—all of Hitchcock and Woody Allen and much more—and still for only $12 a month. When you come to think of it, that's really just pennies a day.

What all this means is that we're mixing feelings and numbers all the time, and often making choices and decisions based on what we best "see" and "feel." But some numbers may just be too large for our emotional comprehension. The American writer and memoirist Annie Dillard made this point effectively in her 1999 work *For the Time Being,* writing about the people of China: "There are 1,198,500,000 people alive now in China. To get a feel for what this means, simply take yourself—in all your singularity, importance, complexity, and love—and multiply by 1,198,500,000. See? Nothing to it."

Dillard is being ironic. Of course we cannot "simply" do this kind of arithmetic and feel anything. The number is too big. Our brains simply can't do the emotional calculations to feel the humanity of China.

Slovic (one of the psychologists who demonstrated the "benign percentage") uses this example to show how our cognitive limitations—and specifically our fallback to the arithmetic heuristic—create the phenomenon known as "psychic numbing." When the scope of the Holocaust was revealed following World War II, moral people around the world vowed it would never happen again. Yet mass murders and genocides continue to take place, and unhappily they are not rare: in Ethiopia, Cambodia, Kosovo, Rwanda, and most recently in the Darfur region of Sudan.

To Slovic, these are not only moral failures but cognitive failures as well—a heuristic trap. Such tragedies are the consequence of a fundamental deficiency of the human brain—and won't be stopped until we understand them that way. Our brains are fundamentally skewed against comprehending very large numbers, and thus we cannot feel large-scale suffering in any real way. In this sense, the phrase *mass murder* is an oxymoron; individuals murder individuals, and we feel that pain and outrage, but (as Dillard demonstrates) we can't simply multiply this heinous human act by a large number and scale up to the proper outrage for genocide. Genocide doesn't compute.

Mother Teresa once said: "If I look at the mass, I will never act. If I look at the one, I will." That's just the arithmetic heuristic put into lyrical language. And this paradox has been demonstrated time and again. Remember Jessica McClure? "Baby Jessica" was eighteen months old when she fell into a deep and narrow well in Midland, Texas, in 1986. For fifty-eight hours the world was riveted by her story as rescue workers tried desperately to reach her. Newspaper reporters and TV cameras flooded her rural town, and people from all over the globe sent donations to save the toddler. The photograph of her jubilant rescue won a Pulitzer Prize, and her tale soon became a made-for-TV movie starring Patty Duke and Beau Bridges.

People have responded with comparable sympathy to the plights of animals. Just think of Michael Vick's dogfighting scandal for a recent example. Such human response is not a bad thing, but perplexing, because the outrage over dogfighting appears to eclipse an emotional response to the victims of Darfur, who are systematically being wiped out by the ruthless Janjaweed gangs of western Sudan. Slovic argues that the 1948 Genocide Convention, which was written to prevent such tragedies, is doomed to failure; it was written at a time when we did not understand the power of our heuristic mind. He is lobbying for participating nations to rewrite the convention in a way that would bypass our inability to feel large numbers, and force intervention. Such a step would in effect translate the arithmetic heuristic into public policy.

⎯⎯⎯⎯⎯⎯⎯⎯⎯⎯⎯⎯⎯⎯⎯⎯⎯⎯⎯⎯⎯⎯⎯⎯⎯⎯⎯⎯⎯⎯⎯⎯⎯⎯⎯⎯⎯

S AY YOU ARE shipping a family heirloom overseas, an antique you are very fond of. How much would you be willing to pay for an insurance policy that would pay you $1,000 if the heirloom were lost? Fifty dollars? A hundred dollars? More? Most people are willing to pay considerably more to insure something they are emotionally attached to, even though that makes no sense. If it's lost, it's lost. A higher premium won't bring it back—and indeed won't even get you more money for your loss. This irrational thinking has been demonstrated time and again in the lab, but this is not just about lab gimmicks. In late 2009, the U.S. Preventive Services Task Force issued new guidelines for the use of mammograms to detect breast cancer. The guidelines stated that, based on risk and benefit, women didn't need mammograms at all before age forty, and that women from age fifty to seventy-four should get the test only every other year. This was a major departure from the existing medical standard and caused a political firestorm. It also focused public attention on the emerging field of health numeracy—the use of statistics to make intelligent health choices. According to Cornell's Valerie Reyna, a pioneer in the field, low health numeracy distorts perceptions of real risk, reduces medical compliance, and leads to adverse health results for many consumers. Even people who are adept with numbers have difficulty estimating true risk with all the variables in play, so we rely on the arithmetic heuristic for better or worse.

Numbers are not just figures on a page. They are emotional quantities. The arithmetic heuristic, like each of the mind's heuristics, rarely operates as a free agent. All of the chapters in this section of the book deal in one way or another with our far-from-flawless inner mathematician—and with the often irrational interplay of emotions and numbers. You will see the idea of delayed rewards echoed in the futuristic heuristic, which adds the element of time to emotional calculation. And the scarcity heuristic—the topic of the next chapter—looks at the tricky interplay of value and desire.

The **SCARCITY** Heuristic

||||||||||||||||||||||||||||||||||||||||||||||||||||||||||||||||||||||||||||||||||||||||||||||||||||||||||||||||||||||||||||||||||||

SUPPLY AND DESIRE

I HAVE A FRIEND who really wants a life partner. She is divorced, and after some dreary years on the dating scene she has come to realize just how much she wants a mate again. Her standards are realistic—someone engaging, kind, decently groomed. But she has had no luck, not even with personal ads or e-dating services or singles dances in the church basement.

With each passing month, her longing intensified, and as her longing got stronger her prospects appeared dimmer and dimmer. Recently her attitude has gone through a major shift. She now believes that there really are no quality men left out there. That's not hyperbole. She believes this in her heart. She has concluded that good men are so vanishingly rare that there is no point in looking anymore. She's throwing in the towel.

Psychologists are very interested in this kind of thinking. The fact is my friend can't know for sure how many good men are out there.

How could she? That's really a probability question, and despite her painful experience she just doesn't have enough information to answer it. Yet she has convinced herself that she knows the answer, and the answer is zero. What's going on in her brain?

This is the scarcity heuristic at work. The scarcity heuristic says that if something is rare, it must be valuable, and if something is valued, it must be scarce. The connection between value and scarcity is something we all know. Gold is precious because there is not much of it to go around, not because you can use it to build skyscrapers or cure cancer. Or how about the Cabbage Patch Kids craze? Cabbage Patch Kids were dolls that Coleco began marketing in the early 1980s. They were kind of goofy-looking, with oversized vinyl heads, wide eyes, and cloth bodies, and they came complete with names and "adoption papers." For whatever reason, the dolls caught on big-time, and once they did, it was quickly apparent that there weren't nearly enough of the dolls to go around. The scarcity fueled a true market panic. Parents were fighting in department store aisles, pushing their way ahead of the other parents to claim one of the prized dolls. Stores began hiring security guards specifically for Cabbage Patch Kids, and even so, several toy stores were trashed. The dolls were soon selling on the black market for $150 or more.

This is an extreme and dramatic example of the scarcity heuristic. Obviously, not every commodity scarcity brings out the worst in humans, but every scarcity has the potential to skew our sense of real value. Psychologists and commodity theorists have demonstrated the perverted power of scarcity with a range of goods. The inverse (sometimes called the value heuristic) is just as perverted in its own way. My forlorn friend was unwittingly subbing something clear and simple—her yearning, what she values highly—for a complicated and unknowable statistic.

And it's not just dating. One research group did a fascinating study of health and disease judgments, which illustrates just how pervasive this heuristic is in our decision making. It was an elaborate experiment involving an entirely fake medical lab. Volunteers were ushered into a lab with all the medical trappings—health posters, stethoscopes, eye charts, "doctors" in lab coats, and so forth. All were told about (and given) a new medical test with the phony but convincing name thioamine acetylase saliva reaction test (or the TASRT for short). According to the elaborate ruse, the TASRT screened for a deficiency in a pancreatic enzyme called TAA. In fact, TAA deficiency was also a bogus disorder, conjured up by the researchers for the experiment.

Here's where the scientists really got clever. The TASRT involves a small strip of yellow paper, kind of like a litmus test. For the purposes of the experiment, some were told that if it turned green, they had the deficiency; others were told the opposite—that green meant they were okay. It was a trick test: the paper always turned green.

So half thought they had tested positive for this unfamiliar disorder, and half thought they were off the hook. At this point, the "doctor" told the volunteers one of two things: some heard that TAA deficiency was a common condition (present in four of five people), while others learned that it was rare (found in only one of five people). The idea was to plant in the volunteers' minds either a sense of scarcity or a sense of ordinariness, in regard to the enzyme deficiency. The researchers wanted to see if priming the scarcity heuristic would affect their decisions about whether to seek treatment.

And it did. Those who believed the disorder was rare also believed it was more serious; that is, they "valued" the disease more in the sense of taking it more seriously. By contrast, those who believed it was common saw it as less threatening. Patients who discount a disorder's seriousness are less apt to seek treatment, so this has clear health implications.

The scarcity principle has been demonstrated in many different contexts over the years, but it's only recently that psychologists have begun seriously exploring the way its flip side can cause havoc—by skewing my friend's romantic judgments, for instance. An international team of psychologists—Xianchi Dai, Klaus Wertenbroch, and Miguel Brendl—have run some surprisingly simple experiments to show the power of this mental bias. For example, in one they had a group of young people look at about a hundred pictures, half of birds and half of flowers, in random order. Then they shuffled them up and showed them again, but this time they offered some of the volunteers money for each flower they spotted. Others were paid for each bird they saw. Then they all were asked to estimate the total number of bird pictures and the total number of flower pictures in the deck.

The results were consistent with the theory. People who were paid for spotting flower pictures thought there were fewer flowers than birds, and likewise those who were made to value birds were sure they were scarcer than flowers. Nobody knew that in fact there were exactly the same number of flowers and birds, so in effect their laboratory-induced "yearning" for something caused them to wrongly perceive scarcity.

This doesn't make sense, of course, but a lot of the brain's shortcuts don't. To replicate their findings, the scientists ran another experiment, this one a little closer to my friend's real-life dilemma. In this case, participants (both men and women, all heterosexual) viewed portraits of both men and women—some attractive and some not. When questioned later, both men and women believed that there were fewer attractive people of the opposite sex than there were of the same sex. When they were shown only unattractive portraits, they didn't perceive a scarcity. So again, the participants were in effect substituting their emotional desire for realistic calculation, and ended up believing that what they wanted was less likely to be found.

And again they were wrong. These cognitive tools likely evolved over eons and served an adaptive purpose long ago. Maybe it made mate seekers less picky—readier to hook up with one of the (perceived) rare partners, rather than keep looking. Being too choosy wasn't adaptive for early humans, since peak reproductive years were limited. But making decisions under uncertain conditions may be trickier in the modern world, and mental shortcuts may be a shortcut to a solitary life—or to an infelicitous choice of mates.

There are, of course, a lot of ways to perceive and estimate value. Think about time. We've all had the experience of sitting through a really boring lecture or meeting and literally counting the minutes as we watch the clock. Time is money, as they say, and this very unpleasant experience is costing us valuable time. The opposite of that is what psychologists call "being in the flow": whatever we are experiencing is so enjoyable and captivating that we lose all track of time.

Psychologists have looked at the scarcity/value heuristic in this way. In one experiment at the Sorbonne University in France, for example, volunteers listened to a short clip of music. Not Verdi's *Requiem* or Miles Davis—nothing that was likely to stir emotions. Think Muzak, as neutral as music can get. Then the researchers asked some of the volunteers how much money they would be willing to pay to hear the music again. Others were asked how much money they would accept as payment to listen to the Muzak again. This is a classic laboratory manipulation. When faced with an ambiguous experience, those who are asked about paying assume that the experience must be enjoyable or valuable—why else would they be asked to pay for it? Those asked about being paid assume the opposite—that the experience is of little value, even undesirable.

Then the psychologists asked all the volunteers to estimate the duration of the music they had just listened to. And guess what. Those who had merely thought about paying for more music thought the musical clip was shorter than did those who were asked about being paid. No actual money was exchanged, but the idea of paying made them perceive value—it primed the value-scarcity heuristic. That, in turn, made them perceive scarcity—that is, less of the highly enjoyable music to listen to.

It's not hard to imagine a real-life example of this experiment. Tickets to rock concerts have become very expensive in recent years. Even aging rockers now charge $100, $200, and up for seats to some venues, so if you're like me, you have to actually think about the value before forking over those big bucks to Ticketmaster. So imagine that you do decide a particular performance is worth it. You buy the tickets, arrange for the babysitter, whatever arrangements you have to make, all the while anticipating this great evening of rock music.

Finally the big night arrives. You settle into the concert hall, and the band begins. Then, after fifty minutes, the band stops playing: "Good night, folks. Thank you all for coming." Huh? That's not nearly enough music. You want way more. You clap until your hands are raw, but not even an encore. You feel cheated, as if a con man had just taken cash from your wallet. You feel a sense of loss.

Now imagine that you wander into a free concert in the park. It's almost over, but you get to hear a few numbers, perhaps half an hour of music. Do you feel cheated, a sense of loss? Most likely not. If anything, you feel as though you got an unexpected bonus. You're not calculating your "money's worth," so you don't perceive any scarcity or deprivation.

Does this mean you undervalue performers who play for free? It sounds mean-spirited and irrational, but there may be some truth to this notion. The same researchers did several other experiments to see if the value heuristic and the scarcity heuristic might act in concert, reinforcing each other in circular fashion. For example, in one study they primed the unconscious link between value and scarcity by having volunteers think about the worth of rare postage stamps. Then, as before, they had them listen to music, but in this case only half listened to Muzak, while the other half listened to classical music.

Then they asked all of the volunteers a bunch of questions, including how willing they would be to work in exchange for the listening experience.

The findings were intriguing. Those who had been primed to think about value and scarcity perceived the classical musical performance as briefer than the others did. That is, they perceived a scarcity of something valuable. Moreover, these same volunteers also said that they were willing to work more for the experience of listening to the music. In other words, valuing an experience led to perceived scarcity, which in turn led to an enhanced sense of value. The circular interplay of the two cognitive biases reinforced the initial belief.

These findings relate to the value of an experience. The researchers also wanted to explore the circular reasoning idea with consumer products. In a separate experiment at the University of Chicago, they showed volunteers different advertisements for bottled water. Some saw the bottled water pictured against a background of desert and camels, while others saw a background of snowy peaks. The desert imagery was meant to stimulate the internal sense of thirst and scarcity.

Then the researchers showed the volunteers two works of art: one by Salvador Dalí and the other by Henri Matisse. They were asked to choose the one they preferred, then to estimate the difficulty of finding another painting by the same artist. Finally, they were asked to estimate the market value of each painting. The findings were consistent: those who had been primed with the desert and camels believed that works of art by their favorite artist were rarer, and they also estimated their market value as greater. In other words, craving water triggered the brain's value heuristic, which created a sense of scarcity in a totally unrelated realm, the market for fine art; this, in turn, bolstered volunteers' estimates of market value for their artists of choice.

What's really interesting here is how this heuristic cuts across areas of human need and desire. You would think that aridity and thirst and water would have little to do with modern art, but apparently the brain doesn't make that distinction. Scarcity and value are so inextricably linked in the brain that experiencing either one, regardless of context, has the potency to trigger and solidify the connection somewhere else.

If all this seems contrived and disconnected from real life, it's not. We all have preferences of all sorts—we value things differently—and we all think about supply all the time, in various ways. What these experiments show is that these two intertwined heuristics work in circular fashion, polarizing and reinforcing preferences—and not always for the good.

Let me describe one more experiment that brings these lofty ideas down to dollars and cents—and real consumer behavior. It has to do with charity. The researchers asked a group of people to donate money to save the endangered giant panda, but they asked them in different ways in order to observe the circular process in action.

Because the researchers didn't know if any of the volunteers really cared about the fate of the giant pandas, they manipulated their level of caring by showing some of them a photograph of a cute panda. They asked some of them to estimate the number of giant pandas remaining in the world. Then they asked some of each of these overlapping groups how much they would be willing to donate to help protect the endangered species.

The heuristic cycle was unmistakable. That is, those who saw the picture started off valuing the giant pandas more than the others. These volunteers estimated that there are far fewer giant pandas in the world—that the species was rarer, more endangered—and they in turn were willing to donate more money to save the panda. Value led to perception of scarcity, which increased the panda's perceived value.

Most of the experiments described so far have to do with commodities—things that you may or may not want (and be willing to pay for) in the marketplace of life. But the value-scarcity heuristic is also at play in a lot of everyday behavior that has nothing to do with money or markets. It may in fact be the foundation for self-control, for saying no to things that harm us.

Think about addiction. There is a saying in many addiction recovery programs that goes like this: "If you keep going to the barber shop, eventually you'll get a haircut." Translated from recovery-speak, that means: stay away from temptation. It's the received wisdom that hanging around saloons or raves or chocolatiers or racetracks—name your poison—just increases the odds that your self-control will fail you someday.

But is this true? Does the mere supply and easy availability of something tempting weaken the will to resist? The answer is of more than theoretical interest to public health experts, and the problem goes far beyond serious addictive disorders. Just think of all those Christmas cookies in your office at holiday time. As our national obesity crisis grows, experts are increasingly focused on widespread and harmful difficulties with discipline and self-control.

Let's focus on sweets, just because these are a common and familiar temptation. Every self-control challenge is a trade-off of one kind or another, and here it's a trade-off between satisfying that sweet tooth and committing to good nutrition. Although it seems intuitively obvious that one should not keep bonbons in every room of the house, another psychological theory argues the opposite, based on the powerful influence of value and scarcity principles. We simply don't much care for things that are commonly available, and we covet what's rare. This is the theory behind the idea of "forbidden fruit," that is, that keeping things hidden away only sharpens our desire.

Three psychologists recently decided to test a paradoxical view of self-control based on the scarcity principle. Kristian Ove Myrseth and Ayelet Fishbach of the University of Chicago and Yaacov Trope of New York University predicted that increasing the availability of sweets would indeed deflate desire for them. They further speculated that this happens because availability of sweets is threatening to the loftier goal of good health and so causes the mind to damp down desire to protect the greater good. In short, by making a tempting sweet readily available, we make it less tempting.

Here's how they tested this counterintuitive notion. They stood at the exit door of a gym and buttonholed young women as they were leaving. They offered them a choice of granola bars or chocolates, and had them rate their desire for each. Simple enough. But some rated their desire before choosing, and others right after choosing but before eating. The idea was to compare desire for chocolate when it was readily available and when the supply was gone.

They figured that young women at a gym would tend to be health conscious and thus conflicted over the choice. They found that the women did indeed prefer the healthy granola bars—that is, they devalued the chocolates. But as soon as they expressed their preference for the granola bar and the chocolate was no longer an option, their preference vanished. So it appears that self-control does in fact operate paradoxically, by actually diminishing desire for what's tempting. And this self-regulation works best when the sweets are right in front of you.

But what if you could just change your mind—ditch the granola bars and scarf down the chocolate? Does the mind keep desire flat for as long as the temptation remains an option? The psychologists decided to test this, but not with chocolates. Instead they created a self-control trade-off involving work and play. They studied a group of graduate students in the University of Chicago's school of business. Unhappily, these MBA students were enrolled in an excruciatingly boring class—but one they really should complete. They had these students rate the desirability of a number of leisure activities, such as going to movies, partying, and so forth.

Some rated leisure activity while they still had the option of dropping the boring class. Others did the same, but after the deadline had passed for dropping the class. In other words, for some the decision was reversible and for others it was not. The scientists found that as long as the students had the option of blowing off work for recreation, they continued to dampen their urge to play. Only after the deadline had passed did they allow themselves to yearn for the lost opportunity for fun. It appears the mind protects itself against succumbing to temptation for as long as it must.

These findings are a bit puzzling, and the authors raise some intriguing questions: Would dieters actually benefit from the sight of the dessert cart rolling by? Should alcoholics keep liquor in the liquor cabinet—paradoxically to help with self-control? The intuitive answer to such questions is no, but the evidence from these studies suggests that it might not be a resounding no. Long-term self-control may actually be enhanced by living with temptation.

I N T H E D A R K L Y funny film classic *Harold and Maude,* Harold is a nineteen-year-old who is obsessed with death and dying. He repeatedly fakes his own suicide, drives around in a hearse, and attends strangers' funerals for fun. He falls in love with Maude, a seventy-nine-year-old with the same morbid hobby. In the end, it is Maude's death that causes Harold to put aside his morbid ways and embrace life anew.

We see this in real life too. People who have close brushes with death often report a sharpened appetite even for the ordinary stuff of life. Some recent research from the University of Missouri suggests that this interplay might be the ultimate example of the scarcity heuristic at work. Death, to the heuristic mind, is a scarcity of life—and makes us value the life that is left to us. Quantities of anything—or at least our perceptions of quantities—are subjective, shaped by our hopes and desires. As we'll see in the next chapter on the anchor heuristic, our irrational relationship with facts and figures shapes our judgments about everything from trivia to others' beliefs.

9

The **ANCHOR** Heuristic

‖‖

WHY THINGS COST $19.95

FOR THE PAST three years, a team of IBM scientists has been working tirelessly on what can only be described as a trivial pursuit. As many as twenty experts in artificial intelligence and natural language processing have dedicated themselves to a computer program called Watson, named for the company's founder, Thomas J. Watson. The project's goal: to create a computerized "contestant" to compete with the regular contestants on the popular quiz show *Jeopardy!*

Why would a company commit so much time and money to such a venture? Well, think about just what it is that *Jeopardy!* really tests in people. It's nothing less than the natural human ability to negotiate a vast amount of general knowledge—to make connections and assess relationships between bits of information and discard useless facts and focus on what's most relevant—and all very rapidly, almost instantaneously. In short, it tests people's intellectual suppleness to make educated guesses.

We all do this every day, of course, mostly outside our conscious awareness, but that doesn't make it any less remarkable. Indeed, playing *Jeopardy!* successfully requires much more cognitive flexibility than the ultimate egghead's game, chess. IBM scientists have already devised a computer program, Deep Blue, that defeated world champion Garry Kasparov. That's because chess is a rule-based game with finite possibilities. Human knowledge may be trivial but it's infinite.

If the IBM scientists are successful, they will have figured out one of the most robust—and trickiest—cognitive tools at work in the human mind, which psychologists call the anchor heuristic. To get a sense of its workings, think of a sailboat's anchor. You decide to take a break from sailing and anchor your craft in a small lagoon. When you drop the anchor, it secures the boat to a specific spot in the sandy bottom below. The anchor holds, but the boat itself doesn't stay in one spot. You give it a fair amount of anchor line, so it can drift a bit, depending on the wind and tide and current. It might drift ten or twenty yards toward the shoreline, or out toward the open sea. It has a range of motion.

The mind has a similar tendency to drift around a firm anchor, depending on the cognitive tides and currents. The anchor can be a fact about the world, a perception, or a point of view about issues or problems—even your attitude toward a friend or partner. The point is that our thoughts are dynamic, in motion, but our mental anchors limit our choices.

Let's stick with the *Jeopardy!* example for a bit, because it's a mini version of the information processing we do every day. Imagine that you are actually a contestant on the show. It's Final Jeopardy, and you're in a dead heat with the two other contestants. The category is Founding Fathers, which is good because you know a bit about eighteenth-century history. Alex Trebek reveals the Final Jeopardy answer: George Washington was elected president of the United States in this year. Uh-oh. You don't know for sure. There is a lot of money at stake, and you have two kids you'd like to put through college. You're going to have to make an educated guess. That familiar *Jeopardy!* tune starts to play.

So how do you come up with your best guess? Other than historians who specialize in the eighteenth century, very few of us actually know precisely when the father of our country was elected. It's not the kind of information you need to keep accessible in your memory every day. When we don't have the precise answer we need stored in our memory, we use the next best thing: a factual anchor. That is, we probably have some other related historical facts stored in our heads. We probably know, for example, that the Declaration of Independence was signed in 1776.

Okay, 1776, so that's at least a starting point. But you know it's not a game winner, and the clock is ticking. So beginning with that mental anchor, you start adjusting—drifting, if you will. You know for sure it wasn't before 1776. Was it the next year, 1777? Five years later? Could it have been as much as twenty years later? What was going on in those years, anyway? When was the Constitution written? Was that the 1780s? In your mind you come up with a range of plausible answers, moving away from the anchor in increments, and as time runs out you jot down the best of the possibilities.

This basic process, known as "anchoring and adjusting," has been studied and reworked for some years, and is holy writ for most cognitive psychologists. But it still leaves a lot of questions begging for answers, most notably: why are our educated guesses wrong a lot of the time? *Jeopardy!* contestants, as a group, get about eight of ten questions correct. That's impressive, but it also means they get almost 20 percent wrong. The fact is, if anchoring and adjusting were a perfect cognitive strategy, not only would *Jeopardy!* be a predictable and uninteresting game show, life would be a lot easier. But it's instead an imperfect process that leads to all sorts of misjudgments and problems.

Unless we are aware of its power. We can monitor and fine-tune our use of this heuristic in daily life, and psychologists have been running a variety of lab experiments to refine the theory and explore how we can best channel our hard-wired tendencies. In one experiment, for example, Nicholas Epley of the University of Chicago and Thomas Gilovich of Cornell had volunteers answer general-knowledge questions similar to those on *Jeopardy!* For instance, from the category of Animal Mothers: the number of months a pregnant elephant carries her baby before birth. In the Potent Potables category: the freezing point of vodka. (The George Washington example comes from that experiment as well.) They discovered, first, that people generate anchors in different ways. Usually, as with the 1776 example, they have a fact stored in their brain that they sense is vaguely connected to the question at hand. If they have nothing in their memory to anchor on, they simply guess blindly.

What's interesting is that even if the anchor is an arbitrary guess, people still adjust around it. A person's original anchor exerts a kind of cognitive drag on the mind as it tries to adjust, so the further one gets from the anchor, the less plausible it feels to keep adjusting outward. Think of that sailboat in the lagoon; it has a range to drift about, but the range is limited by the length of the anchor line. As a result, what the students in the experiment did was adjust as far as they could, until they reached a date that seemed plausible enough to settle for.

You'll recall from the introduction that scientists label this "satisficing"—as in the answer is satisfying enough to suffice. Much of life is "satisficing" because we often don't have the exact answer we need—not just in factual knowledge but in all sorts of problem solving. And we often need to make choices under less than optimal conditions—under time pressure, emotional stress, or with all sorts of distractions. Epley and Gilovich did some experiments to see if they could illuminate a satisficing version of anchoring. They wanted to see why some people might be better at this than others.

For instance, in one study they used a standard personality test to sort out the most reflective students from the least, figuring that the ones who tended to mull things over would do better at making educated guesses than those who answered more impulsively. That's exactly what they found. It appears that simply slowing down and pondering makes the anchoring process more accurate. Then, in a second experiment, they asked the same *Jeopardy!* questions of students who had spent the day boozing, and then compared them to sober students. You can probably guess who did better. Finally, they did the laboratory version of *Jeopardy!* with some students who were distracted and others who were not. They found, not surprisingly, that the sober students and the less distracted students did better at adjusting their guesses and approximating the correct factual answers. Basically, what they demonstrated with this series of studies is that making educated guesses takes a lot of mental effort, and many things can sabotage that effort.

Back to Final Jeopardy, just to see how you're doing. You're a reflective type, or you wouldn't even be up there. You sure didn't need a psychologist to tell you not to have a martini before testing your wits on national television, and the only thing competing for your attention this moment is George Washington's election. You anchor, you adjust, and you take your best shot: what is 1788? We've got a new *Jeopardy!* champion.

But I know what you're thinking. This is great for trivia games, but how much time do we spend on such pursuits? A lot, actually, but you may not recognize this common cognitive strategy in its many different guises. We're anchoring and adjusting all the time, sometimes more successfully than others. We do it when we attach prices to values, when we bid and barter.

Let's turn to an entertaining but perhaps more relevant example of how we use cognitive anchors in real life. Remember the Alfred Hitchcock espionage thriller *North by Northwest*? One of the famed director's most enduring bits of comedy is the auction scene. Cary Grant plays Roger Thornhill, a businessman who has been mistaken for a CIA agent by the ruthless enemy spy Phillip Vandamm. At a critical juncture, Thornhill is cornered by his enemies inside a Chicago auction house, and the only way he can escape is by drawing attention to himself. When the bidding on an antique reaches $2,250, Thornhill yells out, "Fifteen hundred!" When the auctioneer gently chides him, he loudly changes his bid: "Twelve hundred!" When the bidding on a Louis XIV piece reaches $1,200, Thornhill blurts out, "Thirteen dollars!" The genteel crowd is outraged, but Thornhill gets precisely what he wants: the auctioneer summons the police, who escort him past Vandamm's henchmen to safety.

Clever thinking, and good comedy. It's funny for a lot of reasons, and one is that Thornhill violates every psychological rule for how we negotiate price and value with each other. So much of life is an "auction" of one sort or another, whether it's buying a used car, making health care choices, or even choosing a mate. But unlike Roger Thornhill, who blatantly defied the rules to save his skin, most of us are motivated by the desire for a fair deal, and we employ some sophisticated cognitive tools to weigh offers, fashion responses, and so forth—all the to-and-fro in getting to an agreement.

But how does life's dickering play out in the brain? And is it a trustworthy tool for getting what we want? Psychologists have been studying cognitive bartering for some time, and it's exactly the same sort of cognitive anchoring and drifting we've been discussing. For example, an opening "bid" of any sort is normally perceived as a mental anchor, a starting point for psychological jockeying to follow. If we perceive an opening bid as fundamentally inaccurate or unfair, we reject it by countering with something in another ballpark altogether. But what about less dramatic counteroffers? What makes us settle on a response?

University of Florida marketing professors Chris Janiszewski and Dan Uy suspected that something fundamental might be going on, that some characteristic of the opening bid itself might influence the way the brain thinks about value and shapes bidding behavior. In particular, they wanted to see if the precision of the opening bid might be important to how the brain acts at an auction. Or to put it in more familiar terms, are we really fooled when storekeepers price something at $19.95 instead of a round twenty bucks?

Janiszewski and Uy ran a series of experiments to test this idea. The experiments used hypothetical scenarios, in which participants were required to make a variety of educated guesses. For example, they had participants think about a scenario in which they are buying a high-definition plasma TV, and asked them to guesstimate the wholesale cost. They were told the retail price, plus the fact that the retailer had a reputation for pricing TVs competitively.

But there were three scenarios involving three retail prices: some of the hypothetical buyers were given a retail price of $5,000, while others were given the price of $4,988 and still others $5,012. When the buyers were asked to estimate the wholesale price, those with the $5,000 price tag in their heads guessed much lower than those contemplating retail prices that were not round numbers. That is, they moved further away from the mental anchor when the anchor was round. What's more, those who started with the round number as their mental anchor were much more likely to guess a wholesale price that was also in round numbers. The scientists ran this experiment again and again with different scenarios and always got the same result. It turns out that a precise anchor is also a stronger anchor— people are more uncomfortable straying from a precise anchor than a round one.

Why would this happen? Well, the Florida psychologists have a theory: people appear to create mental measuring sticks that run in increments away from any opening bid, and the size of the increments depends on the opening bid. That is, if we see a $20 toaster, we might wonder whether it's worth $19 or $18 or $21; we're thinking in round numbers. But if the starting point is $19.95, the mental measuring stick would look different. We might still think it's wrongly priced, but in our minds we are thinking about nickels and dimes instead of dollars, so a fair comeback might be $19.50 or $19.25.

The psychologists decided to check these lab findings in the real world. They looked at five years of real estate sales in Alachua County, Florida, comparing list prices and actual sales prices of homes. They found that sellers who listed their homes at less rounded prices—say, $494,500 as opposed to $500,000—consistently got closer to their asking price. Put another way, buyers were less likely to negotiate the price down as far when they encountered a precise asking price compared to a round number. So, bottom line: one way for a seller to deal with a buyer's market may be to pick an odd list price to begin with.

This scientific work has implications that go beyond TVs and real estate—and certainly beyond winning at *Jeopardy!* Think of the realm of medicine, where the stakes can be life and death. Cognitive psychologist Roberta Klatzky of Carnegie Mellon University has shown that people will schedule important medical checkups more dependably if they are provided with a mental anchor in the form of a guide to what is normal and advisable. For example, for your age and this condition, every six months is advisable. The patients don't follow the physician's guidelines perfectly, but they come closer to the ideal if they start with an anchor and adjust around it.

Or consider how doctors give patients medical information. A physician might say, for instance, that your chance of responding to a particular blood pressure medication is "good," or that your chance of responding is 80 percent. Patients are often confused by these assessments. The percentage sounds more precise, so patients probably don't stray too far from that numerical anchor. But many studies have shown that patients prefer vague generalities like "good," and doctors tend to use them. But what happens with an anchor like "good"? Remember that life is an auction: in his mind the patient is dickering with the doctor, so why not negotiate "good" up to "excellent"? The patient may "round" good to excellent and conclude that a medication is more effective than it in fact is. When treatment choices are on the line, the auction house can indeed be a perilous place.

These examples from personal finance and health are illustrative, but one shouldn't get the idea that anchoring and adjusting is always so targeted. Anchoring and adjusting permeates just about every life activity—and every relationship—we have. Epley and Gilovich ran a fascinating series of experiments on perspective taking—the basic act of trying to understand what other people think and believe—and demonstrated the crucial role that this cognitive heuristic plays throughout every ordinary day in simply trying to understand someone's else's thoughts.

Consider the ordinary life of Tom Reton. Tom is just an average guy who lives in Chicago, where he often hangs out with his two close friends Steve and Gina. One night the three of them are having dinner, and Gina is urging them to go to see a new comedian who has just opened a new show in the area. "You've *got* to see him," she pleads. "I heard he's just hilarious."

Tom trusts Gina's tastes, so he goes to see this new comedian. And indeed he is very funny. In fact, Tom laughs so hard his stomach hurts.

Or he hates the comedian. He finds him tedious and arrogant.

Tom is an imaginary Chicagoan created by the psychologists, and both scenarios are part of an experiment they designed to explore how cognitive anchors influence perspective taking and empathy. Some University of Chicago students read the first scenario and others read the second. Then they all listened to a voice mail message

Tom left for Steve after seeing the show. Here's the whole message: "Steve, this is Tom. How are things going? By the way, remember that comedian Gina mentioned at dinner? I just saw him yesterday. All I can say is that you have to see him yourself to believe how hilarious he really is. Well, call me back when you get a chance and we'll make plans for the weekend."

Tom's tone is flat, matter-of-fact. So what do you make of his message? What is he really saying about this new comedian? What's going on in his mind?

The voice mail is ambiguous—like a lot of things in life. That was the experimenters' intention. They figured that the volunteers would use the scenario, negative or positive, as an egocentric anchor. That is, if they knew Tom had hated the show, they would interpret the voice mail as sarcastic; if they knew he had loved the show, they would interpret the voice mail as sincere. That makes perfect sense. But how about Steve? How would he interpret the ambiguous message? Remember that he doesn't have the privileged information you have; he doesn't know how Tom really feels about the comedian. Will he also hear the message as sarcastic or enthusiastic, without any inside information to anchor him?

There is no "correct" answer. The idea was to see how capable the volunteers were of getting out of their own head and into someone else's—and how much this was helped or hindered by cognitive anchoring. The results were interesting. Most did realize that Steve lacked the privileged information they had, and so figured he would not be as certain of Tom's true meaning. But their adjustments were inadequate. That is, those who knew that Tom had hated the show were more apt to think Steve would (like them) hear the sarcasm in the message. The others thought he would detect the sincerity.

But Steve couldn't possibly guess what Tom meant. He didn't have enough information. These findings illustrate both the ubiquity of anchoring and adjustment in relationships, and its failings. We do adjust away from our own point of view if we take the time and think it through, but that anchor has a strong tug on our thinking. True empathy takes work, and this is true of intimate relationships as much as casual friendships.

The psychologists did a series of similar experiments to see what influences the accuracy of anchoring and adjusting. One idea is that once we have a clear anchor—a date, an amount, a point of view—we move away from it in short cognitive "jumps." Each time we jump away from the anchor, we stop for an instant to test the hypothesis that this is the best stopping place. If we decide it's not, for whatever reason, we jump again, test again, jump again, and so forth.

All this hypothesis testing takes place very rapidly, of course. Various things can influence the decision to stop—that's the satisficing mentioned earlier. If you're too tired, too busy, or too distracted by a beautiful summer day, any of these can make you say, "That's good enough, at least for now." It follows, then, that prematurely stopping the adjusting process will result in less appreciation for others' points of view. The researchers tested this notion in an intriguing experiment.

Remember the old Queen song "Another One Bites the Dust"? It's one of those songs that is said to contain an encrypted message celebrating illegal drugs. Specifically, some listeners have argued that the chorus, if played backward, can be heard as "It's fun to smoke marijuana." Such alleged encoding of illicit or immoral words is called "backmasking," and it's a fiction. No one intentionally inserted any coded messages into any rock lyrics; they simply aren't there. Yet people swear that they hear them—if they are told what to listen for. It's a way we impose order on randomness—a fundamental psychological urge.

Given this tendency for self-deception, Epley and his colleagues used the supposed backmask in "Another One Bites the Dust" for an experiment. They had a large group of Cornell University students listen to the song backward; some they told about the supposed drug message and others they did not. When they asked them what they heard, almost all who had been told about the backmask said they heard the words. Of those who had not been told in advance, zero heard the illicit drug message.

That part's unsurprising. But they also asked everyone to estimate how many randomly selected Cornell students would say they heard the message if they were told nothing about it. They figured that the anchor—belief in the hidden message or not—would influence their ability to get inside the heads of others. But here's the twist. The researchers interrupted the anchoring-and-adjusting process prematurely. They figured that if the volunteers didn't have time to adjust sufficiently, they would be further off the mark—meaning more egocentric and less empathetic.

And that's just what they found. The students who believed (wrongly) that they had heard the pro-drug message buried in the Queen tune made a cognitive leap to the view that many others must also share their belief. They probably would have corrected—or at least adjusted—this unreasonable view, given time, but because they were interrupted, they ended up with a distorted perspective of normal thinking.

Every social interaction involves this kind of perspective taking, and we're constantly being interrupted before we can adjust perfectly. Lovers, parents, teachers, business partners—everyone bases his actions in part on what he thinks others are thinking. But most of us seriously overestimate what we know about others' thoughts. Because of the ancient but imperfect anchoring and adjusting heuristic, we think others share our perspective when often they do not. The consequences can be much more consequential than simply walking away from a game show with no cash.

THESE LABORATORY SCENARIOS can be entertaining, but the inability to take another's perspective can be the source of a lot of misunderstanding and sorrow in real life. Think of couples trying to negotiate a shared life, or business partners agreeing on strategy. Our initial, fast, and automatic judgment is that someone else's view or desire or perspective is exactly the same as ours, just because that's what is most prominent in our mind. But communication depends on how well we can adjust our egotistical anchoring view away from that automatic perspective. If we can't learn to see a range of possible views, we are likely to misunderstand—and be misunderstood. Perspective taking is the foundation of fairness, which is also wrapped up in the calorie heuristic, the topic of the next chapter. The calorie heuristic is about exchange and currency—but currency broadly defined to encompass hunger, money, deprivation, and our basic human sense of human decency.

10

The **CALORIE** Heuristic

||||||||||||||||||||||||||||||||||||||||||||||||||||||||||||||||||||||||||||||||||||||||||||||||||||||||||||||||||||||||||||||||||||||

"WILL WORK FOR FOOD"

I GREW UP WITH a brother who was very close to me in age, and we were both hypervigilant about getting our fair share. It didn't matter what was at stake, but we were at our most deadly serious when it came to dessert. My mother had all sorts of clever tricks for dealing with this constant competition. If we were bickering over a last piece of pie, for example, she would randomly pick one of us to cut the slice of pie in half. But before the cutting started she would add: "And your brother gets to choose the slice he wants."

Damn. With those few words, she took all the fun out of holding the knife, and indeed she probably shifted the competitive advantage. In any case, she made a muddle of self-interest and fairness in our young minds.

Well, it turns out my mother didn't invent the pie-slicing gambit. Indeed, humans have been dividing up pies of all sorts, actual and metaphorical, for eons. For our earliest ancestors, food was the original cash. In the eons before minimum wages and credit cards and 401(k)s and Wall Street bailouts, the closest thing to earnings and savings was bounty from the hunt. Food was more than nourishment; it was an asset, a currency of exchange. So it's no wonder that the two resources remain inextricably connected and interchangeable in our modern minds today. Food equals money equals food.

So it's probably no mistake that economists use so many pie diagrams to represent money and wealth and budgets. That's a reflection of the calorie heuristic, the brain's tendency to entwine food, cash, and fairness. Even though my mother did not originate the fairness trick, she was recognizing in her competitive children a well-established (and fairly cynical) view of life. That view assumes that we all act like rational calculating machines, governed entirely by utilitarian self-interest. But is this true? Is fairness simply a ruse, something we adopt only when we secretly see an advantage in it for ourselves? And do we expect no more than self-interest of others? Or is there such a thing as fairness for fairness' sake?

Many psychologists have in recent years moved away from the purely utilitarian view, dismissing it as too simplistic. But the trick is in demonstrating genuine fairness in action, uncontaminated by self-serving motives such as greed and need. Recent advances in both cognitive science and neuroscience now allow psychologists to approach this question in some different ways, and they are getting some intriguing results.

I'll get to the calorie connection shortly, but first let's look at a simple study of fairness and self-interest, this one using a classic psychological test called the "ultimatum game." UCLA psychologist Golnaz Tabibnia and her colleagues used a version of the game that goes like this: Person A has a pot of money, say $23, which he can divide in any way he wants with person B. All person B can do is look at the offer and accept or reject it; there is no negotiation. If he walks away from the deal, there is no deal and neither person gets any money. In the laboratory experiment, there is no real person A: it's secretly the experimenter, making a range of offers from generous to fair to stingy. The experimental subjects get to weigh the offers and respond.

Whatever person A offers to person B is an unearned windfall, even if it's a miserly $5 out of $23, so a strict utilitarian would take the money and run. But that's not exactly what happens in the lab. The UCLA scientists ran the experiment with different dollar amounts, so that sometimes $5 was stingy and other times fair, say $5 out of a total stake of $10. The idea was to make sure the subjects were responding to the fairness of the offer, not to the amount of the windfall. When they asked the subjects to rate themselves on a scale from happy to contemptuous, they noted some interesting findings: even when they stood to gain exactly the same dollar amount of free money, the subjects were much happier with the fair offers and much more disdainful of deals that were lopsided and self-centered. Indeed, many people actually reject very unfair deals, even though they lose out on free money, suggesting that their sense of decency trumps their rational, calculating mind. They respond emotionally to the idea that someone would take advantage of them.

That's interesting in itself. But it could simply mean that we don't like being treated shabbily, which wouldn't be all that surprising. The psychologists want to know if, beyond that, there is something inherently rewarding about being treated decently. They decided to look inside the brains of these people to find out. They scanned several parts of their brains involved in aversion and reward while the subjects were in the act of weighing both fair and miserly offers, and they found that, yes, both parts of the brain light up during the ultimatum game. The brain finds self-serving behavior emotionally unpleasant, but a different bundle of neurons also finds genuine fairness uplifting. What's more, these emotional firings occur in brain structures that are fast and automatic, so it appears that this impulse for fairness is primitive and ingrained, not rational. Faced with a conflict, the brain's default position is to demand a fair deal.

So unfairness is fundamentally jarring to the brain, and fairness is fundamentally rewarding. This internal sense of equity is so basic, in fact, that scientists recently discovered it in dogs. Researchers at the University of Vienna studied well-trained and obedient dogs, rewarding them (or not) for shaking hands. When the dogs were tested alone, they offered their paws even without "payment" in the form of sausage or bread. But when they were next to another dog that got a reward when they did not, they became less and less inclined to obey the command. It was not the lack of reward itself but the perceived sense of inequity that disturbed them.

Yet people do accept offers every day in real life that are less than equitable, and indeed they did so in the ultimatum game studies. When the scientists scanned the brains of those who were "swallowing their pride" for the sake of cash, the brain showed a distinctive pattern of neuronal firing. It appears that we can temporarily damp down the brain's contempt center, in effect allowing the rational, utilitarian brain to rule, at least momentarily. So it seems contempt does not go away when the economic pic is sliced unfairly; it just goes underground.

So how are all our basic needs and behaviors—hunger and gluttony and frugality and charity and stinginess—connected in the brain? Put simply, could comfort food translate into feelings of financial security? Might there be a link between satiety and generosity? Can we literally be hungry for money? Psychologists at Katholieke Universiteit Leuven in Belgium have been exploring this dynamic. Barbara Briers and her colleagues did a series of three experiments designed to tease apart the connections between nourishment and personal finances. In the first, they deprived some people of food for four hours, long enough that they wouldn't be starving but would almost certainly have food on their minds. Others ate as usual. Then they put all of them in a simulation where they were asked to donate to one of several causes. Those with the growling stomachs consistently gave less money to charity, suggesting that when people sense scarcity in one domain, they conserve resources in another. Put another way, people with physical cravings are in no mood to be magnanimous.

In the second study, Briers let the participants eat as usual, but with some she triggered their appetites by wafting the scent of baked brownies into the lab. Then they played a computer game that, like the earlier simulation, tested their generosity. Again, those with food on their minds were less willing to part with their cash. Interestingly, in this study none of the participants was actually hungry, meaning that the desire for brownies alone was powerful enough to make them into tightwads.

That's pretty convincing evidence. But the psychologists decided to look at it the other way around. That is, they wanted to see if a heightened desire for money affected how much people ate. They had participants fantasize about winning the lottery, but some imagined winning big (the equivalent of about $25,000) while the rest thought about a much more modest prize (about $25). The researchers then had the winners further fantasize about what this imaginary windfall would buy them—sports cars, stereos, and so forth. They basically made some of the participants greedy and not others.

Then they had all the participants participate in a taste test of two kinds of M&M's, although, unbeknownst to them, the scientists were actually measuring how much they ate. And yes, the greedy people scarfed down significantly more candy. It appears that the desire to accumulate money (and stuff) is a modern version of the ancient adaptation to accumulate calories. (Significantly, however, people who were watching their weight did not break their diets, even if they were salivating for a large-screen TV: evidence that we can indeed trump our automatic thinking if we're motivated and thoughtful.)

That last experiment echoes a classic study from the 1940s. In that study, poor kids consistently overestimated the size of coins, while rich kids did not. The new findings are also consistent with cross-cultural studies showing that men's preference for the curviness of women's figures varies directly with the men's economic status. Psychologists Leif Nelson and Evan Morrison demonstrated this intriguing connection in the lab. In one experiment, they recruited a large group of students from campus and asked them how much money they had in their wallets. They figured that those with no cash would be less satisfied, financially, than those with spending money. Then they asked them about their preferences for body weight in a dating partner. When they analyzed all the information, they found that men without money desired women who were significantly heavier than did men with bulging wallets. This was the first laboratory evidence that thinking about one's financial situation affects dating preferences.

The psychologists decided to take another look at these initial findings in a slightly different way. Instead of asking about ready cash, they asked the volunteers how much money they had socked away in the bank. But they asked some of them to place themselves on a scale of $0 to $500, while others placed themselves on a scale from $0 to $400,000. The idea was to manipulate their sense of relative deprivation: some would feel kind of rich compared to others, while others would feel somewhat deprived. Then they again asked them about their preferences in partners, and again they found that those feeling flush wanted skinnier women. The men with a sense of life's scarcity wanted their women to carry some extra pounds, almost as if their partner's fat could protect them against starvation.

What's the dynamic here? What explains this odd mental link? Nelson and Morrison think it has to do with actual hunger; that is, lack of cash or savings triggers the physiological state we all associate with too little food, and that sense of want triggers a basic need for more calories, more fat. To test this idea, the researchers parked themselves at the door of the Stanford dining hall and handed out questionnaires about dating to diners, some as they entered and others as they left. The idea was that some would be satiated when they thought about dating, while others would have food on their minds. And indeed, the hungry men preferred more full-figured women.

The calorie heuristic is the brain's ancient link among food and money and fairness. Both food and money are rewards, they give pleasure, and it's possible that both (and perhaps other rewards as well) are processed in the same clusters of neurons devoted to savoring rewards. Whatever the underlying neurology, the findings could help explain a phenomenon that has long perplexed public health officials: the high prevalence of life-threatening obesity among society's most disadvantaged. It seems counterintuitive that those with the least money should be consuming more calories. But it may be, Briers suggests, that material success has become so important that when people fail in their quest for money, they get frustrated and their brains switch between two intertwined rewards. In effect, they're reverting back to a primitive state, when high-calorie food was the common currency. So those living hand to mouth do indeed work for food—just not nutritious food.

This ancient and automatic entwining of food and money can skew our diets in other ways as well. Consider this bit of trivia: Americans typically eat yogurt out of eight-ounce containers. By contrast, the typical yogurt in a French market is less than five ounces. This seemingly pointless fact may hide a fundamental psychological truth about how humans regulate their consumption—and, in fact, how we make all sorts of choices in life.

That at least is the theory of University of Pennsylvania psychologist Andrew Geier and his colleagues, who are studying what they label "unit bias." The number one, they argue, is a "natural unit," and in the realm of food and diet that means one serving. The French don't double up on their tiny yogurts to get the same volume of food or caloric intake as Americans. Instead, they simply stop eating after one serving, and therefore eat less overall, and therefore are more slender and healthier than overweight Americans.

That's a heavy social burden for a simple yogurt container to carry. So Geier and colleagues decided to test the power of one in everyday settings. They did three similar experiments: In one, they put out a bowl of Tootsie Rolls for public consumption; some days the Tootsie Rolls were large, and other days they were small. They did the same test with Philadelphia-style soft pretzels; some days they put out whole pretzels, while other days they cut them in half. Finally, they put out a large bowl of M&M's, alternating a tablespoon-sized serving spoon with a spoon four times that size.

The results were indisputable. Whatever their junk food of choice, people helped themselves to substantially more when they were offered supersized portions. Conversely, offering small portions effectively controlled how much people ate.

Why are snackers so mesmerized by the number one? It's probably because the idea of one is so fundamental to identity and all the basic tasks of life. Each of us is one person, and most of us have one partner, one shelter, and so forth. But this deep-seated bias is probably reinforced by the forces of experience and culture. Many American children, for instance, are indoctrinated from early on to "clean their plates," reinforcing the notion that a plateful is the appropriate amount to eat at a meal. And people may also limit themselves to one serving so as not to appear greedy or gluttonous.

Whatever the dynamic at work, the researchers believe that the unit bias affects many choices we make every day. We typically go to one movie, not two, whether the movie is ninety minutes long or three hours. We only ride the roller coaster once at the amusement park, regardless of the ride's length. The unit bias is also the foundation of the most successful drug and alcohol recovery programs, which recognize the deep-seated need to focus on "one day at a time."

But the most obvious implications of these snack food experiments are in the public health arena, where overeating and obesity increasingly threaten Americans' well-being. Remember the Dagwood sandwich? Some readers will know the comic strip *Blondie,* in which the lazy husband and father, Dagwood Bumstead, eats very tall sandwiches, layers upon layers of lunch meat and cheese and vegetables and bread. It's a caricature of the unit bias in action.

Interestingly, food marketers appear to have picked up on this bit of psychological insight—in both good ways and bad. Many restaurants continue to attract customers with enormous Dagwood-sized "units," as if those were normal, healthy helpings. One minor-league ballpark in Michigan sells a four-pound, 4,800-calorie cheeseburger for $20—that's about twice the calories I consume in an entire day. That gross example of a "meal" might be dismissed as a publicity stunt, but the fact is that many offerings at fast-food chains are only a bit less exaggerated in their notion of a serving.

But a few food companies are capitalizing on the unit bias in healthier ways. For example, a couple of years ago Nabisco started selling junk food in 100-calorie "snack" units. Weight-conscious Americans loved them to the tune of $100 million a year, and many other food companies soon followed suit. Now we can get everything from Pringles to Sprite to Chips Ahoy in prepackaged 100-calorie snacks. Chips are still chips, but it's better than pigging out on a family-sized unit.

My mother also knew this intuitively. My family was always pinching pennies when I was growing up, and my mother was a very frugal grocery shopper. One thing she did was buy snack food in "economy size" or "family size" packages; she didn't need a calculator to know that this was a smarter way to buy pretzels and chips by the ounce. But she didn't stop there. As soon as she got home and had put away the perishables, she would repackage the snacks, dividing the contents of the economical bags into much smaller units, which she would seal up in plastic sandwich bags. By doing this, she was in effect telling us the proper portion or serving to eat at any given time. To her, moderation and fairness were the same thing.

I GO TO A spinning class a couple of days a week, and I recently noticed something interesting. We exercise to music, and all the instructors use songs as units of measure. They shout things like "Three songs left! Give it your best!" Or "Last song now! Leave it at the gym!" Songs, of course, are not really meaningful units, because a song might be three minutes and twelve seconds, or five minutes and thirty-three seconds, or something else. But all of us spinners know what the instructor means: he means units of motivation and work and—well, calories burned, energy. It's the flip side of food, but it's currency nevertheless. All this is driven by the calorie heuristic, which commingles money, energy, food, and need. At its root, the calorie heuristic is a fear of doing without. In the most basic sense, fear drives many of the choices we make—and even choices we fail to make. The very act of choosing is a terrifying necessity of life, and we will do a lot to avoid choosing. The decoy heuristic, coming in the next chapter, is one of our mind's tools for easing the anxiety of choosing badly. It may explain why you're living in your current home, why you voted for a Democrat in the last election, and maybe even why you find a particular stranger attractive.

11

The **DECOY** Heuristic

||||||||||||||||||||||||||||||||||||||||||||||||||||||||||||||||||||||||||||||||||||||||||||||||||||||||||||||||||||||||||||||||||||||||||||||||||||||

PLEASE DON'T MAKE ME CHOOSE

YOU'VE JUST MOVED to town and need a place to live. You've narrowed your choices to two apartments that seem suitable. The first is spacious, 800 square feet, but it's a good fifteen miles from your new job. That's a long daily commute. The second is much closer, only about seven miles away, but at 450 square feet the space is a bit cramped. It's a trade-off, and you're torn.

Then you open up your newspaper to the classifieds and notice a third apartment, newly available. This one is 350 square feet and ten miles from work. Now you've got three choices, but you have to make a choice pronto. You start your new job in a week. Which do you choose?

Well, if you're like most people, you will choose the second apartment. That may be a perfectly fine choice, and chances are you'll be happy there. But it's not a completely rational choice, and here's why: Eliminating the third apartment is a no-brainer. Just compare it to number two. It's both smaller and more remote. So that should still leave you with a toss-up between two decent places, and you should be just as likely to choose one as the other. But you're not. Because you compared it to number two, you are still swayed by that comparison. You pick the second not because it is better than the spacious apartment, number one, but because it's superior to the loser apartment, even though you ruled that one out.

Cognitive psychologists call that third apartment a "mental decoy." It is so clearly inferior to the other two, neither spacious nor well located, that it really shouldn't even be in the mix, but dinging it does not make it go away entirely. It exerts what psychologists call an "attraction effect," lingering in your mind, tugging you toward apartment number two. The decoy heuristic is a potent choosing tool, even if it is flawed and illogical. We make choices like this every day, some trivial but some momentous. We decide what to have for dinner, which movie to see, where to go to college, even whom to date and marry. And a lot of the picks we make are irrational, influenced by irrelevant decoy information.

Nobody knows for sure why the heuristic brain operates this way, but there are theories. Think about that same apartment dilemma pushed back a couple of million years in time. You're an early hominid, part of a primitive tribe, and you're trying to secure your place in the group. Should you put your energy into claiming the plot of ground near the river, the water supply? Or the smaller one on the ridge, which offers a better view of approaching threats? Which one makes you safer overall? Which gets you closer to the seat of power? Perhaps you should opt for the small one right in the middle of the neighborhood. It's clearly the safest.

Choices matter. Some matter a lot, and they mattered even more back when our minds were adapting for survival. Originally, our ancestors were primarily motivated to protect against loss, and we continue to feel that risk aversion in our gut. The wrong choice—

of property, friend, husband or wife—could cost us a lot, even our life, so it's not hard to understand why we might have a strong bias for quick and conservative choices that do no harm. So in this sense we're programmed to make choices based on fear of danger.

Two marketing professors, William Hedgcock and Akshay Rao, believe that trade-offs are so threatening and unpleasant because they always involve taking a loss of some kind. We hate and fear having to pick. The decoy lets us off the hook, emotionally, by allowing us to make an easier and less stressful choice instead, a no-brainer. Hedgcock and Rao decided to explore this idea in the neuroscience laboratory.

They used a brain scanner to observe the brain in action—to see which regions of the brain are firing and which are quiet during a specific task. For this experiment, the task was a choice very much like the apartment dilemma above, only it involved a trade-off between price and safety: higher rent came with less crime in the neighborhood, and vice versa. (This dilemma is actually more akin to the one our ancient ancestors faced, because their choice of shelter really was a calculation of physical safety.)

The researchers gave volunteers this choice and watched their brains light up. Then they introduced the third, or decoy, option—a place slightly inferior to number two on both safety and price—and watched again. The findings were striking: the brain regions known to process fear and other negative emotions lit up during the trade-off between the original two apartments but calmed down once the decoy became an option. In other words, difficult choices actually trigger the brain's fear centers, and decoys turn the fear off. No wonder the attraction effect is so powerful. Hedgcock and Rao ran this experiment with more dilemmas, many decidedly modern: career choices, day care options, hotels, car repairs. In each case, they got the same results.

But here's the rub. A conservative cognitive strategy made sense when survival was more precarious, but it's often inappropriate for the choices we make in the modern world. As with a lot of heuristics, we apply the decoy heuristic reflexively, and in circumstances that really require more reasonable, deliberate thinking. The attraction effect was first identified by Duke University professor Joel Huber in research on consumers and consumer choice, and much of the experimental work has looked at how people compare products that aren't easily compared—and often make regrettable buys. From restaurants to cars and TVs, we're constantly making bad consumer choices because we're deep-wired to avoid loss and are unduly swayed by a world of decoys.

But what about major life choices? We save our biggest regrets for bad choices related to career, romance, and health, which can be equally irrational. Consider this example of physicians' illogical medication decisions. Scientists asked forty residents in internal medicine to examine three patient cases, one each describing the symptoms of depression, sinusitis, and vaginitis. These are pretty common complaints for an internist to see, so one would expect textbook diagnosis and treatment. And indeed, if they were given two options for prescription medication—different but neither wrong—they chose about equally. But if they were given a third treatment option that was clearly inferior to one of the original medicines, they irrationally changed their minds. The decoy created a cognitive pull in the brain, resulting in a strong preference for one of the medicines over the other. These findings were published in the journal *Medical Decision Making* as a caution to physicians to be aware of their own cognitive biases when choosing a sinus medication or an antidepressant.

So more choices is not always better, even when we think it is. Consider politics. American voters face classic choice dilemmas with almost every primary or election, and every third-party candidate is a potential decoy. Think back to the 2008 Democratic primary, when Barack Obama and Hillary Clinton were locked in a passionate contest for the minds of Democrats. Did the candidacy of John Edwards make a difference? Did the North Carolina senator siphon off votes from Clinton or Obama, or was his candidacy irrelevant? How about Ralph Nader's Green Party candidacy in the hard-fought 2000 contest between George W. Bush and Al Gore?

Classic political theory says that third-party candidates hurt the candidate they most resemble, because they split the votes of like-minded voters. That's why Democrats railed at Nader for handing the election to Bush. But cognitive psychology suggests that the opposite is probably true. Indeed, Nader's candidacy may well have tilted voters toward Gore rather than away from him, according to American University psychologist Diane Lowenthal. That is, voters who considered Nader and then decided not to vote for him probably voted for Gore rather than Bush.

Lowenthal actually simulated such an election in her laboratory by giving volunteers this hypothetical congressional face-off: The Democrat promises to bring 2,000 new jobs and $500,000 in new business to his district, while the Republican is promising 1,500 jobs and $900,000 in new business. If you are unemployed, you may be swayed by the Democrat's job creation program, but if you're a small businessman, you may find the Republican promise more attractive. Either way it's a reasoned decision, and when Lowenthal had people vote, 61 percent voted for the Democrat and 39 percent went for the Republican.

Enter a third-party candidate—for fun, let's say a Green Party candidate. She's promising a thousand new jobs and $800,000 in new revenue. How will the voters choose now? The Green candidate isn't going to appeal to anyone, neither the unemployed worker nor the entrepreneur. But she may sway voters: her promises feel more like the Republican's, and so voters now end up comparing those two—and voting Republican. Indeed, that's exactly what Lowenthal found: even though neither the Democrat nor the Republican changed his campaign promises in the slightest, with the third-party candidate in the race, a full 58 percent said they would pull the lever for the Republican—enough of a shift to tilt the election from a Democratic victory to a lopsided Republican win.

So the stakes are higher than just buying the wrong TV. In fact, there is no reason why the same heuristic trap shouldn't affect choices in dating and marriage. Consider this hypothetical from psychologist Constantine Sedikides of the University of Southampton, England: Lori is a young woman who is being courted by two young men, Antawn and Serge. Antawn is a knockout, one of the best-looking men she knows, but he's not the sharpest knife in the drawer. Serge is pretty average-looking, but he's known for his clever wit. For Lori, this is a classic case of comparing apples and oranges. A pretty face or intelligence? She really wants both, but she can't have both. She's torn, but she must choose.

Enter Trajan. Trajan is also very good-looking, though he's no Antawn. He is, however, about as clever as Antawn, which is to say not very clever at all. So Trajan doesn't make the cut; that's a no-brainer for Lori. But that doesn't mean Trajan hasn't shaped her thinking. He's a cognitive decoy, and in fact his mere presence in the mix will tilt Lori toward Antawn and away from Serge—as unfair as that is to the witty Serge.

At least that's the theory, which Sedikides and his colleagues decided to put to the test. They created a whole variety of dating possibilities like this one, but with many more traits for consideration: In addition to physical attractiveness and intelligence, the potential dates varied on honesty, sense of humor, and dependability. In other words, the dilemma was more like real life, where each of us has a mix of positives and negatives.

They recruited a large group of college students to participate in a study. Most were young women in their early twenties, so they probably had dating on their minds, though most were unattached at the time of the study. The psychologists created a number of triangles like the Lori-Antawn-Serge triangle, with the volunteers playing Lori. That is, each volunteer had to decide if being funny trumped being reliable, or whether honesty trumped good looks, and so forth.

Then they complicated matters by introducing decoys. Like Trajan, the decoys were clearly inferior, but they varied in how similar or dissimilar they were to the others on the mix of traits. One might be slightly less trustworthy, another funny but not a laugh riot, and so forth. As predicted, the decoys swayed the choices of most volunteers, tugging them toward the one the decoy most resembled. In other words, they had an irrational attraction to one dating partner or the other, based only on the false comparison to some guy they would never consider dating.

The scientists aren't saying that our choices of partners are entirely random. But they are arguing that at the early dating stage, our choices are imperfect and irrational, and these choices could theoretically trigger a cascade of other psychological processes that have long-term repercussions. Say you end up dating the person you have chosen irrationally. This often leads to familiarity, which could breed liking, which could lead to commitment and some kind of bonding, perhaps even wedding vows. And all because a decent-looking stranger with a lousy sense of humor happened into the room.

We are of course capable of making deliberate, logical choices as well. We can stop and reason ourselves out of the irrational attraction caused by decoys. But what determines how we will handle a particular choice in life? How do we know what part of our cognitive repertoire will be in play today?

A couple of Florida State University psychologists may have part of the answer to that. If the brain truly is like a hybrid engine, E. J. Masicampo and Roy Baumeister reasoned, then why not look at the fuel system? All of that cognitive crunching doesn't come cheap, and effortful deliberation is especially greedy for energy. This is not just a metaphor: they wanted to see if the brain's supply of fuel—blood glucose—might determine whether we make logical choices or irrational ones. They decided to explore this in the laboratory.

The experiment was fairly simple. They started by having all the subjects do an exercise meant to deplete their power—both their willpower and the glucose that fuels self-control and decision making. Specifically, they had them watch a silent video of a woman talking. A series of words also flashed on the screen, but they told the subjects to ignore the words; if they did find themselves distracted by the words, they were to refocus their attention on the woman. This is actually very hard to do; it requires a lot of mental effort to not read the words right in front of you.

The purpose here was to mentally exhaust the volunteers, much as doing wind sprints would deplete their muscles and lungs. Once the researchers had all the volunteers in this depleted condition, they reenergized some of them with sugar. They actually had all of the subjects drink some lemonade, but only some were getting real sugar; the others were drinking lemonade artificially sweetened with Splenda. The idea was that the Splenda drinkers would remain cognitively drained while the sugar drinkers would be restored to normal intellectual functioning.

Finally, the psychologists confronted the subjects with a classic decoy choice task, very similar to the apartment dilemma. In theory, the depleted subjects should at this point have been mentally "weaker" and therefore less capable of making effortful, deliberate decisions. And that is precisely what they found. The subjects who were running on empty were much more likely to be swayed by the decoy apartment—and thus to make a poor judgment. Those who had recently been reenergized didn't waste any time or energy on the inferior decoy and didn't allow it to sway them in their real choice:

they chose the spacious apartment and the better-located apartment about equally.

This is obviously not about lemonade and apartment hunting. But it is about the intricate interplay of mind and body in so many of life's dilemmas. A lot of things can compromise us cognitively— stress, distractions, multitasking. These findings raise a question that can be asked of much of our heuristic thinking: Do we have the capability to overrule such rapid, automatic processing if it's irrational or harmful? Can we learn to damp down irrational thinking and sub in our more deliberate, analytic thinking strategies?

Two University of Toronto psychologists have done a study that offers some hope in this regard. Sunghan Kim and Lynn Hasher wanted to look at the effects of normal aging on decision making, so they recruited hundreds of college students and senior citizens from all over the country. They gave them two different dilemmas, one involving grocery shopping and one involving getting extra credit in a college course. The task was just like the other decoy tasks, with two options and a decoy, and the idea was to see who would think rationally and who would think irrationally in each scenario.

The psychologists anticipated that the older volunteers would do better—that is, be less distracted by the decoy—in the grocery store, because their age would likely make them more experienced shoppers. Similarly, they expected that the college students would do better in the extra-credit scenario, because that was their territory.

They were half right and half wrong. The college students did think rationally in their area of expertise, and irrationally in the less familiar domain, grocery shopping. But the senior citizens did well in both. That is, they ignored the decoy and made rational choices. They appeared to have a generalized ability to trump their own automatic heuristic judgments, regardless of the life task. It may just be that this acquired skill—recognizing fast choices based on impulse and correcting them—is what we call wisdom.

CHOOSING A HOME, choosing a partner—those are big life choices. And, sad to say, most of us don't have the wisdom to make those choices soundly at the time in life that we make them. But simply being aware of the power of decoys—and irrational attraction—should be able to help us avoid some unreasonable tugs on our mind. These choices are tough enough when they are frozen in time, but most of our judgments and choices are not such snapshots. They involve anticipating how circumstances will shift over days or months or years, and how we might change as well. The futuristic heuristic offers some insight into the difficulty of mental and emotional forecasting—and how we might make better judgments for what's around the corner.

CHAPTER

12

The **FUTURISTIC** Heuristic

||||||||||||||||||||||||||||||||||||||||||||||||||||||||||||||||||||||||||||||||||||||||||||||||||||||||||||||||||||||||||||||||||

A WRINKLE IN TIME

EVERYONE HAS A favorite image from election night 2008, a moment seared into memory. For me, it was the spontaneous outpouring of young celebrants, black and white, into Washington, D.C.'s U Street corridor, not far from my house. U Street, home to the famed Lincoln Theatre and Ben's Chili Bowl, was once the center of African American culture in D.C., until it was burned and gutted by the race riots of the 1960s. It has taken decades for this historic neighborhood to recover from those divisive times, so to see it throbbing with youthful hope was poignant and exhilarating.

I am writing this just a few days after the election of Barack Obama as the forty-fourth president of the United States, a historic event no matter what your political stripe. But you are reading this much later. As I write I am filled with hope and expectation, like much of America, yet even as I write, I wonder how I will feel a year or two from now—how the country will feel. Can we carry that excitement and goodwill into the future? Are our expectations too high?

Psychologists are very interested in how the mind processes events like Obama's election, and how it turns these events into either hopeful anticipation or regret and disappointment. How powerfully do our experiences today shape our emotions of tomorrow? How good are we at seeing the future and using what we see to guide us today? In short, what predicts future happiness?

Researchers call this "emotional forecasting." Humans are arguably the only animals capable of imagining what doesn't already exist, conjuring up detailed future scenarios. That's a trait of our highly evolved brains. But evolution apparently stopped short—because we're not all that talented at predicting our own state of mind. Indeed, study after study has shown that we're usually way off the mark with our predictions. We believe that winning the lottery will make us blissful, and it rarely does. We think being jilted will devastate us, yet we almost always bounce back.

Why are we so bad at this? A growing cadre of psychologists—Daniel Gilbert of Harvard, Timothy Wilson of the University of Virginia, and others—have been exploring the cognitive machinery of emotional forecasting, and its failures. Their studies point to a few possible reasons for our failures of imagination, which might be collectively called the futuristic heuristic.

There appears to be a fundamental asymmetry in the way we think about the future and the past. The future is more interesting, more important, and more valuable than the past, even if we're thinking about the exact same event. Just think about something coming up in the weeks or months ahead, something you're excited about—a new job, a big date—or something you are dreading. Now think about the same event in the past; you know it was important once, that it stirred emotion for you, but it's hard to get excited or upset about it now.

This makes sense from an evolutionary point of view, because even our very primitive brain had this sense that the future was important in terms of survival. The past is gone and carries no threat or promise. The future has both.

At least that's the theory. Gilbert and Wilson, working with Eugene Caruso of the University of Chicago, ran some experiments to examine this premise in the lab. They asked a large group of Harvard students to imagine that they had agreed to spend five hours entering data into a computer; they deliberately chose something that was dull but not dreadful, and certainly not intriguing. Some imagined taking on this drudgery in a month, while others imagined that they had already completed the task, exactly a month before.

So it was the same task and the same distance away in time, but guess what. When the psychologists asked the volunteers to make a bid on the job—to say how much they should fairly be paid for five hours of monotonous work—those who were projecting into the future thought they should be paid 101 percent more than those who, in effect, were billing their clients for work already completed. That is, they viewed the identical workload as twice as valuable a month into the future than a month into the past, which is to say that they valued future time more than past time.

The psychologists call this asymmetry a "wrinkle in time," an allusion to the award-winning Madeleine L'Engle children's book in which people travel through the folds of time and space. They have run some more experiments to verify it. They especially wanted to see if we make this kind of judgment automatically, even though we "know" it's irrational. We know that five hours of data processing is five hours of data processing, in the past or in the future, but our judgment is distorted by the wrinkle in time. That's the nature of cognitive heuristics: they're ingrained and rapid, but if we slow down and analyze our thoughts and behavior, we can often see that they don't make sense.

There is a tried-and-true way of testing this in the lab. It's an elaborate statistical analysis, but think of it as the "I-know-that's-crazy test." Here's an example: If you ask someone to choose between the health of migrant workers and the health of endangered animals, they almost always place a higher value on the lives of the workers than the animals. But if you ask people to place a value on just one of these at a time, without mentioning the other, and compare all the ratings from a lot of people, it turns out that people rate the health of endangered animals higher than they do the health of migrant workers. I know—crazy but true. The contradictory answers indicate that on some level we *know* it's a crazy thought to value animals over people.

So the researchers ran the I-know-it's-crazy test on the emotional forecasting findings. In one experiment, volunteers imagined that a friend had offered to let them use his vacation home at the beach. But, as before, there were two different scenarios. In one, they imagined that they had just returned from a week at the beach house, and in the other they imagined that they would be heading to the beach in a week. Then all the volunteers were shown descriptions of eight wines and told to select the one that was the most appropriate gift for their gracious host. The wines varied in price from $10 to $400.

The wine was just a proxy, a way to get the volunteers to value the future and the past. And when they analyzed all the volunteers' answers, this is what they found: The "guests" who were looking forward to the beach house stay selected a wine that was 37 percent more expensive than the wine chosen by guests for whom the beach sojourn was history. But here's the interesting part: when they ran the I-know-it's-crazy test, it was clear that the guests saw their asymmetrical thinking as irrational and distorted. But they did it anyway.

The psychologists ran this test many different ways with various scenarios—compensating a woman who was injured by a drunk driver, for example. In every case they saw the same automatic but irrational thinking pattern. That is, in every case future events were valued more highly than equivalent events in the past. Why would this be? Well, one possibility is that when we ponder future events, we do so with much more emotional baggage than when we contemplate what's done and gone.

To test this idea, the researchers had volunteers imagine helping a friend move into a new apartment. Now, unlike the drudgery of data entry, helping a friend move is an aversive task. We all live busy lives, and we almost never would choose hoisting sofa beds rather than, say, watching Sunday football games on TV—even when it's a really good friend. So it was not surprising that they imagined their friend giving them a fairly nice bottle of wine for their time and self-lessness, and a more expensive wine in the future than in the past. But what's more, when they asked the volunteers about the past and future moving days, those who were anticipating a future event described being more exhausted, more stressed out, and more full of dread about the prospect. Put another way, they were paying themselves more because they saw the future moving day as much more unpleasant as the identical day gone by.

And they knew this was irrational. It appears that the brain has a natural, deep-wired tendency to compare events, and this is an obstacle to fair and accurate forecasting. Here is a fascinating demonstration of this bias. In this experiment, psychologists had volunteers contemplate a plate of potato chips—to imagine eating them. For some of the volunteers, there was a tin of sardines sitting nearby; it was just sitting there, without explanation. Others pondered the potato chips while also eyeing a fine Swiss chocolate that was on the table, technically not part of the experiment.

Here's what happened: those who were sitting near the tin of sardines predicted that the chips would taste much better than did those eyeing the chocolate. That in itself is not surprising. They were obviously comparing the chips to the canned fish (or to the chocolate), and it's not a shock which one won out. But here's the intriguing part: when they actually ate the chips, there was no difference in their enjoyment, whether there was fish or chocolate nearby. In other words, the predicted pleasure or disappointment was illusory. In the scientists' words, their "miswanting" was based on a meaningless comparison. The reality of actually munching chips trumped the imaginary version that had been conjured up.

Such failures of imagination happen all the time in the real world, Gilbert says, and they affect our life choices and our happiness. Consider this hypothetical in which people have a choice of jobs. One job pays $30,000 the first year, $40,000 the second, and $50,000 the third. Not bad. The other offers $60,000 at first, but then only $50,000, and finally $40,000. Inexplicably, most people choose the first job, even though in the long run they will make less money. Why? The simple answer is that people hate pay cuts. The more complicated answer has to do with perversity of the human mind, which for unknown reasons favors relative numbers over absolutes; that is, the relative increase in the first job scenario is more appealing than the greater total income in the second. In order to avoid the psychological discomfort of taking a pay cut, people fail to imagine themselves three years hence, when their actual (and completely avoidable) loss of thirty grand will almost certainly make them very unhappy.

Here's one more example from Gilbert's Harvard lab. Why is it, the psychologist asks, that most of us would drive clear across town to save $50 on a $100 radio, but wouldn't consider the same inconvenience to save $50 on a $100,000 car? The answer, again, is that we think in relative terms, not absolutes. Getting a good radio at half price is a bargain. Getting that fancy car for $99,950 doesn't feel like a bargain at all; the savings are trivial. Such reasoning and behavior drive economists crazy, because to an economist $50 is $50 is $50. But paradoxically, it takes an act of supreme imagination to get to this obvious truth.

Think back on that election night euphoria and some of the revelers' outsized hopes. Why did we have such a hard time keeping it in some kind of perspective? In addition to our strong preference for comparisons, people are also thrown off by what psychologists call the "durability bias." That's just a jargony way of saying that when we have an emotional experience, we automatically assume that the emotion—optimism and excitement, say—will continue at the same level of intensity for the foreseeable future. Again, it's a bit irrational, but apparently the brain is not wired to imagine the gradual dissipation of emotion over time: slightly less excitement tomorrow, even less the next day, and so forth. The fact is most people's emotions, good and bad, gradually head back toward a preset emotional baseline, but it's very difficult to see that when you're in a peak experience. When I was watching the crowds on U Street, the furthest thing from my mind was the notion that all this wonder would evaporate. We're not wired for cynicism.

Indeed, we may be wired for the opposite, for unfounded expectations, both good and bad. Our brains are clever enough to know the future is coming, but not nearly clever enough to automatically project ourselves into it and analyze future events dispassionately. This distortion is compounded by another deep-wired cognitive tendency—the tendency to view events in a vacuum, without any context. With the Obama victory, in order to realistically project ourselves into the future, to view the Democratic victory in some kind of historical perspective, we would have needed to say something like this to ourselves: "This is an amazing event, unprecedented in history, but there are inevitable political realities and obstacles. Plus tomorrow I have to revise my resume because work isn't going so well, plus my kid may be coming down with the flu, and my old Saab's transmission is likely to give out," and on and on. In other words, there is a lot going on in our lives, but the brain can only do so much, and when you're celebrating a historic event, it pretty much eclipses all the other stuff. But all that other stuff will creep back into focus over the days, weeks, and months ahead. And so we get the inevitable letdown.

But is it inevitable? Is there anything we can do to avoid these cognitive pitfalls? Well, perhaps. Gilbert and Wilson and their colleagues believe that people can train themselves to avoid the errors of emotional forecasting. They did a series of experiments that offer some hope. They studied college students at the University of Virginia and Virginia Tech just before and after a big football game between these longtime rivals. They asked them to predict how happy (or sad) a victory (or loss) would make them in the future, and then they actually measured the volunteers' sense of well-being later on.

But here's the twist. They had some of the students keep a prospective diary before the game. That is, the students projected themselves into the future and wrote down everything that they imagined they would be doing either after a victory or after a defeat: studying for exams, partying with friends, writing papers, playing video games, and so forth. They found that those who did this—who basically put the prospect of a depressing loss (or joyful victory) into the perspective of daily life—had much more realistic expectations for their future happiness. The event lost its potency, good or bad. You might not want to do this for life's little victories—why not savor the joy of a football victory?—but it offers a tool for tempering the emotions of a big disappointment.

Now, we don't have to actually write such diaries, although that may not be a bad exercise if you have the time and inclination. But short of that, we can apparently talk to ourselves, and with such mental work we can become capable of keeping peak experiences in proper perspective. These psychologists have also begun exploring another technique that may prove valuable in avoiding disappointment. They call it the "George Bailey effect." George Bailey, you'll recall, was the fictional small-town banker in the beloved Frank Capra film *It's a Wonderful Life*. Frustrated by financial problems at the bank and his own squandered ambitions, Bailey decides to end it all by jumping from a bridge into the icy waters of Bedford Falls. He survives only because his personal angel intercedes, and this angel takes him on a tour of what life would have been without him. He witnesses the absence of all the joys his family and community might have had, and in this process his hope is restored.

The film is a perennial favorite at Christmas, but new research suggests we may be able to re-create the same psychological process any time, with or without an angel. Psychologist Minkyung Koo of the University of Virginia had the idea that mentally "undoing" positive events by thinking about the absence of those events—basically following George Bailey's lead—could be tonic. It's counterintuitive, because thinking about losing out on good stuff is inherently unpleasant, but she speculated that such negative thinking would make positive experiences seem better. In other words, the count-your-blessings philosophy of gratitude may be fundamentally flawed.

To test this idea, she asked volunteers to think of an event for which they were grateful, and then to write a narrative of how the event came about. These events could have to do with health, possessions, job success, and so forth, but they had to be specific. Others also wrote about such an event, but they wrote about how, hypothetically, the event might never have occurred—and how surprising its occurrence was to them when it did happen. Then afterward, she assessed the volunteers on such measures as gratitude, joy, and appreciation, as well as distress and melancholy.

The findings? Those who had gone through the George Bailey exercise came out higher on every measure of positive emotion than the others. They were uniformly happier. Koo and her colleagues believe that thinking about the absence of an event in effect renews its surprise value. Over time, we adapt emotionally to good things that happen to us—we can't sustain the high levels of joy and gratitude and excitement. But imagining life without the blessings helps us "unadapt" and see our condition as new and surprising once again.

This might work with romantic relationships as well. The psychologists did a similar experiment with people who had been in long-term relationships—almost fourteen years on average. Again, they had some recall the basic history of the relationship—how they met, how the relationship progressed, how they made a commitment to each other. Others imagined how it might never have happened, how unlikely their meeting really was, and how they might have gone through life without each other. They then asked a battery of questions about their relationship—satisfaction, desire, problems, and so forth.

Again, the psychologists found that mentally subtracting the good things in life led to increased satisfaction across the board. It may be that just spending a few minutes a day "undoing" our good fortunes can reinvigorate them—and make us feel better. This does not mean we shouldn't savor the vivid emotional memories of election night or not root for our favorite football team. Peak experiences bring joy to life. But we need to keep elections, football games, and relationships—and more—in perspective, and counting our blessings may not be enough to do that.

NUMBERS AND ROMANCE? We don't like to think of ourselves being calculating in our most intimate relationships, but in fact we are all romantic oddsmakers. Numbers are not just the figures printed in your mathematics textbooks. They are part and parcel of our political choices, our career decisions, our emotional responses to human indecency, even genocide. These numerical heuristics don't operate in isolation, of course. They are interwoven with another set of powerful cognitive tendencies that shape the high-order thinking that makes us uniquely human: the ones that shape our sense of ourselves in the universe, our curiosity about the unknown, our beliefs. These meaning-making heuristics make up the final part of the book.

Three

HOW THE MIND MAKES MEANING

13

The **DESIGN** Heuristic

||||||||||||||||||||||||||||||||||||||||||||||||||||||||||||||||||||||||||||||||||||||||||||||||||||||||||||||||||||||||||||||||||||||||||||||||||||||||||||||||||||||||||||||||

SIMPLICITY AND PURPOSE

CONSIDER THIS RATHER wild scenario. Imagine you are a very early human, trying to eke out a living on the savannas of eastern Africa. You wake up one morning and head out to forage some breakfast, but you discover that your path is blocked by a robot. That's right, a gleaming silver robot, with lots of knobs and flashing lights. What do you do?

Well, first off, you've got to make sense of this thing. Remember, you're a primitive thinker. You've got a couple hundred thousand years of evolving to do before you'll even know the word *robot,* much less what an algorithm is. But right now your primitive brain wants to put it in a category. So what do you ask yourself? Do you wonder how and what it eats? How it moves? How it reproduces? Or do you instinctively ask yourself: "What is this thing's purpose? How can it serve me?"

It may surprise you to know that psychologists study this

question. They want to know how the modern human mind deals with the world's seemingly infinite diversity—basically, how we discover the universe and put it all into some kind of sensible order. What do we know intuitively about the world and our place in it? How do we think about design and purpose?

The short answer is that we have a powerful impulse for simplicity and order—the design heuristic. One crucial part of the human discovery process is learning to categorize and label things—to differentiate between an animal, a plant, a cloud, and a bicycle. One way psychologists explore basic explanatory processes is to study the minds of preschoolers who are just beginning to make sense of unfamiliar things. Kids are analogous to early humans in their naivete about the world around them, so they can often offer insights into the fundamental psychological processes of all humans. Consider these experiments by psychologist Marissa Greif and her colleagues at Yale University.

Greif showed a group of preschool children pictures of both animals and man-made objects. The animals were real, but unfamiliar, even to many adults: pangolins, for example, and saigas. The objects, on the other hand, were made up but quite detailed, complete with names and purposes. A garflom, for instance, looks like a wooden foot massager, but its official purpose for the experiment was to flatten towels. A riepank (which looks awfully like a woodworker's C-clamp) is used to make holes in play dough. And so forth.

The children, who averaged about four and a half years old, were encouraged to ask questions about these things. Their questions (and guesses) were revealing. For example, when the kids asked about action, some questions were appropriate for either an animal or artifact (does it turn?), while others would only be asked sensibly of animals (does it climb trees?) or artifacts (is it for cutting?). Remarkably, the children almost never made mistakes. That is, they never asked inappropriate questions of either animals or objects. They never asked of a tarsier or pangolin: How does it work? Similarly, they never asked how riepanks reproduce or what garfloms eat, though they did ask such survival questions of the unfamiliar animals.

What this suggests to the scientists is that children have a rich and intuitive understanding of these two fundamental categories of things in the world. At four and a half they are too young to articulate this sensibility, but they appear to know the distinct qualities of animals and artifacts. What's more, it appears that humans have an innate sense that the world is designed—and that the essence of being an animal (and human) is survival. The essence of artifacts is to serve humanity, to be tools.

This is obviously a species-centered view of the world. The point is not that it is a correct interpretation of the world but that it's common, perhaps universal. It's the heuristic mind at work. We are all meaning-making creatures, intuitive taxonomists. We instinctively explain (and evaluate explanations) in order to navigate an incredibly complex and threatening world. The readiest explanation is that the world is simple, it makes sense, and we're at the center of it.

But it's not that easy. The world's complexity constantly challenges our basic impulse to simplify. Dividing the universe into animals and artifacts is one thing, but what about finer distinctions? How does the human mind link together things as varied as hippos, lichens, mosquitoes, and rhododendrons? And how do we sort this diversity into meaningful categories? In short, how do we think about life?

How the mature mind sorts the living world, and where we put ourselves in relation to other life forms—that's the stuff of philosophy and religion and morality. But it's not as obvious as one would think. Take motion, for example. Many living things move, but so do rivers, clouds, and rocket ships. And some living things, such as coral, don't appear to move at all. So it's not just the fact of motion that defines life, but the why and how. Young children find this confusing and make a lot of mistakes about what's animated and what's not. Only over time do we outgrow our primitive, childish ideas and replace them with a sophisticated view of the natural world.

Or do we? Do we really discard all our naive thinking as we experience the world and learn about its complexity? University of Pennsylvania psychologists Robert Goldberg and Sharon Thompson-Schill have been exploring these questions in the laboratory, with intriguing results. Here's one of their experiments.

The psychologists showed a group of college students a long list of words, one at a time and very rapidly. Some were the names of plants, others animals, and still others nonliving things. The nonliving things were further divided into nonmoving objects, such as brooms; nonmoving natural things, such as boulders; moving artifacts, such as trucks; and finally, natural moving things, such as rivers. The idea was to see how quickly and accurately the volunteers used movement and "naturalness" to classify these various things as living or nonliving.

The scientists were particularly interested in how we think about plants, where we put them in the grand scheme of things. Plants are an interesting anomaly because—at least to young children—they don't "do" anything; instead, we do things to them, like climb them and water them and prune them. If they move at all, their movement is very subtle. Not surprisingly, kids often misclassify plants as nonliving.

But how about college students? Well, it appears that they too make mistakes, even with all that formal education. The volunteers in the study were much more hesitant in classifying plants, suggesting that they had to slow down to deliberately overrule their naive taxonomy, and they also made more outright errors. They were also slower to size up moving things in general, and nonliving natural things—suggesting that movement and naturalness were the features that stymied them.

To be fair, these weren't biology majors. And we all know that kids can slip into college without much in the way of rigorous scientific training. But here's the really interesting part. The psychologists ran basically the same experiment with biology professors, people who make their living teaching university students about the natural world. Indeed, the volunteers in this second study had been teaching college-level biology for a quarter century, on average, and at highly prestigious schools. And guess what. The profs did better than the undergraduates, but not as brilliantly as one might from the scientific elite. Even these experts were significantly worse at classifying plants than they were at categorizing animals. That is, even a lifetime of advanced scientific training didn't trump the naive impulse to view plants as artifacts.

Some readers will remember *The Secret Life of Plants,* a 1973 book that made a fleeting claim to fame by arguing that plants are sentient, even spiritual beings. The book lacked scientific merit, but it struck a chord by challenging humans' claim to uniqueness and centrality in the world. Psychological research now explains the odd appeal of that cultural sensation: it challenged our deeply wired bias for design and purpose.

So we're all natural-born taxonomists, but we're not perfect by any means. The design heuristic is a deep-wired urge to see the world as designed and simple, and to be at the center of it all. This is basically the cognitive process called diagnosis. One of the most popular shows on TV right now is *House,* in which Hugh Laurie plays Gregory House, a misanthropic but brilliant medical doctor, the chief of diagnosis at a hospital. The episodes all begin with the onset of a mysterious medical condition, and they almost all end with House figuring out what's wrong, but along the way he makes lots of missteps and wrong turns. The intellectual challenge is always basically the same: to inventory an assortment of symptoms and find the most parsimonious answer.

We're all diagnosticians in our own worlds. We may not be as brilliant as the curmudgeonly House, but we use the same intellectual methods. And like House, we have a powerful yen for the simplest, cleanest explanation of things. Consider the plight of poor Treda.

Treda lives on Zorg, a small planet with only 750 permanent residents, and at the moment she is feeling punk. She has purple spots and her minttels are sore. It falls to you, a visiting physician, to diagnose her, and this is what you know: Tritchet's syndrome has been known to cause both sore minttels and purple spots. Morad's disease always causes sore minttels, but the disease never causes purple spots. When a Zorgian comes down with a Humel infection, the patient invariably breaks out in purple spots—but there is no known case where the infection caused sore minttels. Those are the only Zorgian diseases known to cause either symptom. So what's the best diagnosis?

Treda and Zorg are the fantasy of psychologist Tania Lombrozo of the University of California at Berkeley. When she describes this hypothetical medical problem to her students, she asks them to pick the most likely diagnosis from these: Tritchet's syndrome, Morad's disease, Humel infection, Tritchet's and Morad's, Tritchet's and Humel, or Morad's and Humel. The overwhelming majority—fully 96 percent—pick the simplest, one-cause explanation, that is, Tritchet's syndrome.

That's not all that surprising in itself. It's pretty easy to see that you don't need more than one cause to explain the symptoms. That is, Tritchet's is sufficient to explain both symptoms. But the fact is, that diagnosis might be wrong. The purple spots might be caused by one disease, the sore minttels by another. Treda could very well have two medical problems, or even three. When Lombrozo asked the volunteers to justify their diagnosis, the answers were revealing: many said their diagnosis was simpler, but many more said it was more likely—even though they had no probability information to support such a belief. What's more, they used terms like "prettier" or "less complex" to describe their judgments. It appears the simpler explanation had an intuitive appeal, which trumped any rational calculation of actual probability.

This bias for simplicity is powerful, as Lombrozo demonstrated in a second experiment. It was basically the same Treda dilemma, but in this case she gave the volunteers some actual information on the incidence of the three disorders. She might add, for example, that fifty Zorgians now suffer from Tritchet's syndrome. These disease rates varied from trial to trial, but there was always enough information that volunteers could actually calculate a true likelihood of one disorder or another if they wanted to make the mental effort. Few did. For most, the simple, intuitive explanation trumped cold calculation.

The volunteers in the Zorg experiments were about twenty years old, students at one of the nation's elite universities, so they were not naive about the world. Yet they clearly preferred to think of the world as simple—or simplistic. Why? And where does such a childlike perspective come from?

Lombrozo decided to explore this question with preschool children to see if this impulse for simplicity emerges early in life. In an experiment in a Boston museum, she presented four-and-a-half-year-olds with an invented toy. It's complicated to describe, but basically the toy used different colored chips to activate different functions—a red globe, a green fan, or both at once. The kids' job was comparable to playing doctor on Zorg—that is, they had to decide which chip (or chips) was most likely to activate which function. But Lombrozo also varied the numbers of chips in a way that the kids could in some cases make a reasoned decision based on probability. In effect, the experiment pitted the kids' power to reason against their impulse to simplify.

Again simplicity won out, but with an interesting twist. The more information they had that enabled them to reason the problem out, the more likely they were to reason it out. But it took a lot of probability information to tip them that way, and they never became reasonable creatures. All things being equal, they still opted for the more parsimonious explanation.

What this suggests is that simplicity is a common heuristic for probability judgments, even for young children. Calculating likelihoods and odds is tough cognitive work, and we only do it when we must.

So is this urge for simplicity and design and purpose wired into our ancient neurons? Do we carry around an inner theory of the world? Other work with children has shown that even very young ones have a natural inclination to see the world as purposeful and things like stars and trees and rain primarily in terms of their function instead of their natural causes. Laboratory tests have shown this again and again: when psychologists ask children why mountains exist, most say they exist so animals have a place to climb. In kids' "theory" of the natural world, trees don't just happen to provide shade; making shade is their primary purpose. And so forth. In fact, unless there is really good evidence to convince kids otherwise, they want to see everything as having a precise function in the grand scheme of things.

But is this childish yearning for purpose and design simply a sign of cognitive immaturity, a primitive habit of mind that we grow out of as we age and our brains sprout new neuronal connections? Psychologists are very interested in how both kids and grown-ups explain the world, because our theories about stars, eyes, and lakes are closely tied to our understanding of creation and a creator—our personal cosmology.

Lombrozo suspected that the strong childhood preference for purposeful design might actually be a lifelong default position, one that is eclipsed but doesn't actually disappear as we gain experience and form beliefs —beliefs in gravity, plate tectonics, and natural se-lection, for example—that constrain our explanations of things. And she figured out a way to test this provocative idea.

Lombrozo decided to study patients with Alzheimer's disease. She figured that dementia would weaken the entrenched causal be-liefs of adulthood, and that with their beliefs so compromised, adults would show their true cognitive colors. To test this idea in the labora-tory, she gave Alzheimer's patients the same cognitive tests that are used with children, basically consisting of a series of questions with two possible answers. For example, she might ask, "Why is there rain? Is it because water condenses in clouds and forms droplets, or does rain exist so we will have water for drinking?" Other questions she used included "What is the sun for?" and "How about trees?"

Well, guess what. Alzheimer's patients think the primary purpose of rain is to provide drinking water, that trees exist to provide shade, and that the sun is up in the sky for the sole purpose of keeping us warm. Healthy adults, by contrast, while they know the sun warms us, also know the sun does not exist for that reason. It's a subtle but important distinction. The Alzheimer's patients' thinking mirrors the rudimentary thinking of children and suggests that the urge for de-sign and functionality is never really outgrown. There is a fundamen-tal human urge to comprehend the world as purposeful.

There is an intriguing twist, however. Lombrozo did a second study with the same people, asking whether the order in the universe was caused by God or by some natural process. In other words, do design and purpose require a designer? The answer appears to be no. Even though the patients tended to see the world as designed and purposeful, they were no more likely to presume that a supernatural designer is behind the natural order of things. So our lifelong im-pulse is to see the world as ordered and purposeful; some of us add on the God part, but it's not necessary to explain the brain's urge for order.

Yet a lot of people—and many societies—do add on the God part as a way to explain this basic cognitive urge. For example, psychologists have found that in cultures where formal education is limited, people often prefer purposeful explanations of things, presumably because they remain scientifically naive. Lombrozo believes the same fundamental impulse explains the appeal of "intelligent design" creationism, a worldview that rejects evolutionary theory in favor of a design explanation of life's complexity. Though scientifically indefensible, this view is understandable as a persistence of the basic human impulse to infer order.

On a lighter note, the new science may also explain why there seems to be a part of all of us, even supposedly sophisticated and educated adults, that still likes the magic of Disney movies and similar modern fairy tales. Two of the most endearing characters in Disney's *The Lion King* are the clownish pals Timon and Pumbaa. Timon is a know-it-all meerkat and Pumbaa a bumbling warthog, and late one night they are out on the savanna wondering about the origin of the stars. "They're fireflies," says Timon, "that got stuck in that big bluish-black thing." To which the less sophisticated Pumbaa replies, "Oh. I always thought they were balls of gas burning millions of miles away."

Pumbaa is scientifically correct, of course. That's why the joke is funny. But many children watching *The Lion King* would probably find Timon's theory more appealing. We may "know" that Pumbaa's mechanistic explanation of the universe is right, but our naive explanatory impulse is right below the surface.

Although the design heuristic is universal, individual minds vary in their need for order and simplicity. That is, some people have a high need for order, while others are freer from this ancient impulse. This manifests itself in everything from personal habits to political views. For example, my office is a cluttered mess and always has been. You can't see my desktop, and my books are not alphabetized. I rarely file anything, though I do make neat piles on the windowsills and floor. I have artwork and mementos, but I have never quite gotten around to actually nailing them to the walls. They sit leaning against the wall. I decorate with Post-it notes.

I have never given much thought to my disorderly life. I figured I was just a slob. But research on the design heuristic suggests that there may be meaning in my mess, indeed that my office disarray may reflect my views about everything from women's reproductive choice to the war in Iraq. According to this view, habits like tidiness and messiness are really habits of the mind; they are meaningfully linked to basic personality traits, and these traits in turn shape political ideology. Put another way, our deepest psychological needs and fears may play a big part in determining where we fall on the political spectrum: left or right, liberal or conservative, blue or red.

That's a lot to swallow, because most of us, left or right of center, like to think we come to our political positions through rational analysis. Our views may be self-serving, but they're at least logical. Well, maybe not, according to accumulating evidence from the laboratory. A team of psychologists has recently been exploring just how deep-wired the core tenets of conservatism and liberalism are, with some surprising results.

Most people would agree on the essential ideas: the conservative tendency to value tradition and authority over change, and the liberal tendency to value equality over hierarchy. New York University psychologist John Jost and his colleagues have been using time-tested instruments to plumb the unconscious attitudes of both self-proclaimed conservatives and liberals. Although most everyone prefers order to chaos, the psychologists found this yearning to be much more potent in conservatives than in liberals. Put another way, conservatives have little tolerance for any messiness, let alone rebelliousness, even on this basic neuronal level. Liberals, by contrast, have a deep-wired preference for flexibility and progress over tradition. The starkest difference between conservatives and liberals was related to feminism, which conservatives believe in their gut to be a threat to their ordered world.

This may seem at first to merely reflect tired old stereotypes. But remember that these laboratory probes are designed to tunnel below conscious thought, suggesting that ideology permeates the most basic cognitive machinery we have. If so, views on civil rights, welfare, affirmative action, and much more are not just politically meaningful but psychologically meaningful as well.

Why would this be? Well, it may be a matter of basic inborn temperament or personality. As Jost and his colleagues (Brian Nosek of the University of Virginia and Samuel Gosling of the University of Texas at Austin) explain, extreme political ideologies appear to fit with certain core personality traits. Specifically, conservatives are more "conscientious" than liberals, who are more "open to experience" than conservatives. In two large studies of University of Texas students, the psychologists found strong liberal preferences for novel experiences like foreign travel and unusual foods and art, plus greater tolerance of everything from tattoos and erotica to street people and drugs. Conservative students favored fraternities and mainstream activities like fishing and watching TV, in addition to traditional religious practices such as prayer.

Again, these may be stereotypes, but stereotypes often have truth to them. The design heuristic offers a psychological explanation for these predictable tastes and attitudes. It's human nature to crave certainty and structure. But individuals crave security to varying degrees, depending on how fearful they are. People who are the most fearful see safety in stability and hierarchy, where more emotionally secure people can tolerate some chaos and unpredictability in their lives. The psychologists gathered data from twelve different countries to test this out, and they found that conservative politics were inextricably linked to several measures of emotional insecurity: intolerance of ambiguity, need for structure, desire for closure, and so forth. They also found that conservatives had a more intense existential fear of death.

So what does all this have to do with my messy office? Another of Jost's colleagues, Dana Carney of Harvard, actually went into people's offices and bedrooms to probe the "secret lives" of liberals and conservatives, and found dramatic differences. The conservatives' rooms were not only tidy and orderly but also full of utilitarian stuff like cleaning supplies, calendars, and postage stamps. The liberals' rooms were painted in bold colors and cluttered with books and art and travel brochures. The red rooms, if you will, were places to hole up and be safe, while the blue rooms felt more like staging areas for exploration.

The urge for simplicity and order is powerful, but it often conflicts with the realities of the complex, modern world. The design heuristic may be intuitively appealing, but it's anti-nuance; it demands black and white in a world that is many shades of gray.

THERE WERE NO political parties in the ancient world, no red and blue tribes. Primitive humans were simply trying to make sense of the world around them—to see patterns in the amazing diversity of clouds and snails and shrubs and stars that they encountered. But this yearning for patterns and design became a hard-wired habit over time, and today it influences everything from our place on the political spectrum to our beliefs about creation. Like our ancient ancestors, we are constantly on the move intellectually, exploring ideas and expanding them and sharing them. The foraging heuristic, the topic of the next chapter, illuminates the creative impulse.

14

The **FORAGING** Heuristic

|||||||||||||||||||||||||||||||||||||||||||||||||||||||||||||||||||||||||||||||||||||||||||||||||||||||||||||||||||||||||||||||||||||||||||||||||||||||

EXPLORING AND EXPLOITING

I ONCE HAD A colleague who collected razors. He had a large assortment of every kind: straight razors, double-bladed razors, primitive electric razors, razors from different countries and different eras. He knew a lot about the history of razor technology, and it was fascinating to hear him talk about these artifacts. I once asked him why he chose to collect razors and how he got started, and after a pause he said: "I have no idea."

Everyone is an expert on something. You may not be paid for it, but somewhere along the line you have no doubt chosen one or two things that intrigue you. You've pursued that interest over years and achieved some level of mastery. Maybe you collect something, or visit Civil War battle sites, or study the game of golf. It doesn't matter what: no matter what your passion, you have triggered your basic foraging heuristic to focus and hone an idea and made it yours.

The foraging heuristic is what makes us explore, peek around new corners, learn new things. But it also makes us stop and focus and enrich our thinking. This is how we pick not only hobbies but careers as well, and the trick is to keep the proper balance in our foraging. We need to explore and we need to focus.

You can see this tension in your day-to-day life. For example, I live in a town with hundreds of restaurants serving many of the world's cuisines: sushi, pizza, pho, tapas, KFC, you name it. My family eats out a fair amount, and we appreciate all these tastes, so we could conceivably explore a different menu every outing. But we don't. Some years ago we discovered a neighborhood café that we all really like, and that's pretty much where we go. It's our place.

I know that other people are different, thriving on variety and novelty and discovery. We're basically opting for certainty and predictability, where others prefer exploration and change. But why do people differ on this trait? What motivates some to constantly seek out the next best thing, the greener grass, while others of us are content to stick with what's known and safe? How do we know there's not a new and better favorite eatery just around the corner? Are we trading off curiosity and novelty for the luxury of not having to make a decision?

The foraging heuristic works its powers far beyond your local watering hole. This powerful heuristic shapes how we dress, whom we hang around with, our hobbies and passions and careers, and even our romantic attractions. Why do so many people wear blue jeans? Why do some people have lifelong partners while others are romantically restless their entire lives?

It's all about strategy. Think of it this way: When our ancient ancestors had to forage in the savanna there was no telling where they would find basic necessities. The environment was patchy, with a watering hole here and an antelope herd there, but no uniformity or predictability. So what was the best search strategy? Once you find a hunting ground with some antelope in it, do you set up camp and make it your own, or go looking for a better hunting ground, then a better one still? Picking the wrong foraging strategy meant dying.

Now fast-forward to modern times. Our challenges are perhaps more complex and intellectual and abstract—and not commonly life threatening—but we still have to decide how to deal with an uncertain world. Faced with a relationship problem or a key decision at work, do we bear down and exploit one idea for all it's worth, or do we move rapidly from one solution to another to another? Or maybe we do both, depending on the problem, switching back and forth depending on what works.

Psychologists Thomas Hills, Peter Todd, and Robert Goldstone of Indiana University have for some time been exploring these questions in the laboratory. They wanted to see if people do indeed have a consistent cognitive style for foraging, whether it's for food or ideas. They also wanted to see if priming those ancient foraging neurons—triggering either exploration or exploitation impulses—influences the way people approach modern problems.

Since they couldn't actually ask people to forage for food in the wild, they used some modern tools: a computer game and a board game. They had a large group of volunteers use icons to "forage" in a computerized world, moving around until they stumbled upon a hidden supply of food or water, then deciding if and when to move on, continue the search, in which direction, and so forth. The scientists tracked their movements.

But the volunteers explored two very different worlds. Some were arbitrarily dropped into a "clumpy" world, which had fewer but much richer supplies of resources. Others happened into a "diffuse" environment, which had many more but much smaller supplies of food and water. Both kinds of environments existed in ancient times, and the idea in the experiment was to prime the optimal foraging strategy for each possible world. Those in a diffuse world would in theory do better giving up on any one spot quickly and moving on rapidly, nomad style. Those in a clumpy world would be more likely to stay put, exploiting the rich lodes of nutrients rather than wandering fruitlessly.

That was the first part of the experiment. Afterward, the volunteers participated in a more abstract, intellectual search task: the board game Scrabble. They didn't actually play Scrabble, but they got letters as if they were going to play, and had to search their memory for as many words as they could make with those letters. As with the board game, they could also choose to trade in their letters for new ones, but in the experiment they could do it whenever they wanted to. The wholesale trading of letters is what the psychologists were actually observing. They wanted to compare the volunteers' Scrabble strategies with their foraging strategies, to see if they stuck with the letters they were given or rapidly abandoned one set of letters for another (more promising) set. In other words, would those who were mentally primed for a clumpy world see their Scrabble letters as rich clumps, worth sticking with, while those primed for a diffuse world quickly abandoned one set of letters for another?

The results were striking. Those whose neurons were primed for exploration in the wild were also more restless and exploratory in Scrabble, while those primed for exploitation were more focused and persevering when they switched to the abstract mental challenge. Put another way, the human brain appears capable of toggling back and forth between exploration and exploitation, depending on the demands of the task. They are flip sides of the same foraging heuristic.

But the psychologists also found that individuals tended to be fairly consistent in their cognitive style. That is, the most persevering foragers were also the most persevering Scrabble players, just as gadabouts in the food search tended to be gadabouts in intellectual matters as well. And presumably in life: the latter would probably be too antsy to settle for a "good enough" neighborhood café. So it appears we inherit the capacity for both cognitive styles, though age and personality may tilt us toward favoring one or the other.

So what happens when you put a hundred, a thousand, or a million foragers together and make them share a world? That's basically what modern life is. Do we enrich one another's lives or stymie one another? How do ancient foraging impulses intertwine to create intellectual progress, creativity, and social harmony? What's the best approach for any one of us to live creatively and meaningfully in a world teeming with intellectual foragers?

These same questions apply whether you're talking about politics or investing or relationships. But think about fashion for a minute, just as an example. There's a great scene in the 2006 movie *The Devil Wears Prada* that captures the gist of this idea. Meryl Streep plays Miranda Priestly, the workaholic editor of a fashion magazine called *Runway*, and Anne Hathaway plays her deliberately unfashionable assistant Andy. Miranda senses Andy's disdain for her world of designer skirts and belts and shoes, and at one point she icily confronts her assistant for her arrogance: "You see that droopy sweater you're wearing?" she asks. "That blue was on a dress Cameron Diaz wore on the cover of *Runway*—shredded chiffon by James Holt. The same blue quickly appeared in eight other designers' collections and eventually made its way to the secondary designers, the department store labels, and then to some lovely Gap outlet, where you no doubt found it. That color is worth millions of dollars and many jobs."

Miranda is an intuitive social psychologist. The fact is that whether people favor droopy sweaters or Manolo Blahnik shoes, very few are original thinkers when it comes to what they wear. There are a few true innovators, of course, but unless you spin and dye the fabric and design your own wardrobe, you are cribbing from someone else's mind. And what's true of sweaters is also true of less trivial ideas, which move through the ether in unpredictable ways. If you think you coined a clever phrase or discovered a new talent, it's almost certain you did not.

That's because we don't really operate as free agents in the world of ideas. We are all entangled in complex patterns of collective behavior, many spontaneously organized and most entirely outside our understanding or awareness. Psychologists are very interested in these circles of ideas, how they grow and how people navigate them. Is there an ideal social arrangement for creating and sharing ideas, for mixing innovation and imitation? Are there perils in "borrowing" from others' minds—being too much of an exploiter—or in the opposite, being too much of a rogue explorer?

The Indiana scientists have been exploring these questions as well, in their computer laboratory, and they're gaining some insights into the collective mind. They used the same kind of virtual environment, an Internet-based "world" in which groups of people—from twenty to about two hundred—simultaneously forage for ideas. They use the word *forage* to make the point that ideas are really just abstract resources, food for the brain. As we solve life's various problems, we observe others' ideas in action, invent a few of our own, trade off ours against theirs—and succeed or fail. The psychologists have been studying these virtual successes and failures to see what lessons they can draw.

Here's an example of how these intriguing experiments work. Participants, interconnected via the Internet, were asked to guess numbers from 0 to 100, and they received feedback in the form of points, depending on whether their guesses were more or less correct. Think of this as the first day on the job in a big corporation where you know none of the cultural rules; all you can do is guess and see if you guessed right. But while you're guessing and getting feedback, you're also watching all your new colleagues to see what choices they make and how well they do. If they do better than you, maybe imitation makes more sense than guessing? Or maybe you'll try another guess? And so forth. Trial and error, borrowing, compromise—until you figure it out. Meanwhile, all the other participants are doing the same thing, including watching you.

The scientists ran this experiment several different ways, each approximating a different kind of real-life social group. We all exist in many social circles simultaneously, some tiny and some very large. This is what the computer game simulated. For example, in local networks, participants were connected only to a few immediate neighbors, while in global networks everyone was connected to everyone in a rich web. In small-world networks, participants were connected locally but also had a few long-distance connections, so they might pick up an idea or two from, say, a distant relative. Facebook is a kind of small-world network, or at least has the potential to be.

The findings were intriguing. When the problems were easy, the global networks did best. This makes sense because such richly connected groups can spread information rapidly and basically speed is all that's needed to spread a simple notion efficiently. But as the problems became trickier, the small-world networks tended to perform better. In other words, the truism that more information is always better proved untrue when life got a little messy. And as the problems became even more complex, the small local networks proved most clever.

No one of us can navigate this complicated world by ourselves. It's too arduous and time-consuming, like designing all your own clothes instead of trusting the Gap. But there is also a hazard in connectivity. If everyone ends up knowing exactly the same thing, you have a world of like-minded people, and this homogenous group ends up acting like a single explorer rather than a federation of ideas. People pile on to the well-known bandwagon, even if it's a really bad idea. It happens in fashion, but also in politics, in musical taste, and just about every other realm of ideas.

So think again about exploration and exploitation. We all explore a lot of ideas superficially—the merits of health care reform, how to bake an apple pie, and so forth—because we have to know a little about a lot of things. But we also exploit certain ideas, and when we do this, our knowledge gets more specialized, and we share it with a smaller circle of others. This is called expertise, or mastery—and it is driven by the human emotion called curiosity.

Here's an example. Fans of the old British TV series *The Avengers* will remember the classic wine cellar "duel" scene. Foppish secret agent John Steed and villain Henry Boardman face off in a tasting of rare wines, each one-upping the other with his impressive expertise about vineyards and vintages. After some minutes of sparring, Steed summarily ends the contest with this pinpoint identification of a wine: "Nineteen-oh-nine," he states drily. "From the northern end of the vineyard."

Touché. Even wine connoisseurs will laugh at this caricature. Nobody understands wines at that level of detail. But the bit is funny precisely because experts do in fact think of wines in much finer categories than the rest of us. Some truly know grape varieties, vineyards, specific harvests, and soil and moisture, while others of us settle for much coarser categories, like red and white.

But what happens in the mind that makes such mastery possible? The obvious answer is that you must be endlessly interested in every nuance of a topic, but that's not a very helpful answer. What does that mean exactly, that it was interesting? Is interest a universal emotion, like fear or pride or bemusement? How does one person come to be fascinated by politics while others are equally entranced by baseball statistics or the early poems of Lord Byron? And if it's possible to find such esoterica absorbing, why not trigonometry and irregular verbs? Can interest be nurtured and channeled in the classroom, the workplace, and elsewhere?

Scientists have shown surprisingly little interest in interest, given its obvious and fundamental connection to learning and education.

That's starting to change. In the past few years a handful of psychologists have started exploring interest in the laboratory, and they are starting to piece together a theory about this curious emotion.

One of the most striking features of interest is that it's all over the map. One person's passion for butterflies is another's huge yawn, according to psychologist Paul Silvia, who has been exploring interest in his lab at the University of North Carolina at Greensboro. Interest also comes and goes; a book you found mesmerizing just a few years ago might leave you bored to tears if you tried to reread it today. Silvia has been trying to dissect this unpredictable mental state.

Much of his work involves exposing people to things in the real world that may or may not be interesting: contemporary poetry, abstract and classical artwork, and so forth. In one experiment, for example, he had people read an abstract poem, but some were given a small hint about the poem's meaning, while the others were left on their own. When asked later to rate the poem, those who had been given the hint found the work much more interesting. In a similar experiment, students who had studied a little about art history found a modern art gallery much more engaging than did students with no exposure to art.

Silvia thinks he knows what's going on in these simple experiments. All of the people in these studies are appraising their experience, trying to make sense of it. That's basic human nature, and we make such appraisals all the time. But they are sizing up the same experience very differently depending on the knowledge they bring to the event. All of them probably find the poem or artwork to be fresh, complex, mysterious—so they are at least curious enough to look more. That's the first requirement for interest. But only some find the experience also to be comprehensible. That is, they have just enough knowledge that they believe they can cope intellectually with this complex and unexpected event; it's not totally beyond their ken.

The combination of complexity and comprehensibility adds up to genuine interest, and genuine interest cannot exist without both.

At its best, genuine interest becomes fascination becomes absorption becomes enrapture. Psychologists call such intensity "being in the flow," a state of mind so focused that not even time can intrude on the experience. This sounds awfully like bliss to me, but Silvia is careful to distinguish even intense interest from happiness. Interest motivates people to explore, to seek out novelty, where happiness serves to firm up existing attachments, whether to a favorite restaurant or a favorite person. Like exploration and exploitation, interest and happiness are the flip sides of the foraging heuristic.

Interest and happiness also have different sources, as Silvia showed in another experiment. He had people look at a variety of paintings, including serene landscapes by Claude Monet and the rather disturbing images of Francis Bacon. The subjects rated both their interest in the paintings and their enjoyment, and then Silvia surveyed the range of their emotional reactions to the different works. The paintings that made people happy were simple, positive, and calm. But they were consistently more intrigued by the works that they perceived as complicated, strange, and upsetting. Interest, in short, requires emotional and mental challenge.

So how do we stay challenged once we have begun to master a topic? Why not just move on to something else and learn a little bit about a lot of things? Well, it appears that interest is self-propelling. Think of wine connoisseurs again. They have the whole map of vintages, years, tastes, and so forth burned into their neurons, so they can now perceive subtleties and nuances and contrasts that are completely lost on the rest of us. Intellectual challenge motivates people to become experts, and expertise in turn allows them to keep foraging for every new bit of knowledge.

But why? Why do some people see nuance where others don't?

I know, because they're the experts—but what is going on in the expert mind when it slices and dices a corner of the world into fine-grained distinctions? What is the cognitive engine that drives nuanced thinking?

Psychologists have been studying thinking styles for some time, and one emerging idea is that such thinking is driven by emotions. Forget wine for a second, and think about something you are an expert on—beach volleyball, Alaskan politics, the late novels of Joseph Conrad, whatever. With enough effort, you could probably make yourself an expert on something you don't like, but why bother? Curiosity and interest not only drive mastery, they make it seem effortless.

Or at least that's the theory, which psychologists Rachel Smallman and Neal Roese decided to test in their University of Illinois laboratory. They suspected that the act of liking actually molds the brain's thinking, opening it to nuances that are unapparent to others. Put another way, preference and taste pave the way for more textured thinking. They ran this experiment to test the idea.

They started by artificially creating preferences in the lab, using hobo symbols. These are the crude symbols that hobos once scratched onto walls and trees to warn other hobos of dangers in particular neighborhoods. One, for example, meant "unfriendly police here," and another signaled "people hand out food." But the psychologists assumed that few people would know those meanings anymore. They showed volunteers a collection of these symbols, pairing them with either pleasant or unpleasant scenes. The idea was that they would learn preferences for some hobo symbols and aversion to others. They in effect created a rudimentary laboratory version of a hobby—an idiosyncratic pleasure in something.

Then the volunteers sorted a deck of twenty cards, each card picturing one of the hobo symbols. They were told to sort the cards into "meaningful" categories of any size, and to label the categories. This is what they found: those who had been conditioned to have positive feelings about the symbols sorted them into much finer categories than did the others. In other words, liking influenced thinking. What's more, the volunteers were clearly guided by their emotions in sorting the symbols, labeling the piles with adjectives such as *inspiring* and *ominous*.

These findings may explain the power of hobbies, but they also sound a warning to those choosing jobs and careers. Hard work and mastery may give us a measure of satisfaction, but pleasure also drives mastery and expertise. There may be good psychology beneath the old saw "Do what you love."

The foraging heuristic may also help explain one of the great mysteries of human psychology: why we even have positive emotions like serenity, gratitude, and joy—and interest. Psychologists are in general agreement that negative emotions exist because they once had survival value: fear motivates escape from predators, and disgust helps us avoid poisons. But how do interest and awe help with survival?

Psychologist Barbara Fredrickson of the University of North Carolina in Chapel Hill has been piecing together an answer to this puzzle. According to her "broaden and build" theory, positive emotions open the mind—literally, almost the way our pupils dilate—to new and varied experience. People who are primed to feel curious or joyful see more possibilities; they look further and wider and have richer mental maps of the world. And over time these positive, opening experiences build up, creating psychological and emotional resilience.

In other words, positive emotions turned early humans into better foragers, and they continue to do so today: more creative and intellectually engaged, less self-focused—and therefore better equipped to navigate and survive in a complex social world.

P RIMITIVE HUMANS DIDN'T collect stamps or fine wines. They were too occupied processing the environment around them. The wellspring of both the design heuristic and the foraging heuristic is a fundamental need to understand the world, to make it work for us. These two potent heuristics work together in shaping human curiosity and imagination and mastery. But our yearning for order and sense does not always result in admirable attitudes and actions. The caricature heuristic is also driven by a need to simplify an overwhelmingly complicated social world, but it often yields attitudes that are hurtful and unfair. As we'll see in the following pages, it is the engine of old-fashioned prejudice and beliefs that are literally unhealthy to both ourselves and others.

The **CARICATURE** Heuristic

||||||||||||||||||||||||||||||||||||||||||||||||||||||||||||||||||||||||||||||||||||||||||||||||||||||||||||||||||||||||||||||||||

ENGINEERING PREJUDICE

I **WENT TO A** very nerdy college. This school was so nerdy that the mascot was an engineer, and at football games students would chant: "Tangent, secant, cosine, sine. Three point one four one five nine." I'm not kidding. This geeky-looking guy was emblazoned on everything from T-shirts to notebooks. He wore a goofy hat and was usually depicted surveying land, harnessing electrical power, or some such. It was an unflattering caricature, and was meant to be funny in a self-deprecating kind of way.

A lot of students and alumni didn't like it, though, and the engineer was eventually replaced with a bird. That's the problem with stereotypes: they contain enough truth to be both humorous and cruel. We all use stereotypes, probably more than we'd care to admit, because the caricature heuristic is one of those fast and efficient cognitive shortcuts that save us a lot of time and energy. The caricature heuristic is essential to sorting out the overwhelming complexity of the world—and sorting it into categories, boxes, and pigeonholes.

You probably have a caricature of an engineer in your mind's eye right now. And there's probably some truth to it. Psychologists are very interested in stereotypes, and in fact have used engineer stereotypes in some classic studies of the power of caricature. Consider this hypothetical situation. Say there's a room with 1,000 people in it, and we know that 995 are lawyers and the other 5 are engineers. We walk into the room and begin milling about, and the first person we meet is Jack. In a few minutes of small talk, we learn that Jack is forty-five years old and has four children. He doesn't appear to have much interest in politics or social issues and is generally conservative. He leads a quiet life. For recreation, he likes sailing on the bay and doing mathematical puzzles.

Is Jack a lawyer, or an engineer? Logically, if you use the statistical part of your brain only, the best educated guess is that he's a lawyer, simply because there are all those lawyers in the room and there's a far better chance of meeting a lawyer in the room than an engineer. Indeed, the odds of stumbling upon one of the five engineers are vanishingly small. Yet a lot of people immediately say engineer because Jack fits a stereotype. It's a convenient pigeonhole. Scientists have run this experiment many times with all sorts of people, and the majority of even highly educated people jump to this caricatured conclusion.

Just to spread the caricature-mongering around, here's another example from the scientific literature. It may seem a bit dated, but it makes an enduring point. Psychologists call it the "Linda problem." Linda is thirty-one years old, single, outspoken, and very bright. She majored in philosophy. As a student, she was deeply concerned with issues of discrimination and social justice, and also participated in antinuclear demonstrations. Which is more likely, that Linda is a bank teller or that Linda is a bank teller and is active in the feminist movement?

Remarkably, fully 85 percent of people who answer this question say that option two is more likely—that Linda is both a bank teller and a feminist. But clearly that's not only unlikely—it's impossible. With just a moment's reflection, it becomes obvious that it can never be more likely that Linda is both, because being both a bank teller and a feminist is a subset of being a bank teller. Some bank tellers may be feminists—probably are—but some may not be.

So what's wrong with the thinking of 85 percent of people? Basically what they've done here is throw statistics out the window—even the most elementary statistics. That's because of the potency of stereotypes: the stereotype of Linda the feminist is so powerful—so easily accessible—that we substitute it for logic.

That's because stereotypes are quick and easy, and what's more, we need them. We humans are cognitive slobs—we're mentally lazy, because we're wired to conserve energy—and stereotypes are energy-saving tools. We need them so we can use our limited brainpower for more useful and important things. This has actually been demonstrated in the laboratory. Three psychologists—Neil Macrae, Alan Milne, and Galen Bodenhausen—gave volunteers two tasks to do simultaneously. First, they had to form impressions of a group of unfamiliar people, based on a list of traits flashed on a computer screen. So, for example, they might see the name Nigel with this list of traits: clumsy, caring, honest, unlucky, forgetful, upstanding, enthusiastic, reliable, passive, and responsible. The order of the traits was mixed up different ways for different volunteers, and they later had to recall as many traits as possible. But here's the experimental part: half the volunteers saw a label as well—Nigel the doctor, say. The psychologists wanted to see if providing the stereotypic trigger made them remember more stereotypic traits of a doctor, compared to general recall.

At the same time that the volunteers were doing this stereotype task, they also had to listen to a really boring audio recording about the economy and geography of Indonesia. The psychologists didn't choose this topic to be cruel; they picked it because they figured that it was highly unlikely anyone would know anything about the economy and geography of Indonesia. Afterward, they quizzed the volunteers on a series of questions to see if they had absorbed the material: Which coast is Jakarta on? What is Indonesia's official religion? And so forth.

They wanted to see two things. First, they measured to see if the volunteers more readily used the stereotypic traits if they were given the tip that Nigel was a physician. They did. They were almost twice as likely to recall traits such as caring and reliable and responsible when they knew Nigel was a doctor. Similarly, with John the skinhead, they were apt to recall John being rebellious, aggressive, and dishonest, and with Julian the artist, they remembered Julian being creative, temperamental, and sensitive. But the researchers also want to see if using stereotypes eased the volunteers' cognitive burden and thus freed them up to listen more attentively to the boring narrative about Indonesia. And this was also true. Given the stereotypical labels to guide their thinking—to carry part of their cognitive burden—the volunteers learned a lot more about Indonesia.

That's quite remarkable when you think of it. Learning boring facts about Indonesia is a kind of proxy for real life. Think of a typical day at the office. A lot of the mental work we have to do every day—the stuff we have to process and use in some way—is not intrinsically fascinating, but we must concentrate and absorb it anyway so we can write that memo or run that meeting. And basically what this experiment shows is that a measure of lazy, caricatured thinking boosts learning. Paradoxically, you are a better worker because you pigeonhole people.

The psychologists reran this experiment a couple of times to clarify the findings. Specifically, they wanted to see if such stereotyping is intentional and conscious or if it occurs automatically. In other words, which part of our mind is at work when we categorize doctors as caring or skinheads as dangerous and aggressive? To find out, they gave the cues to some of the volunteers subliminally, by flashing the labels—doctor, skinhead, artist—so rapidly that it was outside the volunteers' threshold of conscious awareness.

They found that the volunteers did indeed use the subliminal stereotypes. Even though they had no recollection of seeing the unconscious cues, they still recalled more stereotypic traits—and still learned more about Indonesia's economy than did the volunteers who were given only the list of traits but no cue. It appears that stereotypes are tools that automatically and effortlessly economize mental resources. They act as built-in categorizers so we can conserve brain power for the (often tedious and mentally demanding) business of life.

So two cheers for stereotypes. Despite the negative connotations associated with the word, they can be very useful in real life. Consider the field of medicine and medical diagnosis. Obviously there are cases where group traits *should* be considered. One *should* consider race when diagnosing sickle cell anemia, for example, or gender when diagnosing complications of certain cancers, or age when considering dementia. In fact, we would all probably agree that it's irresponsible for a physician not to use these categories, even if we accept that racial, gender, and age stereotypes are harmful in other contexts.

But what about more ambiguous medical conditions? Bodenhausen (one of the three psychologists just discussed) has done other studies of stereotypes in medical judgments, both justified and misguided, and he offers this example: What if a physician has an elderly patient, and what if the physician believes that elderly people as a group are cantankerous and forgetful? What if the physician assumes, furthermore, that as a direct result of these traits, it is unlikely that elderly patients will take the medications that are prescribed for them? This is obviously a stereotype, but is it a fair and useful one? Should the doctor assume that the patient will not take the necessary medication, and opt for some other treatment?

Well, that would clearly be unfair to some elderly patients, and perhaps even dangerous. Noncompliance with drugs is a complex interplay of memory and attitude and behavior. Even so, the stereotype of the elderly as incompetent is widespread, and what's more, it reinforces itself. Bodenhausen has shown this in a study. A large group of physicians saw 150 young patients and 90 elderly patients in random order, over time. Fifty of the young patients failed to take their prescribed medication, while thirty of the elderly patients did so. When the physicians were asked about the caseload later on, they consistently overestimated the rate of noncompliance among the elderly but not among the youthful patients. In fact, the young and the elderly blew off their meds at exactly the same rate—33 percent—but the physicians' stereotyped thinking shaped their expectations about the elderly and actually distorted what they remembered as fact. So the stereotype in effect reinforced itself, creating the "evidence" that it is fair and accurate.

Caricatures are stubborn and difficult to shake. That's because these stereotypes—even some of the cruelest—are deeply rooted in our biology. Bodenhausen showed this in a clever study of "morning people" and "night owls." These categories are not just folk wisdom. They are actually legitimate scientific categories: The world is indeed divided into those who think well in the morning (I'm writing this at four-thirty in the morning) and those whose cognitive powers peak later in the day. Bodenhausen used this biological fact to study people's propensity for stereotyping.

He recruited a large group of college students, who contrary to stereotype are not all night owls, and had them solve the Linda problem. He figured that students would be more apt to think heuristically—to use common stereotypes—when they were not at their mental peak, so he tested the students at both 9:00 a.m. and at 8:00 p.m. And that's precisely what he found: self-described night owls were much more likely to "fail" the Linda problem in the morning, while morning people were much more apt to get it wrong in the evening. Put another way, the volunteers were much more likely to fall back on lazy, stereotypical thinking when they were biologically compromised.

Before you dismiss this as a mere laboratory game, consider the implications for courtroom trials. One of the presumptions of the legal system is that juries can make fair and reasonable judgments based on facts, not irrational thinking. Bodenhausen decided to explore this idea, to see if in fact our circadian rhythms shape our judgments of guilt. He did a mock jury experiment in which college students were asked to judge the guilt of fellow students accused of different kinds of misconduct. One defendant was accused of cheating on an exam, while another was charged with physically attacking his roommate, and yet another stood accused of selling illegal drugs on campus.

The researcher had pretested certain stereotypes related to these different crimes. That is, he knew that students (however unfairly) viewed jocks as more likely to cheat on college exams, Hispanics as more likely to be physically aggressive, and African Americans as more likely to deal drugs. He wanted to see if the jurors' biological wiring determined their use of these common stereotypes in making judgments of guilt and innocence.

So, as before, he tested both the night owls and the morning types at different times of day. He gave all the jurors various facts in each case, some pointing toward guilt and others toward innocence. Then some of the jurors got a tip about the defendant's group membership: they were given the additional fact that the alleged cheater was a "well-known star athlete," and in the cases of assault and drug dealing they were given the defendant's name, Roberto Garcia (or

Robert Garner) in the assault case and Marcus Washington (or Mark Washburn) in the drug dealing case. That is, they were supplied with a handy caricature to shape their thinking.

The jurors were then asked to judge the likelihood that each defendant was guilty of the charges he faced, and they were also asked to rate the seriousness of the crime. This is akin to the sentencing portion of an actual trial. The results were alarming: across all the cases, jurors were much more likely to find the stereotypical defendants guilty as charged—and to consider the crime more serious—if they were doing the judging at their less-than-optimal time of day. In other words, they were better jurors when at their mental peak, disregarding irrelevant information such as the defendant's ethnicity or athleticism.

These findings have obvious and serious implications for jury trials, and provide further evidence for the biological roots of stereotypical thinking. When we stereotype people, basically we're denying them the opportunity to be individuals. Imagine yourself as a parole officer and consider this case: The prisoner is serving prison time for robbing a convenience store. In his argument for parole, he doesn't deny robbing the store. But he does testify that he was under extreme stress at the time; his pregnant wife was seriously ill and they had no money to pay for the medicine she needed.

Most people would take these extenuating circumstances into consideration when judging this man. There is no evidence that he's a menace to society—no pattern of convenience store robberies, or any other serious crime for that matter. He seems like a dedicated family man, and you can even think of him as a victim. Doesn't he deserve a second chance at life?

Not if he's Latino. When Bodenhausen gave this hypothetical to a group of "parole officers," he got distressing results. They were lenient in their judgment of the prisoner in general, but not if they knew him as Roberto Garcia. Once they had this additional fact, the leniency vanished into thin air. It was almost as if they had never heard any of his story about his pregnant wife and her illness and the expensive medication; now he was simply a Latino guy who robbed a store. And indeed, when the researchers asked the volunteer parole officers to recall the details of the case, those primed with the Latino stereotype were much less likely to remember any of the extenuating circumstances. They apparently never even inscribed the details in memory once they were under the powerful sway of an ethnic stereotype. The automatic caricature heuristic trumped the basic brain processes involved in remembering.

Those findings are pretty scary. Does all this mean we're hopelessly doomed to wrongful judgments of our peers? Or is there a way to avoid falling back on broad caricatures, to police our own lazy mental habits to avoid harming others with simplistic stereotypical thinking? In other words, do we know that stereotypes are wrong yet find them too psychologically tempting to avoid?

Psychologist Wim De Neys of Leuven University, Belgium, decided that the best way to explore these questions was to actually look at the brain in action. Past research has shown that a particular region of the brain's frontal lobe becomes active when we detect conflict in our thinking—between an easy stereotype, say, and a more reasoned and complex view. But actually overriding stereotypical thinking requires another part of the frontal lobe. De Neys basically wanted to see if stereotypical thinking is a detection problem or a self-control problem. That is, does the brain actually fail to see a stereotype for what it is, or does it accurately see caricature and act on it anyway?

To see, he watched these two brain regions during stereotypical thinking, to see what lit up. To prime the volunteers' stereotypical thinking, he went back to the quiz about the five geeky engineers in a ballroom full of lawyers. A minority of people who take this little quiz actually do (logically) say lawyer, not engineer. In fact, they answer so quickly that it seems instantaneous—but the question is whether the brain needs to quash that powerful caricature of the geeky engineer in order to give the more reasoned response.

De Neys watched volunteers' brains as they puzzled through this and similar problems. He found that the brain's stereotype detector lit up regardless of whether the subject answered stereotypically or rationally. So apparently we all detect the stereotype and recognize that it is out of sync with reality. But the brain's inhibition center, the part of the brain that says, "No, I am not falling for that simplistic idea," lit up only when the subjects actually reasoned that Jack was most likely a lawyer—that is, only when they overrode the stereotype and made a calculation based on probability. Apparently some of us find the ready caricatures too tempting and use them anyway, against our better judgment, but we all carry the potential to trump our own caricatured thinking.

This caricatured thinking may hurt us as well as the people we're oversimplifying. Think back on those stereotypes of the elderly. Ageism is rampant in America, and surprisingly, many old people themselves trade in unflattering stereotypes of the elderly, especially images of helplessness and incompetence. Such caricatures are not only false and cruel but also unhealthy. New evidence suggests that young, healthy people who stereotype old people may themselves be at risk of heart disease many years down the road.

Becca Levy of the Yale School of Public Health (with colleagues at the National Institute on Aging) examined data on hundreds of men and women who have been studied for almost four decades as part of the Baltimore Longitudinal Study of Aging. Back in 1968, when scientists first began studying these volunteers, they were fairly young and in very good health. At that time, scientists gathered all sorts of information about the volunteers, including their attitudes toward the elderly. Their images of being old covered the gamut from very positive to very negative.

Levy and her colleagues examined the health histories of all the volunteers, focusing on cardiovascular disease: heart attacks, congestive heart failure, stroke, and so forth. There was a striking link between ageism early in life and poor heart health later on. That is, those who viewed old age as a time of helplessness were much more likely to experience some kind of cardiovascular disorder over the next four decades. The episodes of heart disease could not be explained by smoking, depression, cholesterol, family history, or any of a myriad other possible risk factors.

What this suggests, Levy says, is that people are internalizing stereotypes of old age when they are still quite young—with far-reaching consequences. This is the first scientific look at people maturing into the very people they have been unkindly caricaturing. It could be taken as a cautionary tale for those who think they'll never grow old. When we trade in unfair caricatures, we literally take them to heart.

The good news is that we can think ourselves out of caricatured views of aging. Imagine that you could rewind the clock twenty years. It's 1990. Madonna is topping the pop charts, and TV sets are tuned to *Cheers* and *Murphy Brown*. Widespread Internet use is just a pipe dream, and Sugar Ray Leonard and Joe Montana are on recent covers of *Sports Illustrated*.

But most important, you're twenty years younger. How do you feel? Well, if you're at all like the subjects in a provocative experiment by Harvard psychologist Ellen Langer, you actually feel as if your body clock has been turned back two decades. Langer did a study like this with a group of elderly men some years ago, retrofitting an isolated old New England hotel so that every visible sign said it was twenty years earlier. The men—in their late seventies and early eighties—were told not to reminisce about the past, but to actually act as if they had traveled back in time. The idea was to see if changing the men's mind-set about their own age might lead to actual changes in health and fitness.

Langer's findings were stunning. After just one week, the men in the experimental group (compared with controls of the same age) had more joint flexibility, increased dexterity, and less arthritis in their hands. Their mental acuity had risen measurably, and they had improved gait and posture. Outsiders who were shown the men's photographs judged them to be significantly younger than the controls. In other words, the aging process had in some measure been reversed.

I know this sounds a bit woo-woo, but stay with me. Langer and her Harvard colleagues have been running similarly inventive experiments for decades, and the accumulated weight of the evidence is convincing. Her theory is that we are all victims of our own stereotypes about aging and health. We mindlessly accept negative cultural cues about disease and old age, and these cues shape our self-concepts and our behavior. If we can shake loose from the negative clichés that dominate our thinking about health, we can mindfully open ourselves to possibilities for more productive lives even into old age.

Consider another of Langer's mindfulness studies, this one using an ordinary optometrist's eye chart. That's the chart with the huge *E* on top and descending lines of smaller and smaller letters that eventually become unreadable. Langer and her colleagues wondered: what if we reversed it? The regular chart creates the expectation that at some point you will be unable to read. Would turning the chart upside down reverse that expectation, so that people would expect the letters to become readable? That's exactly what they found. The subjects still couldn't read the tiniest letters, but when they were expecting the letters to get more legible, they were able to read smaller letters than they could have normally. Their expectation—their mind-set—improved their actual vision.

That means that some people may be wearing the wrong glasses. Perhaps they don't even need specs. But that's the least of the health consequences. Here's another study, this one using clothing as a trigger for aging stereotypes. Most people try to dress appropriately for their age, so clothing in effect becomes a cue for ingrained attitudes about age. But what if this cue disappeared? Langer decided to study people who routinely wear uniforms as part of their work life and compare them with people who dress in street clothes. She found that people who wear uniforms missed fewer days owing to illness or injury, had fewer doctors' visits and hospitalizations, and had fewer chronic diseases—even though they all had the same socioeconomic status. That's because they were not constantly reminded of their own aging by their fashion choices. The health differences were even more exaggerated when Langer looked at affluent people: presumably the means to buy even more clothes provides a steady stream of new aging cues, which wealthy people internalize as unhealthy attitudes and expectations.

Langer is not advocating that we all don uniforms. Her point is that we are surrounded every day by subtle signals that aging is an undesirable period of decline. These signals make it difficult to age gracefully. Similar signals also lock all of us—regardless of age—into pigeonholes for disease. We are too quick to accept diagnostic categories like cancer and depression and let them define us. Doing so preempts the possibility of a healthful future.

That's not to say that we won't encounter illness, bad moods, or a stiff back—or that dressing like a teenager will eliminate those things. But with a little practiced awareness, we can try to embrace uncertainty and understand that the way we feel today may or may not connect to the way we will feel tomorrow. Who knows, if we're open to the idea that things can improve, we just might wake up feeling twenty years younger.

THE BRAIN STUDIES cited in this chapter are hopeful. They show that we are capable of catching ourselves in the act of caricaturing, which suggests that we can with effort trump this strong heuristic impulse. And the provocative mindfulness studies show that we can indeed alter our state of mind to defuse our prejudiced views. But it's not always easy. The heuristic mind evolved for a reason—for many good reasons—and defusing and detoxifying these biases takes vigilance. In the next chapter, we explore the playfully named cooties heuristic, which is basically a different kind of stereotyping—the labeling not of people but of substances that may (or may not) be physically harmful. As we'll see, what was once a healthy fear of the natural world's poisons can today poison even our basic sense of nationality and identity.

16

The **COOTIES** Heuristic

|||||||||||||||||||||||||||||||||||||||||||||||||||||||||||||||||||||||||||||||||||||||||||||||||||||||||||||||||||||||||||||||||||||||||

CONTAGION AND MAGICAL THINKING

MINE IS A tea-drinking family, and I will sometimes sweeten my cuppa with an artificial sweetener. A couple of years ago, I read that this sweetener was discovered by accident: A chemist was working on developing a new insecticide, and he inadvertently let some of his solution touch his lips. It tasted remarkably like sugar, so he just switched course and developed a new sugar substitute instead. Now, if my wife is making me tea, she will call from the kitchen: "Cream? Insecticide?"

Does this disgust you? Does it seem unnatural to you? If so, you are experiencing the cooties heuristic, an ancient aversion to impurities that has some surprising ways of expressing itself in the modern world. A lot of people hate the idea of putting any kind of contaminant into their body and will go to great lengths to avoid chemicals and additives in their food. The food industry long ago noticed this aversion: marketers have slapped the label "all natural" on everything from sugary drinks to red meat to grab the attention of purists.

But what does "natural" mean to us, really? It obviously doesn't mean that it occurs in nature. Arsenic is number 33 on the periodic table, yet we all know not to add it to our elderberry wine. So when we say something is "natural," what do we mean?

University of Pennsylvania psychologist Paul Rozin has studied this question at some length. In one revealing experiment, for example, he decided that the best way to define "naturalness" was to see what destroyed "naturalness" in people's minds. That is, he picked things that most people would consider natural when they come out of the ground, and perverted them in various ways, to see what was acceptable and what was not.

He chose water and peanuts. You could argue this, but they're pretty good choices. After all, everyone drinks H_2O in one form or another; otherwise you die. Rozin chose mountain spring water, which has a special claim on naturalness in many people's minds. And peanuts are not a bad food choice: they grow inside shells, so they're somewhat protected, and they are ubiquitous in "health foods" like granola bars, organic peanut butter, and so forth. For the purposes of this experiment, the peanuts were grown without fertilizers or insecticides.

So he started with a diet of spring water and peanuts. Then he changed this natural diet in many different ways, and asked people how they felt about each of the transformations: is it still natural, or is it unnatural, or is it somewhere in between? With water, for example, how about mixing water from two mountain springs? Is it still pure? Or freezing it, or boiling it? How about adding a trace amount (0.001 percent) of minerals? And so forth. He made similar changes to the peanuts, and collected people's reactions: Would you mind mixing peanuts from Georgia and peanuts from North Carolina? Removing or adding fat? Grinding them into peanut butter? Freezing them, and then grinding them into peanut butter? And so forth.

In general, Rozin found that people didn't mind physical transformations nearly as much as they minded chemical changes to their food and water. So, for example, most say it's okay to mix water from two springs (or peanuts from two farms). And they don't care too much if these things have been frozen, especially if they have been frozen outdoors by Mother Nature. But they do see even trace amounts of additives as contamination. More than half objected to adding trace minerals to water, even if they were precisely the same concentration of minerals that exist in natural water. People similarly felt that adding mineral additives in their peanut butter destroyed its naturalness.

This is interesting, but Rozin wanted to look at a diet that more closely resembles what people actually eat day to day—or what they might eat in the future. So he gave people a long list of foods that had been processed or altered a wide variety of ways, to see what people viewed as unnatural. Here's just a partial list of the many foods they chose from: "fresh squeezed" orange juice, OJ with a calcium supplement, milk fresh from a cow, milk fresh from a zebra, pasteurized milk, skim milk, a steak from a free-range cow, wild strawberries, commercially grown strawberries, a wolf, a German shepherd, an elephant, an oak tree, a penguin, corn with a gene from a cow to make it insect-resistant, a pig with a corn gene to make it grow faster, and a pig with a penguin gene to make it more tolerant of cold.

You get the idea. Most of us eat some of these foods every day, even some of the "transformed" foods. But some of us are more adventurous than others, and everyone has his own personal taboos. Is "wild" preferable to "domesticated"? I may be perfectly okay with something that you find repulsive, and vice versa. When Rozin analyzed the data from this study, he discovered a few patterns in people's preferences and prohibitions. Most notable, people object to processing much more than they care about the actual content. So, for example, fresh zebra milk is much less objectionable than cow's milk that has had fat removed or added to make skim milk or cream. People will stretch their boundaries about unusual food choices as long as the food isn't tampered with too much.

The bottom line is that we simply don't like fooling with Mother Nature. Perhaps unsurprisingly, people reserve their harshest judgments for genetically modified foods, and again it was the idea itself that people found objectionable, rather than the particulars. Whether it was moving a plant gene to an animal, an animal gene to a plant, or even a plant gene to a plant, it didn't matter. We see this kind of manipulation as undermining the natural state of what we put in our bodies.

All of this points to a hard-wired aversion to contagion, an automatic neuronal bias for things in a pure and natural state and against impurities and unnatural essences. It's a simple rule: avoid contaminants. Other Rozin findings support this idea. He found, for example, that people don't much care how much of a foreign ingredient is added to their food. Even a trace amount renders it unnatural and therefore unappealing. And it appears to be additions more than subtractions that ruin food—a cognitive bias that would help explain another popular marketing phrase, "no additives."

This contagion bias almost certainly originated in prehistoric times, long before our ancestors understood modern germ theory. It was (and remains) deeply entangled with feelings of disgust, which helped early humans avoid infection, food poisoning, and so forth. But the heuristic remains deep-wired in our brains, and as with a lot of heuristics, its modern-day expression is not always rational. Here's the thing, though: we *know* in our modern minds that the beliefs are irrational. How else do you explain the "five-second rule"? This widely accepted cultural "rule" says that if you drop some food on the floor, it's still okay to eat if you pick it up within five seconds. Some say three seconds, other ten, but the rule is ubiquitous; the Russians simply say: "Quickly picked up is not fallen." It's widely popular because, medically, it *is* okay. It may gross out some people's ancient sensibilities, but you're almost certainly not going to come down with a disease from a brushed-off pretzel.

When Rozin and his colleagues asked people to explain their preferences for things that are natural, they got an intriguing answer—two answers, really. Many say they prefer naturalness because it is healthier and kinder to the environment. That's the modern mind talking. These are sensible answers, based on evidence—or at least what we think is true. But just as many people say they prefer natural things because they are inherently "better"—more moral, more aesthetic. Natural things are simply "right." This is the ancient heuristic talking. The bias is so deeply ingrained that it doesn't require rational explanation.

One could argue that these ancient contagion beliefs are still adaptive—that what feels "right" is also in most cases healthier. Indeed, many vegans describe their preference as both a moral choice and a healthy one. But what about when these deep-rooted impulses emerge in other realms of life, having nothing to do with food or nutrition?

Many of the contagion beliefs that linger in the modern mind are a form of magical thinking. Think of cooties. Cooties are fictional germs that spread on contact; they are disgusting and they are everywhere, and nowhere are they more prevalent than in the vivid imagination of just about every American child. They are often carried by unpopular kids, and almost always by kids of the opposite sex, and they clearly have a moral dimension. Indeed, one is much more likely to "catch" a classmate's unpopularity from cooties than to come down with a fever.

Cooties are part of the harmless magical thinking of childhood.

But the adult versions of cooties are often not as benign. Just think about sweaters.

There is a whole line of contagion research involving adult sweaters. Imaginary sweaters, all thoroughly laundered. What psychologists do is ask people which sweaters they would be willing to wear, or not. For example, would you wear a sweater once worn by Adolf Hitler? A lot of people would not, and psychologists take this as evidence for the potency of the contagion heuristic. Merely touching something once touched by evil "essences" can potentially infect one with those essences.

There is no actual Hitler's sweater. It's hard to even imagine him in a pullover. It's a laboratory paradigm. Researchers have used the sweater paradigm to study various kinds of contagion and, more important, to explore the nature of the essences that people tend to avoid. For example, one team of psychologists used such fictional sweaters to study attitudes toward people with AIDS. It's long been known (and many surveys have shown) that people's aversion to AIDS victims is both moral and medical, and anecdotal evidence suggests that this prejudice is rooted in misguided contagion beliefs. People are reluctant to buy houses owned by AIDS victims, to work in the same workplace, and to have their child go to school with a classmate who has AIDS.

These attitudes were documented long after HIV transmission was well understood, so they are clearly irrational, uninformed by science. Psychologists have since shown the heuristic roots of such magical thinking. They asked people how likely they would be to wear a sweater worn by someone with AIDS, or a gay man with AIDS, or a man who got AIDS from a transfusion. For comparison, they also asked about other hypothetical sweater owners. Would you wear a sweater worn by a man who had tuberculosis? A man who lost his limb in an automobile accident? And so forth. In every case, the researchers make it absolutely clear that the sweater has been thoroughly washed, to make sure that their aversion is not an actual fear of real germs. The idea was to sort out the components of contagion beliefs: How much of the aversion is based on irrational fear of disease? How much on moral disapproval? How much on aversion to any misfortune? The findings were interesting and disturbing. People didn't stigmatize TB; they just didn't want to catch it. But *all* of these biases—against disease, immorality, and misfortune—appear to be active in the stigmatization of AIDS victims, which makes it particularly difficult to overcome.

Psychologists have also studied the sweaters of good and admirable people, like Mother Teresa. And they do find that people believe they can pick up the good essences as well. That may explain in part why people wear and cherish their grandmother's wedding ring. But in general the good essences are not as powerful as bad essences. That is, you can't undo the evil contagion of Hitler's sweater simply by wearing Mother Teresa's sweater later on.

There may be one exception to this rule, however, and that is land. Consider the enduring land disputes in Israel and the Gaza Strip. Such disputes are as ancient as mankind, but the notion of national land is relatively new in human history. In prehistoric days, emotional attachments to place were more personal and sacred than abstract and legalistic, as they are today. Why is that? What is it about a particular plot of land that stirs such deep passions in us? Rozin, working with his University of Pennsylvania colleague Sharon Wolf, decided to explore the role of contagion beliefs in the ongoing land disputes of the Middle East, specifically the land of Israel. They figured that land, at least as much as sweaters, could be perceived as having either good or bad essences. Indeed, ancestral Jewish land could be imbued with associations so powerful that they would make trading or forfeiting the land taboo, even for a similar plot of land elsewhere. Enemy-occupied land would similarly be imbued with negative essences, thus creating a fundamental psychological conflict over the land of Israel. How, they wondered, does this primeval cognitive battle play out in the modern Jewish mind?

As part of this research, the psychologists devised a laboratory tool to measure people's propensity for positive and negative contagion beliefs, and they used it to study Israelis and American Jews. They asked them specific questions about their attachment to the land of Israel: Would they trade any part of East Jerusalem? The Temple Mount? An unoccupied parcel of Israeli land? And if so, to whom? Syria? Jordan?

In general, both Israelis and American Jews considered the land of Israel "untradeable." This was true not only for sacred sites such as East Jerusalem but also for unnamed parcels of border property. When asked about Har Herzl, a Jerusalem burial ground for the Zionist leader Teodor Herzl and assassinated prime minister Itzak Rabin, fully 83 percent of Israelis and 70 percent of American Jews said they "would never trade it for land, or anything else." The majority of respondents put the land of Israel in a category with one's children or one's religion—completely off the table.

But Rozin and Wolf (who did this study before the 2009 Gaza dispute) wanted to sort out the psychology underlying such strong land attachments. So they asked some hypothetical questions about Har Herzl. First, they told the volunteers to imagine that an earthquake hit Jerusalem, destroying the cemetery and wiping out fifty feet of soil in the process; all of the bodies have been moved to a different burial site. Would you now trade Har Herzl? Then they added another wrinkle: Imagine that after the earthquake a prison was built on the site of Har Herzl, specifically for Palestinian political prisoners. The prison has existed for a decade. Would you now trade the land?

The idea was to see what it is about the land that Jews are really attached to emotionally and what it would take to sever those attach-

ments. And it appears it's the soil itself that contains the positive ancestral essences. Following the hypothetical earthquake, significantly
fewer were rigidly opposed to trading the land (39 percent of Israelis,
compared to 85 percent before the earthquake). Even fewer were
opposed to trading after the land had been "contaminated" by the
enemy presence in the imaginary prison.

Yet a significant number of participants held steadfastly to their
no-trade views even following the presence of a perceived enemy for
ten years. Land that has long been occupied by an "enemy"—not
only in Gaza but in various other Mideast regions—should be in-
fused with negative associations and Jews should not be attached to
it. Indeed, if the Hitler–Mother Teresa finding holds true, the negative associations should overpower the positive ones. Yet many Jews
remain attached to enemy-occupied land, just as many Arabs have
strong emotional ties to parts of Israel. One possible explanation, the
psychologists say, is that original positive associations establish prior-
ity, trumping negative essences that come later.

There are of course a lot of other issues at work in the conflicts of
Israel and the region, but the scientists went to great pains to control
scientifically for many of them—feelings of vulnerability, political
views about Israel, and so forth. These other factors didn't diminish
the positive, primal attachment to the land itself. It seems the ancient
contagion heuristic stakes a psychological claim that is hard to shake.

|||||||||||||||||||||||||||||||||||||||||||||||||||||||||||||||||||||||||||||||||||||||||||||||||||||||||||||||||||||||||||||||||||||||||||||||||||||||||||||||||||||||||||||

I DON'T CONSIDER MYSELF a superstitious person, generally
speaking. I open umbrellas in the house and walk under lad-
ders, and I think it's silly that hotels often don't have a thirteenth
floor. But I would be hard-pressed to wear Hitler's sweater, for the
same reason I am finicky about cleanliness. I came by my aversions

naturally, because nature is often perilous—a lesson our ancestors probably learned the hard way. But our earliest experiences in nature also bequeathed to us a bounty of psychological riches, including an invaluable source of tranquility and spirituality. Scientists are just beginning to appreciate the power of this attachment, also known as the naturalist heuristic.

17

The **NATURALIST** Heuristic

||||||||||||||||||||||||||||||||||||||||||||||||||||||||||||||||||||||||||||||||||||||||||||||||||||||||||||||||||||||||||||||||||||||||||||||||||||||||||

BACK TO THE GARDEN

TRAVIS THE CHIMPANZEE grabbed the TV news headlines for a couple of weeks in the winter of 2009. The fourteen-year-old ape was a pet, raised from infancy in his home in Stamford, Connecticut, and according to reports he was thoroughly domesticated: Travis used door keys, had a place at the dinner table, watered the plants, and used the Internet. He even drank an occasional glass of wine. Then one cold day in February, the two-hundred-pound chimp turned on his next-door neighbor unprovoked, mauling her face and leaving her in critical condition before the police arrived and shot the animal to death.

The talk shows were full of moral outrage. What were the owners thinking? Chimps are wild beasts and will always be wild at their core, experts testified. Connecticut might make it legal to own pet apes, but does that make it moral and sensible? Who would want a pet ape anyway?

I was captivated by the sad story of Travis. Just a few days before, my wife and I had visited the National Zoo, near our Washington, D.C., home, to see another ape. Mandara, a western lowland gorilla, had recently given birth, and we were among the hordes who wanted a peek at the newborn. And we lucked out. The accommodating mother nursed her baby while the crowd oohed and aahed and took snapshots.

Some people find zoos morally objectionable too. But the fact is that more Americans visit zoos every year than go to all sporting events combined. Leaving aside the knotty ethical issues of domestication and captivity, the fact is that Travis' owners and zoo goers share a common and powerful urge to affiliate with other living things, even wild things.

Especially wild things. Although many of the heuristics discussed in this book probably have some ancient evolutionary roots, the naturalist heuristic is completely defined by that prehistoric experience. It springs from adaptations that our species made to be safe in a particular environment, the vast savannas of eastern Africa. Our connections to the natural world were not cultural and aesthetic but fundamental to survival, yet they shaped our culture and aesthetics indelibly. Also called "biophilia," this deep-wired genetic impulse continues to mold our modern preferences for all sorts of things unrelated to survival: our choices of shelter and landscaping, our conservation efforts, and our pervasive attachment to pets. It's a basic yearning to get back to the natural world that's imprinted in our neurons.

I feel this. But because I've been a city boy for decades, I generally have to make do with substitutes for the real thing. I go to the zoo, take my hound to the park, and head to the ocean whenever I can. I also watch TV. For example, one of my favorite wintertime activities is holing up and watching nature shows on television. I am mesmerized by rare footage of snow leopards in the Himalayas and wild stallions in the Rockies. I am especially addicted to *Man vs. Wild,* in which the well-named Bear Grylls strands himself in the world's most inhospitable places and challenges Mother Nature with his wits. I want Bear to eat tarantulas and drink his own urine so I don't have to.

I know these videos are a poor substitute for the real thing. Not only is our wilderness shrinking, but the time we have available to enjoy it is dwindling too. Nonetheless, even city people like me look for some sense of primal connection and emotional uplift through these vicarious video experiences. But is it possible to get the psychological benefits of wilderness through technological recreations, such as nature TV, or do we actually need to feel the crunch of the snow and smell the pine needles? And what is it exactly that nature contributes to the human experience when we do get out in the elements?

Peter Kahn is one of a handful of environmental psychologists who have begun systematically exploring these questions. He and his colleagues at the University of Washington ran a series of experiments to see what benefit, if any, people get from high-quality technological versions of nature. To what extent do people distinguish between highly sophisticated versions of wildlife and the real thing? And what traits, specifically, does our "naive biology" see as properties of living things?

Many of the studies involved children, because children are the most naive humans. They offer a "pure" view of the naturalist heuristic in action. Kahn did a series of experiments involving kids' interactions with Aibo, a robotic dog made by Sony. This is one of the most advanced robotic "pets" available on the market. It has a doglike metallic form, moveable body parts, and sensors that detect distance, acceleration, vibration, sound, and pressure. It is programmed to initiate interactions with humans—offering its paw, for example. And it's even capable of rudimentary "learning": that is, petting Aibo will reinforce certain behaviors, and swatting it will discourage them. The result is that over time, different Aibos develop different personalities.

But it's not a dog. It's clearly a machine, at least to any adult. It's not even soft, so it lacks the virtues of a stuffed animal—the comfort of hugging and so forth. The idea was to make its *behavior* as doglike as possible and see how kids respond. The studies involved extensive interviews with kids about Aibo's attributes, observations of their interactions with Aibo, and tests of the children's reasoning about Aibo and other animals and artifacts. Specifically, they wanted to know if and how kids saw Aibo as something separate and apart from ordinary stuffed animals, and how their play was different from imaginary play.

That's where Shanti comes in. Shanti is an ordinary stuffed dog. For every session the kids had with Aibo, they had another one with Shanti for comparison. Kahn studied kids ranging in age from three to six years old, allowing them to interact with the two "pets" for a total of about forty-five minutes. Afterward he asked them questions like these: "Is Aibo alive? What makes him happy? How do you know? Will Aibo eat this biscuit? Can Aibo feel happy? Could he be your friend? Could you leave him alone for a week? Can Aibo die?"

Some clear conclusions emerged from the mass of data. One in four kids acted and talked about Aibo as an animate being, and at least half gave Aibo some biological properties. Even more—two of three—thought that Aibo had thoughts, social rapport, and moral standing. But—and it's a big but—the kids said much the same thing about Shanti. So it appears much of their play and relations with Aibo were part of kids' normal imagination.

Their behavior told a slightly different story, however. Most notable, the kids were much more fearful of Aibo than they were of Shanti, flinching when he approached. So they clearly sensed something beyond the traits of an ordinary toy. What's more, they were much more likely to mistreat the stuffed dog. In fact, they very rarely mistreated Aibo, even though they were apprehensive around him at times. So they were clearly making some kind of fundamental distinction between the two—evidence of the naturalist heuristic's power, even early in life.

These findings were further supported by a simple card-sorting task. When asked to categorize Aibo along with other artifacts and real dogs, the kids seemed to know that Aibo was something in between a living thing and an inanimate object. They saw the robotic dog as less like a desktop computer and more like a robot, stuffed animal, or real dog. Interestingly, most of the kids saw Aibo in moral terms: large majorities said it was not okay to hit Aibo, to abandon him for a week at a time, or to toss him in the trash.

Does that mean that Aibo might promote moral development? Is that one of the roles of nature in human life? It's possible, but Kahn believes that moral relationships with robotic pets will always be impoverished in several ways. What does it mean to have a moral relationship with something you clearly recognize as nonliving? Is it any different from loving your trusty old Buick? He concedes that relations with robots may become more complex as technology advances and they become more and more animal-like, but the existing evidence suggests the relationships will always lack a moral dimension.

We should be careful not to romanticize nature too much. After all, our relationship with wilderness and wild animals has always been a mix of awe and fear. This is reflected in our language. Just think about the epithets we commonly use. Long before pop culture turned *bitchin'* into a synonym for *cool*, *bitch* was one of the more derogatory epithets you could hurl at a woman. Indeed, man's best friend doesn't fare well in the human vocabulary of hate: *mongrel, cur, dog* itself—they're all common insults. And it's not just canines. Pig, rat, cow, mule, ape—if you want to malign your enemy, borrow freely from the animal kingdom. As I write this, there is a major brouhaha in the news about a *New York Post* cartoon that allegedly compared President Obama to the dead ape Travis.

Why is this? If you want to suggest that someone is less than human, why take it out on the beasts of the earth? You could just as easily marginalize a foe by comparing him to a machine, yet you never hear "Get lost, you robot!" or "You son of an android!" Psychologists believe the vocabulary of epithets is just the flip side of our intense love and desire for affiliation with animals. In fact, two Australian psychologists examined this idea in the laboratory. Stephen Loughnan and Nick Haslam of the University of Melbourne decided to look behind overt insults to see if we do in fact malign others in a variety of ways, some more "natural" than others.

They hypothesized that while animals and machines are both less than human, they are less than human in very different ways. That is, dogs and apes lack traits that are unique to humans, such as high intelligence and moral sensibility, while androids and robots lack traits that form the very foundation of "human nature": warmth, flexibility, animation. That is, despite our differences, we're much more closely entangled with animals, mentally and emotionally. That's the naturalist heuristic.

They studied this idea by having volunteers take a common word association test to see how readily they linked different traits with different types of people and with different nonhumans. The volunteers were exposed very quickly to a lot of words, for example, *briefcase*, *fun-loving*, *hard-hearted*, *platypus*, and *software*. They had to decide instantaneously whether to link *briefcase* (or *suit* or *boardroom*) with *fun-loving* or *hard-hearted* or *platypus* or *software*. Or instead of *briefcase*, they might be flashed *easel* or *surrealism* to see if they mentally linked it to *trusting* or *rude*, *kangaroo* or *machine*.

You get the idea. The rapid response times were important, because the scientists were trying to get as close as possible to automatic, unconscious associations. They wanted to see the automatic, heuristic brain in action. And guess what. Predictably, mechanical imagery was closely associated with commerce and its modern-day trappings; in other words, we have no ancient link to these later cultural developments. They're business, and the province of our calculating, analytic mind.

But animals and animal imagery were strongly linked to artists and artistry, suggesting a deeper and more emotional connection. Furthermore, androids and businesspeople had stronger mental connections to rational thought and sophistication, while animals and artists were more strongly linked to feelings and animation—the stuff of the experiential mind.

Or so the theory goes. Some of the most powerful evidence for our "biological bias" comes from studies of vision—how we actually see the natural world. Our mind's eye has a special and intimate connection to all things natural. Consider this hypothetical encounter with a natural landscape.

You arrive by bus at a vacation spot you've never been to before. You get out and look around. What do you notice at first glance? Well, you can't miss the large lake right in front of you; should be some good waterskiing there. There's a snowcapped mountain rising in the distance, and a copse of hemlock trees just to the left. The lodging must be in that chalet down to the right. The screened porch looks inviting, and the weather's perfect.

Now imagine you're a criminal on the lam, and you step off the same bus. What do you see in a glance? Well, mostly you see a vast open space. Other than that small stand of trees, there is very little place to hide. You feel exposed, vulnerable. The water is simply an obstacle between you and freedom on that mountain beyond. Is there a path? You notice a man-made structure, always a threat. At least it's not cold.

Same landscape, yet two very different perceptions. And this is not a matter of interpretation or judgment; a glance is way too rapid for that. It's what the vacationer and the criminal actually see. That's because even something as basic as vision is intimately rooted in our fears and in our ancient strategies for survival. Our brains evolved when there were threats everywhere, so we are highly tuned to extract the most meaningful information with even the first fleeting glance. A long lingering glance might prove fatal. The escaped convict (like our ancient ancestors) doesn't have the luxury of noticing details like hemlocks and verandas or even lakes and mountains. The need and desire for safety trump all other detail in the mind's eye.

We all have a bit of the escaped convict's vigilance deep-wired into our neurons. At least that's the theory, which a pair of MIT scientists decided to test in the lab. Psychologists Michelle Greene and Aude Oliva wanted to explore how we see the natural world in the split second of a first encounter. What information is so essential and so privileged that it's processed instantaneously? And what's mere gilding that can be added later, as we continue to scope out the new territory?

The psychologists had volunteers look at hundreds of color photographs of various natural scenes and very rapidly categorize them. Sometimes they were asked to categorize the landscapes according to common physical features such as oceans, forests, fields, and rivers. Other times they classified the landscapes according to fundamental survival features—ease of navigation, openness, naturalness, and temperature. The researchers timed how long it took the volunteers to categorize each vista, down to the millisecond.

It's remarkable how fast the mind "sees" what it needs to see. The survival features of these landscapes were processed most instantaneously as quickly as nineteen milliseconds, much faster than a finger snap. The common geographical features were also processed fairly quickly, but almost as an afterthought compared to the automatic perception of things such as open space and escape routes. This makes sense, since categories like "mountain" and "lake" came much later to humans, as the slow and analytic mind evolved. They are linguistic luxuries that entered the brain much later in evolutionary time.

But here's the most interesting part. The brain was at its absolute fastest when categorizing landscapes simply as natural, as opposed to man-made. Eons of evolution appear to have linked the brain intimately to the natural world—but not yet to the civilized world, which still requires some (relatively) slower analysis to comprehend. This raises the intriguing possibility that we can know a landscape is natural even before we "see" the mountains, meadows, and waterfalls that give it its nature.

But how do we stay connected to these natural forms in the modern world? Kahn and others have been studying our interactions with mountains, oceans, and forests—or at least their likenesses. In one experiment, for example, they installed plasma TV "windows" in workers' otherwise windowless offices for a period of sixteen weeks and then took various measures of psychological function. They found that those with the "views" of parkland and mountain ranges had a greater sense of well-being, clearer thinking, and a greater sense of connection to the natural world.

All that means, of course, is that HDTV is better than a blank wall. To see if the televised version stacks up against the real thing, Kahn ran another experiment in which some office workers had an actual view of a natural setting through a window—the old-fashioned glass kind—while others got the plasma version and still others the blank wall. They exposed all the workers to low levels of stress, but enough to make their heart rate go up; then they waited to see how long it took them to calm down.

The results were indisputable. Only the actual view of the outdoors had a calming effect; the plasma window was no more restorative than the blank wall. In other words, the technological version of nature—even when it came in HDTV quality—couldn't fool the neurons.

But what exactly is being restored by such immediate connection with nature? Or, put another way, what are we missing without these experiences? An entirely different experiment sheds some light on this question. University of Michigan psychologist Marc Berman believes that nature actually shifts our brain from one processing mode to another. That is, when we walk around city streets with a lot of stimulation, we need to employ a very focused and analytic kind of attention; that's how we process rush-hour traffic, police sirens, and other urban noises. That's also the kind of attention we need to study for exams, make financial decisions, run meetings, and so forth—the business of daily life. Some scientists label this kind of attention "executive control."

But this kind of attention can get depleted. Interacting with nature shifts the mind to a more relaxed and passive mode, allowing the more analytical powers to restore themselves. At least that's the theory, which Berman and his colleagues tested in a clever experiment. They gave a group of volunteers a very difficult cognitive test that measures the kind of focused attention needed for school and work. They then gave them an additional task to further deplete their normal ability to concentrate. This was the laboratory equivalent of having one of those hectic, demanding days at the office. Then all the volunteers took a three-mile walk. But half the volunteers took a leisurely stroll through a secluded part of the Ann Arbor Arboretum, while the others walked down Huron Street, a busy thoroughfare in downtown Ann Arbor. When they got back to the lab, the psychologists again measured their focus and concentration. Those who had been on the nature walk had significantly better focus and attention than those who had been required to negotiate the city streets. It appears that interacting with nature requires a different and less demanding form of attention, and that the temporary switchover allows workaday concentration to replenish. Getting into the woods and away from the hustle and bustle actually equips us to cope better with the cognitive demands of daily life.

So does living in our modern civilization have serious and permanent psychological consequences? Some scientists think it might—and perhaps already does. Kahn has done extensive cross-cultural studies of children's values and attitudes about open space, animal life, forests, plants, and water, and the degradation and disappearance of all these things. He has traveled the globe to see just how universal these feelings and attitudes are, interviewing kids from the Amazonian rain forests of Brazil to urban centers of Lisbon and Houston.

Here's just one example from that extensive work. When he talked to African American children in inner-city Houston about air pollution, most seemed to grasp the idea of pollution and to know it was not a good thing. But when he probed them further, the kids showed no concern about their air. That is, they did not think that Houston was a polluted city, even though it was at the time (and remains) one of the most polluted cities in the country.

These kids ranged in age from seven to eleven years old. They knew about environmental degradation in the abstract—the idea was in their analytic brain, from lectures or books or whatever—but they weren't experiencing it. They had no idea that the air they breathed was a far cry from the cleaner air their grandparents breathed.

Kahn finds this worrisome. He believes that with every generation, kids are losing some of their experiential knowledge of the natural world and their expectations for what is a normal interaction with nature, creating a kind of generational amnesia. If nature is indeed a source of mental and emotional replenishment, this could emerge as one of the most compelling psychological issues of the not-so-faraway future.

Dr. Seuss wrote about this kind of amnesia in 1971. In his children's book *The Lorax*, a child ventures into a desolated region to seek out the Once-ler. The Once-ler is both the environmental villain and the institutional memory for society; only he recalls when the region was forested by colorful Truffula trees, which his greed eventually destroyed. The book is guardedly hopeful, because while the child suffers the kind of generational amnesia Kahn has documented, his inner naturalist is still alive, deep in his neurons.

The concern of environmental psychologists is not that people can't adapt to change and loss in the natural world. It's that we *can* adapt. We have adapted to all sorts of environmental change over the eons. It's possible that right now our brains are rewiring to disconnect with the rudiments of the natural world and to bond with civilization. The question is whether, because of our deep heuristic need to affiliate with nature, we will suffer unknown psychological costs. Aibo and plasma windows may make up for some of the loss, but they may not restore us to a full measure of human flourishing.

THE NATURALIST E. O. WILSON coined the word *biophilia* to capture our powerful yearning to get back to the garden—not the biblical garden of Eden but the ancient environment where our collective mind took shape. He believed that we actually carry around in our neurons an image of the ancient savanna, which still shapes our aesthetics. The naturalist heuristic has a spiritual and moral dimension. But our moral impulses are also shaped by other forces, notably by the whodunit heuristic. This is the compulsion to deconstruct moral dilemmas, to tell right from wrong, to assign culpability and mete out punishment. We're intuitively moral beings, with consequences that we'll be exploring in the following pages.

18

The **WHODUNIT** Heuristic

MURDER AND MORALITY

I AM AN AVID reader of mysteries, everything from Rex Stout to Arthur Conan Doyle. One of my favorites is *The Nine Tailors,* Dorothy Sayers' convoluted 1934 tale of greed, betrayal, murder, and retribution set in the moors of England. It's skillfully plotted and the characters are vividly drawn, but it's also psychologically challenging. Although hero/detective Lord Peter Wimsey does solve the difficult crime in the end, the reader must settle for a lot of moral ambiguity: the killer really doesn't intend to commit murder, and indeed he is not even at the crime scene when his victim dies. What's more, he himself dies in a fluke accident and thus avoids punishment.

This fuzziness violates all the rules. Not literary rules, but psychological and moral ones. We all have a hard-boiled detective in our neurons, and this detective wants certain things, including a motive, an actual act of wrongdoing—preferably bloody—and a punishment that fits the crime. These psychological needs are fundamental and universal, which is why hundreds of thousands of mysteries have honored them over many years. Sayers makes us do a lot of mental and emotional work for our moral equilibrium.

There is something primal about uncovering wrongdoing and meting out punishment. Figuring out whodunit is not mere entertainment. We *need* to know—our very brains insist on it. At least that's the idea emerging from years of research on moral intuitions and moral judgments. And it's more important than crafting a psychologically satisfying story. These rules guide our own behavior and our judgments of others every day for crimes ranging from child abuse to Ponzi schemes to environmental degradation. Whether we're sitting in an actual jury box or simply watching someone steal from a penny tray, we all sit in judgment of others for crimes both heinous and ambiguous.

Happily, most of us will never be involved in a real murder case. But murder's a good crime to study in the lab because it's extreme and brings out our most exaggerated moral responses. Here's a moral dilemma that many psychologists have used over the years. Imagine that you are the operator of a trolley. One day the car's brakes go out, and you're careering down the tracks at ever-increasing speed. Ahead you see five students directly in your path, crossing the track on their way home from class. You have no way to stop the car or warn the students. The only way to avoid killing all five is to throw a switch and turn the trolley onto another track. But if you do that, you will run over and kill another student who is straggling behind the group. What do you do?

This is a version of what philosophers call the "trolley dilemma," which is used to explore how people deal rationally with morally ambiguous situations. The hypothetical situation also reveals how people react on a gut level, which is interesting because one of the main ideas in moral psychology today is that we do both: We respond intuitively to a dilemma—automatically, rapidly, heuristically—and only later switch over to our more deliberative brain to contemplate our impulses. As an afterthought we craft a rationale for what we've done, one that matches some systematic moral code. This is the dual-processor brain at work—the methodical brain "explaining" the quick response of the rapid, heuristic brain.

The trolley dilemma is like Moral Decision Making 101. It's pretty straightforward, and indeed the vast majority of people who face this dilemma in the lab don't ponder it all that long. Most decide readily—in seconds, not minutes—that it's okay to throw the switch, even though that means killing the innocent straggler. Think about this for a second: It's still homicide, yet most of us don't agonize over it at all. There must be something powerful going on in the brain that makes this particular kind of killing okay.

The rationale is what philosophers call "utilitarianism"—it's okay to take a life if it's for the greater good. It's practical—and morally defensible. But the brain has to make a calculation to reach this conclusion. If you do nothing, five innocent people die; if you take action, only one dies. Even though it's elementary arithmetic, it's the complex, reasoning brain at work: we have to "prove" to ourselves that it's okay, that it adds up morally. The rational brain is double-checking the intuitive brain's automatic judgment and signing off: "Yes, it's okay; that makes sense."

But why isn't our gut screaming, "No, no, no" at taking a life, whatever the justification? There is apparently no powerful moral rule that overrules this utilitarian reasoning. Why is that? Well, consider this alternative dilemma, which moral psychologists also use in the lab. It's called the "footbridge dilemma," and it's a bit more nuanced. In this case, a runaway trolley is again heading toward five innocent victims. But you're no longer the driver. You and a fat man are standing on a footbridge overlooking the track, and you realize that the only way you can spare the five students is to push the fat man off the bridge, onto the track below, to block the trolley. Do you push or don't you?

This dilemma is harder for most people. We know this because it takes most people longer to respond in a lab situation; they're pausing a millisecond to think it through. The "greater good" rationale still seems to apply in a way, but our moral intuitions make us balk. Why is that? The dilemmas are fundamentally the same. In each, you can sacrifice one life to save five. Yet people react very differently to the two situations. People automatically see the logic in the trolley dilemma, and almost all opt for the utilitarian solution. But given the footbridge dilemma, most are morally repulsed by the idea of pushing the fat man off the bridge. They won't do it. This seeming inconsistency has intrigued both philosophers and psychologists for years.

Harvard University psychologist Fiery Cushman has been studying the trolley dilemma and the footbridge dilemma—and many other variations as well—to try to sort out the moral heuristics underlying such quandaries. Why does the human brain process these two dilemmas so differently? Why does our practicality, our moral reasoning, falter on the footbridge? To answer this, Cushman created the Moral Sense Test website.

At this Harvard-based website, volunteers can contemplate and respond to all sorts of moral dilemmas. For example, consider this one involving the fictitious Evan. Evan can also save five people, but to do so he must pull a lever that opens a trap door and drops a fat man in front of the trolley. This is obviously very similar to the footbridge dilemma, but the crucial fact in this case is the lever: Evan does not have to touch the fat man, just operate a mechanical device.

Why should that matter? Isn't this semantic and ethical hairsplitting? He's still killing the poor fellow. Well, apparently it's meaningful hairsplitting—at least to our primitive mind. When Cushman tested middle-aged volunteers on this dilemma, he found that they were much less likely to push the fat man than to pull a lever that gets the identical result. It's apparently the actual physical contact that we find intuitively repulsive, the act of putting your hands on another person's body and pushing. And indeed, when Cushman asked the volunteers to rationalize their behavior, they made precisely that distinction: the lever made the act mechanical rather than personal, and that was enough to tip the balance.

Or consider yet another version from the Moral Sense Test website. This is Jeff's dilemma: He can save those five people by doing nothing, because the fat man is going to fall onto the tracks without any intervention from him. But he can save the fat man if he chooses to. He can pull a lever that prevents the man from falling, saving his life—but of course killing the five hapless students on the track. Is it okay to do nothing?

Most say yes. In this scenario, this issue is passivity. Both Evan and Jeff can merely throw a switch. There's no pushing, no wrestling, no sweat. But in Jeff's case, no action is required—zero, zip. He doesn't have to lift a finger to save the five students. And that distinction is fundamental in the brain. Crimes of omission feel less morally reprehensible than crimes of commission, even if the act is throwing a mechanical switch.

So our moral intuitions say no physical contact and no active involvement. Anything else? Here's one more dilemma from Cushman's experiment, this one for Dennis. It's a bit convoluted, but stay with me. Like all the others, Dennis has the power to save the lives of the five students on the track, but to do so he must pull a lever that redirects the moving trolley to another track. So far it sounds like the basic trolley dilemma, but here's the rub: if he pulls the lever to redirect the trolley, his action also drops the fat man through a trap door, in front of the redirected train, killing him. Would you pull the switch?

If you're like most people in the study, you would. When Cushman asked these people why it was okay to pull the switch, he found that their rationales almost always had to do with intent.

That is, the fat man's death was a mere side effect of an action that was well-intentioned and indeed lifesaving. The death was simply unfortunate—the bad luck of being in the wrong place at the wrong time.

If these seem like rationalizations, they are. But they are rationalizations of fundamental rule-driven impulses that are enormously powerful. Many of these insights derive from theories of University of Virginia psychologist Jonathan Haidt, who argues that our quick automatic moral intuitions—moral heuristics—come first. Only after the fact do we bother to make sense of our intuitions. And apparently our intuitions say we must place a high value on three things in weighing a moral dilemma: intention, action, and physical contact. If you lack all three, you get a get-out-of-jail-free card. But if the facts regarding any of the three are unclear, so too is the morality of the action—even if it saves lives.

That's what makes *The Nine Tailors* so psychologically edgy. The victim was trapped in a bell tower during the long hours of New Year's Eve bell ringing, and the intolerably loud ringing killed him. A freak accident, really. No lead pipe in the conservatory. Except . . . the "killer" had tied him up in the bell tower, intentionally holding him prisoner for a time. Then the killer got a crippling case of the flu, which prevented him from releasing the victim as he had planned. Now it starts to sound like one of Cushman's twisted trolley dilemmas. To complicate the situation further, it turns out the victim was himself a criminal and an immoral man. Is his death justifiable? Should the killer be punished as a murderer? He didn't intend to kill the man, he didn't cause the action that did kill him, and he wasn't physically present at the death. Intent, action, and physical contact are all missing. Yet we're uneasy.

Questions of justice and punishment also grow out of moral heuristics. Cushman gives this example: Two friends are drinking at a local bar all afternoon, and they drive home separately. One falls asleep at the wheel and drives into a neighbor's front yard, destroying some shrubbery. The other driver also falls asleep at the wheel and drives onto a neighbor's front lawn, but the neighbor's five-year-old daughter happens to be playing on this lawn. He runs her over and kills her. Identical behavior, most would agree, but do the two friends deserve the same punishment?

Not under the law. For example, Cushman lives in Massachusetts, and under his state's laws, the first driver can expect to pay a $250 fine for driving under the influence of alcohol. A slap on the wrist, really. The second drunk driver faces anywhere from two and a half to fifteen years in prison for manslaughter. Is this fair? Isn't their wrongdoing identical?

Yes and no. When it comes to judging what's right and wrong, intent matters a whole lot, as the various trolley dilemmas show. But when it comes to punishment, consequences matter. When Cushman gave volunteers this hypothetical in the laboratory, most agreed that the two friends were equally wrong. But they did not believe that a driver should do a long stretch in prison for destroying a mere shrub, nor did they think a driver should get off the hook for killing a child. And most of us would probably agree: different consequences, different punishments.

So if there is a detective in our neurons who makes decisions about guilt and complicity, there is apparently also a lawyer in our neurons, and the two don't seem to talk to each other all that much. The detective just wants to know if a crime occurred and who did it, while the lawyer is concerned that the punishment fit the crime. To make this point, imagine that there was a third friend drinking at the bar that afternoon. But this guy is evil—a real sociopath. He leaves the bar actually intending to run the little girl over with his car and kill her, but because he's drunk, he falls asleep and crashes into the shrubbery instead. No harm, no foul? Almost everyone would say that he is infinitely more immoral than the other drunk who ran into the shrubs, even though the incidents look identical. Indeed, he's more reprehensible than the drunk who accidently committed manslaughter. But the law doesn't see it that way.

That's because the law is a product of the plodding, deliberate, rational part of the brain. Laws were written down by civilized societies—by a collection of rational brains—to codify our collective moral reasoning. But they don't adequately capture our moral intuitions, the gut responses to the visceral nature of crime and to evil intent. Judging something as wrong is a moral intuition, a heuristically driven rule. Judging the harm to others and how to even the score—that is a slower, more deliberate act.

The primacy of moral heuristics can lead to other questionable judgments as well. Consider terrorist attacks. When al-Qaeda terrorists destroyed the World Trade Center on September 11, 2001, the criminals were a tragic real-life version of the sociopathic drunk driver above—except they didn't fall asleep and fail in their mission. They had evil intent *and* they succeeded, and their act had horrific consequences—more than three thousand innocent people dead. Guilt was so clear and outrage so justified that the inner detective didn't have much to do.

But what about the 1993 al-Qaeda attack on the World Trade Center? It failed out of ineptitude, but the intent was no less evil. The terrorists did kill six people, but they botched their larger goal of bringing down the towers. It's very much like the evil drunk falling asleep and running into a shrub, and indeed it was treated that way. No overreaction against Muslims, no recriminatory war, very little public outrage at all. It's hard to muster outrage for a failed crime—even when the intent was to kill thousands, just as their compatriots did on 9/11.

It's also hard to muster outrage when there is no evil intent or action, as Cushman demonstrated in his trolley experiments. That's probably why even a much smaller terrorist attack—such as the 2008 attacks on Mumbai's posh hotel district, which killed about two-hundred—stirs more public indignity than a tsunami or cholera epidemic that kills many more. We may feel great horror and sympathy over natural disasters, but far less moral outrage.

Moral conflicts involve much more than murder and death, of course. Our moral instincts and our reasoning often conflict over cultural taboos as well. UVA's Haidt calls this conflict "moral dumbfounding." Dumbfounding occurs when we feel strongly that something is wrong but cannot explain why. Here's an example from Haidt's studies: Julie and Mark are brother and sister. They are traveling in France during summer break from college, and one night, alone in a cabin near the beach, they decide it would be interesting and fun if they tried making love. Julie is already taking birth control pills, but Mark uses a condom just to be extra careful. They both enjoy it but decide not to do it again. They keep that night as their special secret, which brings them closer to each other. End of story.

Was this okay? Most people immediately condemn Julie and Mark's behavior as morally wrong, but when they try to explain why, they are dumbfounded. Inbreeding is not an issue, because of the care they both took with contraception. They obviously haven't been harmed psychologically; in fact, making love brought them closer. When Haidt presses people to explain, they usually say something like: "I don't know. I can't explain it." I just know it's wrong. This is the subterranean moralist talking—or trying to. But heuristics don't translate very well into language, because they are so instinctual and emotional.

This is why it's so hard for conservatives to make a case against gay marriage. The argument is not rational, it's intuitive. At its core, the argument is simply that homosexuality does not seem "right" to some people. Many controversial social issues have the potential for moral dumbfounding. This is what satirist Stephen Colbert calls "truthiness"—things that people know intuitively, from the gut "without regard to evidence, logic, intellectual examination, or facts." Haidt believes that such misguided moral intuitions have their roots in primitive emotions like disgust. In one of his experiments, he asked volunteers how they felt about hypothetical situations, such as this: A family is poor and hungry, and its pet dog, Herman, is killed on the highway. The family cooks Herman for dinner. How do you feel about that?

Again, a lot of people feel dumbfounded. It feels wrong—disgusting to some—but they can't articulate why. Disgust probably evolved as an emotion when early humans switched from a vegetarian diet to an omnivorous diet. There were risks that came with eating meat (including ancient roadkill), and disgust evolved as a psychological deterrent to eating rotten meat. That fear no longer keeps people from eating meat, but the rule remains etched in the brain and shapes our behavior and our ethics. Most people I know—including myself—wouldn't eat roadkill at all, much less a pet dog named Herman.

Much of the crime and immorality that affects our lives these days has to do with greed, cheating, and lying—immoral acts benignly dismissed as white-collar crime. New York financier Bernie Madoff is locked away after pleading guilty to eleven felony counts in one of history's largest investment frauds, and sad to say, this is just one of many recent stories about captains of industry and finance behaving badly with other people's money. There have been so many revelations like this recently that it's enough to make the average taxpaying citizen wonder whether anyone actually plays by the rules anymore. And if people who already have plenty of money can't help skimming (or just hauling away wads of cash), it's fair to ask how an ordinary person is supposed to resist the temptation to skim on her taxes or pad his time sheet at work when times are tight.

So why do some people cheat and others don't? The classical explanation is that it's a rational choice, a cold calculation of cost and benefit: "Can I get away with it, and how much can I get away with before I risk getting caught?" But some scientists have begun questioning this cynical view of human ethics and suggest that the decision is much more complex than this simple calculation.

Three psychologists recently decided to explore these knotty ethical questions in the laboratory. Francesca Gino of the University of North Carolina and Shahar Ayal and Dan Ariely of Duke University set up an elaborate hoax to see if they could actually make people cheat, in order to illuminate the psychological forces at work in the dishonest mind.

Here, briefly, is what they did. They asked a large group of university students to solve a set of complex math problems in a very short time. They made it hard enough that none could realistically solve all the problems, and they paid them for whatever ones they did solve. The math exercise was just a pretense for the real experiment: Shortly after the students began on the math problems, one of them (actually a paid actor) loudly announced to the room: "I've solved everything. What should I do?" Everyone in the room knew this was impossible, so the student-actor was a clear example of blatant cheating. He also took all of the cash, as if he had a perfect score, and—very important—he left without any consequences.

The idea was to see how many of the students followed the cheater's example—to see if blatant dishonesty boosted cheating among students generally. And it did, dramatically. But the psychologists added another twist to the experiment: sometimes they had the actor wear the T-shirt of a rival university, other times not. They wanted to see if the cheater's group identity—classmate or outsider—influenced the level of copycat cheating. That is, would students cheat more (or less) when they saw a rival cheat, as compared to seeing a compatriot cheat?

The results? Fellow classmates had much more influence than outsiders. Indeed, seeing a rival cheat actually lowered the level of overall cheating slightly compared to students who simply cheated on their own initiative, without any prodding. These findings argue against the "cold calculation" theory of cheating. After all, if the students only weighed the can-I-get-away-with-it factor, then they would have been influenced equally by the successful cheating of both compatriot and outsider. And they weren't.

The psychologists decided to double-check these findings with another small experiment. It was basically the same setup, but in this scenario the actor didn't do anything; he simply asked out loud of the proctor: "Is it okay to cheat?" I know, stupid question. Nobody would really do that. But the idea was simply to nudge the inner moralist in the students' minds, to bring the issues of cheating and dishonesty front and center. And when they did this, the students cheated noticeably less. There were no role models, good or bad. Just priming the idea of unethical behavior was enough to keep the students honest.

So it appears our inner moralist doesn't really want to cheat. It's wrong on a fundamental, heuristic level. Yet it also appears that dishonesty can be contagious if we witness one of our own committing the public act of dishonesty. These findings point to a possible strategy for preventing a wave of unethical contagion. If cheating in general declines when cheaters are perceived as outlaws, then it should help to stigmatize public cheaters as just that—outlaws, bad apples. Of course, Bernie Madoff and the rest of Wall Street's alleged fraudsters have already done a lot of that work for us.

So if our moral heuristic is so forceful, why is there such widespread immorality? What's going on with Ponzi schemers, presidential aides cheating on their taxes, industrialists spoiling the environment? Is there a widespread erosion of social responsibility? Are these cheaters simply bad people? Are our educational and religious institutions failing? Are the rewards of being a good and honest person simply not enough to curb our darker impulses? Or are we all both sinners and saints, depending on the circumstances?

Psychologists have been looking into these questions, specifically the idea that we all toggle back and forth constantly between righteousness and immorality. Is it possible that we have a set point for morality, much like we do for body weight? Three Northwestern University psychologists recently explored this question with some intriguing results.

Sonya Sachdeva, Rumen Iliev, and Douglas Medin had the idea that our sense of moral self-worth might serve as a kind of thermostat, tilting us toward moral stricture at one time and moral license at another, but keeping us on a steady track. They tested this by priming volunteers' feelings of moral superiority—or their sense of guilt—and watching what happened.

In one experiment, for example, they had the volunteers write brief stories about themselves. Some were required to use words like *generous, fair,* and *kind,* while others wrote their stories using words such as *greedy, mean,* and *selfish.* This was the unconscious prime, well known to activate feelings of either righteousness or regret. Afterward, all the volunteers were given a chance to donate money to a favorite charity, as much as $10 or as little as zero. The volunteers didn't know their charity was being measured as part of the experiment, and the results were striking. Those who were primed to think of their moral transgressions gave on average $5.30, more than twice that of controls; those who were primed to feel self-righteous gave a piddling $1.07.

These results suggest that when people feel immoral, they "cleanse" their self-image by acting unselfishly. But when they have reason to feel a little superior, that positive self-image triggers a sense of moral license. That is, the righteous feel they have some latitude to stray a bit in order to compensate. It's like working in a soup kitchen gives you the right to cheat on your taxes later in the week.

The psychologists ran a version of the experiment related to moral responsibility toward the environment. They wanted to see if the same feelings of moral superiority and moral transgression shape the trade-offs we make between self-interest and the health of the planet. They used the same primes, and then had all the volunteers pretend they were managing a manufacturing plant. As managers, they had to choose how much they would pay to operate filters that would control smokestack pollution. They could simply obey the industry standard, or they could do more or less; that is, they could choose social responsibility or choose to cheat the common good.

Those who were feeling morally debased were much more communitarian, spending more money for the sake of clean skies. The morally righteous were stingy, and what's more, they took the view that plant managers should put profits ahead of green concerns. They saw it as a business decision, not an ethical choice. So it appears that our inner moralist deals in a kind of moral "currency." We collect chits through our good deeds and debts through our transgressions, and we spend our chits to pay off our moral debts. That way, we keep the moral ledger balanced.

I HAVE ON MY bookshelf at home the *Road Kill Cookbook,* a gift from a native West Virginian. The souvenir makes playful fun of hillbillies, a heuristic-driven caricature. And it also brings into play both the cooties heuristic and the whodunit heuristic. Our sense of rectitude is basic but complex, involving not just basic repulsion but also higher-order intuitions about right and wrong. We can't abide anything disgusting, whether it's roadkill or incest or murder, and that impulse drives us to keep our hands clean—physically uncontaminated, ethically and morally righteous. As we have seen again and again, many of the forces at work in the heuristic mind are driven by threats and fears, even if they now have taken on more abstract and modern forms. The biggest threat and fear we all face is ultimately the fear of death, of extinction. It's so basic to the human condition that we have a very old and deep coping mechanism known as the grim reaper heuristic.

The **GRIM REAPER** Heuristic

LONELINESS AND ZEALOTRY

IN THE 1975 movie *Love and Death,* Woody Allen's spoof of the brooding sensibilities of Russian literature, Allen plays the cowardly soldier Boris to Diane Keaton's Sonja. At a critical juncture in the film, when the Russians are under assault by Napoleon's troops, Boris asks his lover: "Are you scared of dying?" Sonja ponders the question for a few seconds. "*Scared* is the wrong word," she finally replies. "I'm frightened of it."

Woody Allen has gotten a lot of laughs out of death and dying, but the fact is, scared or frightened, we're all in the same boat. We instinctively don't want to die, yet know we must. We are the only animals on the planet who can contemplate our own death, yet we'll do pretty much whatever we can not to, including playing semantic games with ourselves. The fact of death is just too terrifying.

Philosophers and scientists have long been interested in how the mind processes the inevitability of death, both cognitively and emotionally. One would expect, for example, that reminders of our mortality—say the sudden death of a loved one—would throw us into a state of disabling fear of the unknown. But that doesn't happen. We weep and grieve, of course, but we're not paralyzed. If the prospect of death is so incomprehensible, why are we not trembling in a constant state of terror over the prospect of perishing?

Psychologists have some ideas about how we cope with existential dread. One emerging idea—"terror management theory" in the social science jargon—holds that the brain is hard-wired to keep us from being frozen by fear. According to this theory, the heuristic brain allows us to think about dying, even to change the way we live our lives, but not to cower in the corner. The automatic, unconscious part of our brain in effect protects the conscious mind.

But how does this work? It's obviously not easy to study existential thoughts in the laboratory, but a group of psychologists has done just that in a series of clever experiments. They start by using a psychological technique to fill volunteers' minds with thoughts of death. They basically prompt them to think about what happens physically as they die and to imagine what it's like to be dead. They conjure thoughts of neurons not firing and hearts beating their last beats and tissue decomposing beneath the soil. It may sound morbid, but the technique has been widely tested and is highly effective. It's the experimental equivalent of ruminating about dying after the loss of a loved one.

Once the volunteers are preoccupied with thoughts of death and dying, they complete a series of word tests, which have been designed to tap into unconscious emotions. For example, volunteers might be asked to complete the word stem JO_ to make a word. They could make a neutral word like *job* or *jog,* or they might instead opt for the emotional word *joy.* Or, in a similar test, they might see the word *puppy* flashed on a screen, and they would instantaneously have to choose either beetle or parade as the best match. *Beetle* is closer to *puppy* in meaning, but *parade* is closer to *puppy* in emotional content. Volunteers must respond very quickly to these tests, so fast that they really can't consciously process their choices. The idea is that the results represent the unconscious, heuristic mind at work.

When psychologists Nathan DeWall of the University of Kentucky and Roy Baumeister of Florida State University ran three experiments of this type, they got unambiguous and intriguing results. The volunteers who were preoccupied with thoughts of death were not at all morose if you tapped into their emotional brains. Indeed, the opposite: they were much more likely than control subjects to summon up positive emotional associations rather than neutral or negative ones. What this suggests, the psychologists say, is that the brain is involuntarily searching out and activating pleasant, positive information from the memory banks in order to help the workaday brain cope with an incomprehensible threat.

So that's good news. And there's more, because these findings jibe with a separate line of research on aging. Studies show that as we get older and approach death, our brains somehow shift gears, craving more upbeat stimulation. We find ourselves averting our eyes from grisly auto accidents and gradually losing our interest in slasher movies. It's not a planned, deliberate change; it's more like an effortless retuning of the neurons, and psychologists believe it has everything to do with the keener sense of mortality that comes with aging.

This emotional reckoning all begins with the eyes. It may seem as if our gaze flits around capriciously, but in fact our eye movements are not as random as one would think. Scientists use sophisticated machines to track the eyes' darting and stopping, and can tell when someone has "fixated" on something out there. We're talking milliseconds here, but these fleeting fixations are a good proxy for a lingering gaze—or for avoidance.

In a series of laboratory experiments at Brandeis University, psychologist Derek Isaacowitz tested the connection between gaze and mood and motivation. He used a standard personality test to separate optimists from pessimists, and then had both look at pictures. Some were photos of emotionally neutral faces, while others were images of skin cancer, unpleasant and graphic in detail. The sunnier volunteers fixated on the cancer images much less than their gloomier peers, suggesting that they were using their gaze as a tool to avoid going over to the dark side. This was true even if the subjects had a family history of cancer and therefore a reason to be preoccupied with the disease.

That part is not so surprising. If Isaacowitz had stopped there, the study would have done little more than confirm that some people are sunnier than others. But he decided to explore the gaze-mood-age connection in more detail. In another experiment, for example, he compared older and younger adults, measuring their gaze as they looked at happy, sad, angry, and fearful faces. The older participants had a clear preference for the happy facial expressions and avoided the angry faces. The young people lingered on the fearful faces. Isaacowitz speculates that older people's gaze may reflect an underlying motivation to regulate their emotions and feel good. As people age, they may increasingly feel like they're living on borrowed time, and so they pursue emotionally meaningful, uplifting experiences. They don't have time for car wrecks.

Isaacowitz wanted to make sure his results weren't being skewed by a general cognitive decline in the elderly. So he ran another experiment comparing two groups who were both young but had very different time perspectives: college freshmen and college seniors. He reasoned that the seniors, with graduation looming, might have a more constrained sense of the future. And indeed, the seniors spent less time gazing at negative images than did first-year students.

There is a theory in psychology that humans are motivated by a desire to control their world. As people age, they tend to focus on goals that are attainable and to disengage from unrealistic goals, which can lead to failure and unhappiness. In a final experiment,

Isaacowitz compared childless women over age forty with those under forty. Though there are exceptions, forty is often accepted as the time when a woman leaves her childbearing years behind, and Isaacowitz wanted to see if gaze and mood were intertwined with age and life planning. He showed both groups pictures of babies, and also (to control for cuteness) pictures of puppies and kittens. The women who were past childbearing age averted their gaze from the babies more quickly than the younger women, suggesting that they were conserving their emotional resources for realistic life choices. (They all fixated on the puppies and kittens.)

So it's too simplistic to conclude that happy people gaze at happy images just to stay happy. After all, cute babies make most of us feel good, so we turn away from them at the expense of our own momentary happiness. It appears that gaze is much more complex and powerful than that, a tool for nothing less than emotional control in life as we age.

I had a personal experience related to this kind of self-protection. A few years ago, a friend dragged me to a major retrospective on Norman Rockwell's work, and I got hooked on the images of kids doing homework, families gathering for holiday dinners, and communities turning out for local sporting events. I know some people find this vision too cloying for our postmodern sensibilities, but for me the images stir up memories of a simpler past. Something inside me responds to the human connection in Rockwell's idealized world.

That's called nostalgia, and it turns out it's not an entirely bad thing. In fact, my response to these treacly images may be etched into my gray matter for a purpose. A growing number of psychologists have become interested in this uniquely human emotion, in particular its connection to loneliness, social isolation, and emotional resilience. Indeed, some believe that nostalgia may be a powerful psychological tool for fostering mental health, a coping strategy we use to protect ourselves against the existential fear of being alone.

People who are chronically lonely perceive themselves as disconnected from others, especially family and friends; they feel isolated from all the traditional sources of social support. Are lonely people more likely to be nostalgic than others? Is it possible that nostalgia—that sentimental longing for the past—might have a tonic effect on loneliness, buffering against these feelings of isolation?

That is the idea that psychologist Xinyue Zhou of Sun Yat-Sen University in China decided to explore in the laboratory. Zhou and colleagues ran a series of experiments to explore the value of nostalgia in counteracting the emotional costs of loneliness, for people from many walks of life. They wanted to see if nostalgic reverie could create symbolic connections with others—connections powerful enough to temper the very real pangs of isolation.

Here's an example. The psychologists recruited hundreds of migrant children who had moved from remote rural areas to a major city just a few years earlier. These kids were about eleven years old on average, so we can all imagine how emotionally disruptive such an experience must have been and how alien their new world must have seemed. They gave the kids a battery of psychological tests to measure just how lonely they were after a few years in the city, how nostalgic they were for the past, and how supportive they saw the people in their world.

The results were paradoxical. The loneliest kids did indeed see the world as unfriendly and unsupportive. But many of these same lonely kids were also among the most nostalgic, and this nostalgia appears to have a buffering effect against the painful effects of isolation. That is, feelings of social isolation seem to churn up nostalgic memories, which in turn salve the pain of loneliness. Nostalgia is self-protective, much like gaze.

The psychologists ran similar experiments with college students and factory workers, using a variety of experimental methods. In some studies they actually induced feelings of loneliness or nostalgic thoughts in order to verify the paradoxical findings. The results were basically the same in all the studies. It appears that, regardless of age or circumstances, the lonely mind has the ability to protect itself from emotional pain by recruiting romanticized memories of the past.

But how? Why do some individuals summon up nostalgic memories to buffer their loneliness, while others do not? Zhou thinks it may have to do with basic personality. Psychologists have known for some time that people differ on a trait called resilience. Resilience is basically the ability to shake off life's insults, to roll with the punches; it's emotional hardiness. The psychologists suspected that people with resilient personalities would be more likely to use nostalgia as a coping strategy. And that's just what they found in yet another study. When they gave the factory workers a personality inventory on top of the other tests, they found that the most resilient individuals were also most likely to use nostalgic memories for self-protection.

These findings have clear clinical implications. Loneliness, at its pathological extreme, is nothing less than existential dread—terror at being disconnected in the universe. Such fear can lead to disabling anxiety and depression. If nostalgia is an antidote to such fear, Zhou argues, perhaps patients might be taught to recruit sentimental memories as a therapeutic tool for creating a healthful sense of human connection.

How all this unfolds in the brain is still unclear, but one idea is that nostalgia increases the accessibility of certain restorative experiences—moments of human connection. The brain may do this by calling up actual visual images, in effect flipping through an internal photo album and reminiscing. Not all that different from strolling through a Norman Rockwell retrospective.

So the heuristic brain has an arsenal of psychological tools to protect itself from existential fear. But is there is a downside to all this deep-wired self-preservation? Some believe that we also protect ourselves against our deepest insecurities by becoming more rigid in our beliefs. When death looms, we bolster our egos by defending our closely held values—and, worse, by deriding the values of others. In capitalist societies, for example, emotional self-preservation may take the form of excessive materialistic striving, the overzealous valuing of money and material possessions over more intrinsic values.

Psychologists Tim Kasser and Kennon Sheldon decided to test this provocative idea. Capitalist culture, they reasoned, sends the message that making a lot of money and consuming a lot of things are the paths to meaningful lives. So priming people for thoughts of their own mortality should heighten these beliefs. They ran two experiments to look separately at the desire to earn a lot of money, on one hand, and the willingness to consume scarce resources, on the other.

In the first study, they had a group of volunteers think about death—the usual laboratory prime for existential fear. Then they asked them to imagine themselves fifteen years into the future. What would their lives look like? What would their salary be, and their spouse's salary? What about the value of their home, car, clothing, and other stuff? How much would they spend on travel and leisure? And so forth. The idea was to get an index of the volunteers' anticipated financial worth.

As expected, they found that those who were thinking about death expected to be worth more overall, and expected to indulge in more of the trappings of wealth. This may seem counterintuitive at first, because we expect those who are facing death to reevaluate their lives and focus on what really matters—family and friends. As they say, you can't take it with you. But apparently that's not the way the heuristic mind operates. At least in capitalist cultures, people apparently find end-of-life meaning in reaffirming the values they've been taught to live by.

Kasser and Sheldon ran a second experiment, this one to explore

the effects of mortality on consumption of the planet's scarce resources. They devised a clever experiment to do this. They had a large
group of volunteers play a forest management game, which goes like
this: Imagine that you own a timber company and you need to bid
against three other companies to harvest timber in a national forest.
You are aware that the forests are being depleted, and especially by
companies making large bids on the lumbering rights. How much
would you like to outprofit the others? How many of the one hundred acres in the national forest do you intend to harvest this year?
What do you expect from your competitors?

The idea was to see how much greedier the subjects became when
they were focused on imminent death. And indeed they were much
greedier than the others. They were more intent on beating the competition, taking more trees and making more money. Apparently
their insecurities and fears were so powerful that they trumped any
concerns about the fragility of the ecosystem.

This is certainly a gloomy conclusion. But it gets worse. Just consider that humans are the only species that systematically murders its
own for ideological reasons. More than 50 million people were victims of mass murder in the twentieth century, making it the deadli-
est century on record. That included the Ottoman Turks' murder of
1.5 million Armenians, the Nazis' extermination of 6 million Jews,
Mao's murder of 30 million Chinese, and the Khmer Rouge's de-
struction of 1.7 million Cambodians. The list goes on.

Some of these deaths had to do with land and water and such,
but most did not. Most were over philosophy. Why would this be?
Philosophy is not threatening in any literal sense; it can't maim or
make you die, even when it's very different from your view. Scientists are intrigued by this paradox. Why is philosophy—or worldview,
or ideology—so threatening? Or to flip the question around, what
are the cognitive and emotional underpinnings of mass murder and
genocide?

One emerging theory suggests that genocide may make sense, at least on an emotional level. It's part of the unconscious self-protection against paralyzing fear. We manage terror by constructing meaning, and we do that by imagining a meaningful world. That's called philosophy—or religion, or whatever. As we saw with the design heuristic, humans are meaning-making creatures at the core.

The problem occurs when our carefully constructed philosophy is threatened. And the greatest threat to a belief system is an alternative belief system. To put it simply, your unfamiliar worldview makes me keenly aware of my mortality. It threatens my carefully constructed sense of meaning and purpose. So why shouldn't I wish you dead? Philosophy is personal.

Scientists have actually been studying in the lab this entanglement of personal mortality and cultural hatred, with some interesting results. Here's a recent experiment by Joseph Hayes and his colleagues at the University of Alberta, Canada. These psychologists wanted to explore whether a philosophical threat could indeed conjure up thoughts of death and, further, whether those thoughts might be quelled by actual annihilation of the philosophical "enemy." To explore this, they recruited devout Christians for an experiment. They had these Christians read an actual news story about the Muslimization of Nazareth. The article described how Jesus's hometown had become largely a Muslim city, and how the dominant (and militant) Muslim population was marginalizing the Christians who remained.

The idea was that this unwelcome news about a holy Christian landmark would threaten the Christian readers' worldview and in turn their personal security. It appears it did. After they had read about Nazareth, they all took a psychological test that gauges preoccupation with thoughts of death and dying. The findings were clear. Those who had read the report were much more morbid in their imagery than those who had not. They were also much more derogatory toward Muslims than were Christians who had not read the news.

So that's pretty unsettling in itself. But here's where it gets really interesting. Hayes and his colleagues then told half of the participants another bit of news, only in this case it was made up. They told them that an airplane had crashed on its way to Nazareth, killing all 117 devout Muslims aboard. When they again sorted through the data, they found that those who had "witnessed" the annihilation of the Muslims were significantly less morbid in their thinking and significantly less derogatory toward Muslims. Put another way, knowing of the violent death of the Muslims effectively undid the perceived threat to the Christians' philosophy and well-being. It restored meaning and security to their lives.

Isn't it possible that the plane crash simply made the Christians more sympathetic toward the Muslims, at least temporarily? The psychologists actually considered and rejected this idea, based on a surprising finding. The Christians who read about Nazareth became increasingly negative not only toward Muslims but also toward Buddhists, Hindus, and atheists. That is, they became antagonistic toward any worldview that questioned the absolute validity of Christianity. What's more, those who read the fabricated story about the plane crash were less disparaging of all these worldviews. Since no Hindus, Buddhists, or atheists perished in the fictional crash, there would be no reason for the Christians to feel sympathy toward these people. These studies could have been done with Christians and Muslims and Buddhists all switched around, and presumably the result would be the same. All worldviews are protective—and in need of protection.

So our brain fights death with death. It reasons that if an enemy dies, his philosophy must have been perverse or weak or just plain wrong, and thus no real threat to our superior worldview—nor to our life and limb. It's a powerful psychological defense. In real life, of course, it just raises the ante. It's tit for tat, and the new century starts counting its genocide victims.

⁣||||||||||||||||||||||||||||||||||||||||||||||||||||||||||||||||||||||||||||||||||||||||||||||||||||||||||||||||||||||||||||||||||||||||||||||||||||||||||||||||||||||||||||||||||||

THE GRIM REAPER heuristic allows us to keep our deepest existential dread at bay. It deals with the ultimate dilemma, and would seem to have little in common with the rudimentary bodily heuristics discussed in this book's opening chapters. But think about what powers our terror: imagining the physical decomposition of the body. The heuristics discussed in this volume have been organized from the most physical to the mental and numerical to the more spiritual—but the fact is that's just a simplification. Every one of the heuristics we've explored here is entwined with others, many others—and all of them are hinged to the most fundamental heuristic of all, the default heuristic. The default is the über-heuristic, the potent cognitive force that flips the on-off switch on all the others—and ultimately gives form to our choices, judgments, and actions.

20

The **DEFAULT** Heuristic

||

NOT TO DECIDE IS . . .

W HEN I WAS a college student in the late 1960s, I earned my spending money by selling stuff to unsuspecting freshmen. During the first few weeks of the fall semester, while they still had all that gift money from well-wishing relatives, I would cruise the dormitories, taking orders for beer mugs, black lights, and especially posters. Posters were a quick and fairly cheap way for freshmen to stamp their personality on the walls, and I sold hundreds. The most popular by far was a sexy photograph of Raquel Welsh in a fur bikini, a promo for the movie *One Million Years B.C.* But I also sold a fair number of a poster that pictured only scribbled words: *I might or I might not. How should I know? What should I do?* The title, in bold-face, read: *Not to decide is . . . to decide.*

I was much too busy being entrepreneurial to give the words much thought at the time. It wasn't until much later that I learned the source of the slogan, which was the liberal Christian theologian

Harvey Cox. In one of his many critiques of organized religion, *On Not Leaving It to the Snake,* Cox had written: "Somewhere deep down we know that in the final analysis we do decide things and that even our decisions to let someone else decide are really our decisions, however pusillanimous." Cox was talking about the moral responsibility of Christians, but the phrase was somehow seized upon by the restless children of the era and made into a political rallying cry, a call for action and a condemnation of passivity.

The activists of the 1960s were intuitive psychologists, as it turns out. The field known as cognitive psychology was in its infancy in the sixties, but that simple slogan is today recognized by scientists as a fundamental truth about how the human mind works—for better or worse. Even our decisions to let someone else decide are really our decisions, and most of us make more life choices in this way than we'd like to admit.

Psychologists have a technical name for this style of decision making. They label it the default heuristic. Given the option of deciding or not deciding, deciding is always the far more difficult and effortful choice. It's cognitively wearying to study options and make choices—literally, much like lifting weights—so it's much more efficient most of the time to simply not decide, to punt, to stick with the status quo, norms, traditions.

Defaulting is one of the simpler cognitive tools we have at our disposal, but that does not mean it isn't powerful in its effects. Consider this real-life example: About 28 percent of Americans are potential organ donors. That is, if they died tragically today, their kidneys, liver, and other organs would be available to the long list of people waiting for transplants. In France, 99.9 percent of the citizens are potential donors. Why would this be? Do the French have a particular character trait that predisposes them to give? Is their early moral training superior to ours? Is there perhaps an altruism gene that runs in the French population?

Well, it's likely none of those. The answer is almost certainly much simpler. In most states in the United States, the default position for organ donation is no donation. That is, you must actively choose to be a donor by signing something. You must make the effort of deciding. In France it's the opposite. Unless you make the effort to opt out, you are by default an organ donor. And because it's easier for the brain to default than not, most of us don't stop to weigh such choices or to question such policies. As a result, it's better to have kidney failure in Paris than in Washington, D.C.

Because the default heuristic basically means doing nothing, most of the time we don't even know we're making a choice or decision. Yet we are—probably many times every day. The transplant example appeared in the prestigious journal *Science* a few years ago, and the same authors have written about other public policies that, in effect, make our decisions invisible. For example, if you live and drive a car in New Jersey, the standard auto insurance does not give you the right to sue for pain and suffering from minor injuries. You can buy that right, for a premium, but in order to do so requires some deliberate actions. First of all, you must make the effort to know about the option; second, you must do some paperwork (and spend more money) to choose it. Only one in five New Jersey drivers actually does this.

Right across the Delaware River, in Pennsylvania, the default heuristic has very different consequences. There, the right to sue comes with the standard auto insurance policy, although you do pay more for it. As with the donor policy in France, you must opt out of it by filling out some additional paperwork. Only one in four Pennsylvania drivers opts out, so by default the vast majority have this right—and pay extra for it.

Now, which is better? That really depends on your perspective. The authors note that Pennsylvanians pay $200 million more on auto insurance than they would if they had a default position like New

Jersey's. On the other hand, if you're driving along the Pennsylvania Turnpike and a reckless driver clips you, you have a much greater chance of getting some compensation for your suffering.

It's all about fit, not fairness. Your brain is not making a moral judgment (about donating organs or about irresponsible drivers); it is merely doing what it does automatically, defaulting. The automatic part of the brain doesn't value one public policy over another; it simply opts not to decide. That may be good or it may be bad, depending on who is making the moral judgment for you, in terms of public policy.

The problem is that policies and rules do not always make sense. MIT psychologist Shane Frederick illustrates this point clearly by pointing to the National Football League's instant replay policy. In NFL games, a coach can challenge a ref's call on the field if he thinks the ref was mistaken. Say the coach saw a dropped pass where the ref did not. The replay official has access to much more information than the on-field ref, including several camera angles and slow-motion video. Yet the NFL policy is to default to the on-field official unless there is "indisputable visual evidence" that he was wrong. It doesn't make sense to have the original call—made rapidly, with incomplete information—trump a more deliberate analysis with much more information, yet that is what the NFL has decided to do.

Think of instant replay as a metaphor. In life, you always have the opportunity to review your automatic decision, to make a more deliberate judgment. And you don't need overwhelming evidence to overrule yourself. Many choices in life are much more momentous than the outcome of a Sunday afternoon football game, yet the same psychological principles are at work. Think about saving for the future. It's not easy, especially when money is tight, to take money from every paycheck and put it into a savings account; there are so many things you could do with that money right now. It's terribly difficult, psychologically, to imagine yourself in the future, at a time when you will be glad you put some money aside.

That's in part because of our powerful futuristic bias. Psychologists and economists have proposed policies that might help you overcome the psychological difficulty of forecasting your future life. For example, economist Richard Thaler and legal scholar Cass Sunstein of the University of Chicago suggest that companies take a different approach to new employees to encourage contributions to 401(k) plans, benevolently "nudging" workers to save, against their heuristic impulse. Instead of having them decide on a payroll deduction immediately—a tough choice when you're just getting a job and a paycheck—have them check a box that authorizes a deduction (and contribution) starting one year later. This is much easier for most new employees to do, since the pain has shifted to the vague future. Yet in a year they automatically enroll in the company's 401(k), probably without even noticing.

Such policies have been proven to work. What these new employees have done, in effect, is change their default position, so that when the heuristic-driven brain chooses "not to decide," the decision has already been made. You can do this for many of life's decisions, and you can do it by yourself in many cases. You don't need a lawmaker or company CEO to decide for you.

Think about exercise. I exercise every day, and I have for some time. But it wasn't an easy habit to establish in the beginning. Like a lot of well-intentioned people, I had made New Year's resolutions to go to the gym, but I always lasted for a few weeks, then failed. Then I listened to Woody Allen.

Woody Allen famously said that 80 percent of the business of life is just showing up. It's a throwaway line, but it shows keen psychological insight and goes directly to the heart of default thinking. After many failed attempts at fitness, I made a vow to go to the gym every day. Just "show up"—no more. I found a gym that was reasonably convenient, so that wasn't a deterrent, then started putting on my sweats every morning and showing up. If I exercised, great, but if I didn't, that was okay too. I would at least make an appearance.

You know what? I never once showed up without doing something, even if it was just hopping on the Stairmaster for twenty minutes. And it was almost always more, just because I was there, and why not? I was already sweaty. What I had done, without even realizing it at the time, was change my brain's default position. I had written a policy for myself, a policy that let my deliberating brain stay home while my automatic brain took over.

So we often default to a policy, social rule, or convention (official or personal) and proceed on automatic. But we also default to every other heuristic at work in the mind unless we deliberately talk ourselves out of it. Think back to the snow-driving lesson I described in the introduction: turn into the skid. Our natural impulse when we go into a skid is to go away—it's physical and irresistible—and it takes huge effort and self-discipline to trump it. But we are capable of saying no to the first impulse.

Here's another example to make the point. It comes from an unexpected source: behavioral economist Ofer Azar's intriguing study of premier soccer goalies. Azar, a lecturer at Ben-Gurion University in Israel, studied penalty kicks. A penalty kick is awarded after a foul and is often used as a tiebreaker in championship games. A designated player stands thirty-six feet from the goal, which measures twenty-four feet side to side. Only the opposing goalie stands between the kicker and the goal, so it's a high-probability shot. In fact, with the typical penalty kick flying at more than sixty miles per hour, the goalie has only a fraction of a second to respond.

Facing such a physical challenge, professional goalies must decide before the actual kick what they will do: go right, go left, or stay put. So Azar decided to study what they actually do—and what they *should* do to be successful. He collected data on more than three-hundred of the top goaltenders in the world in action, and found a clear pattern: goalies had the best chance of stopping a penalty shot if they just stayed put, smack in the center of the net. If they did this—that is, moved neither left not right—they were able to stop the opponent's shot 33.3 percent of the time. That's not great, but it's a lot better than the other odds: goalies who made a guess and jumped left stopped only 14.2 percent of the shots, and goalies who dove right stopped a dismal 12.6 percent. That's one in eight, which means seven of every eight penalty shots flew past for a score. That can't feel good.

Indeed, it felt lousy. Azar interviewed the goalies about their decisions in the net, and he found that their emotions played a major role in goaltending strategy. Despite the clear statistical advantage of staying put in the center, only about 6 percent of goalies actually choose to do this. Why? Because they feel worse if they fail standing still—worse than they feel if they fail diving. In other words, taking any action, even one doomed to failure, is better than inaction, because doing nothing and still failing is emotionally unacceptable. That's the heuristic mind that makes movement an emotional choice, and as with snow driving, it takes a lot of effort to alter the impulse.

Azar doesn't care all that much about soccer. In fact, he published these results in the *Journal of Economic Psychology*, because his real interest is how and why people make irrational choices in business and personal finance. And it's clear that most of us are just as irrationally biased toward action as these world-class goalies. We have a powerful urge to "do something" even when the something doesn't make a great deal of sense. This almost certainly derives from an ancient and powerful message to deal with threats through action.

Just think about the stock market meltdown of 2008. This may have been an extraordinary economic downturn—economists are still navel-gazing over that question—but in the summer of 2008 the reality was that a lot of people had to make a lot of financial decisions, with huge amounts of money riding on those choices. This was equally true for fund managers and for personal investors wondering what to do with their 401(k)s. Move or stay put?

The received wisdom of investing is to take the long view. Don't overinterpret every sell-off as a warning of something dire; stay the course and the market will correct itself. But the primitive brain says to do something. What if this time is different, historically unprecedented, as many economists were wailing? Won't you feel the fool for doing nothing—fiddling while Rome burns, as the phrase goes? So you act—you sell, or buy, anything. Like the goalie, you leap just for the sake of leaping.

This reiterates the main point of this volume, which is that our automatic, heuristic thinking is neither good nor bad. It's all about fit. Hundreds of times a day we are faced with choices—some life changing—that we can and should make thoughtfully. Think back on the avalanche that buried Steve Carruthers. Carruthers and his fellow skiers had several opportunities to talk themselves out of their perilous default position, but it would have taken a lot of effortful self-questioning: "I know this looks safe at first glance, but is that just because it's familiar, my home territory? Am I staying the course here just because it's what we planned? Because bagging the plan would be disappointing? Am I not speaking my mind because of the others, because it's not just me out here? Is that pure and rare white powder seducing my mind and skewing my judgment?" And so forth. Carruthers—and one or all of the others—would have had to ask these questions about human nature, all while standing out on the cold slopes overlooking Gobbler's Notch, and answer them honestly.

We can do this. We are capable of detecting what our automatic brain wants to do and either affirming or trumping that impulse. The point is that we're faced every day with choices to do something or do nothing—take action or default. Many of these choices are trivial: shall I continue to use the same brand of gasoline that my father used his whole life, just because he did? For me growing up, it was Esso, and it was unthinkable that we would drive around the corner and fill up on Texaco instead. I was an adult with my own car when I finally shook this cognitive bias—but it's still lingering there in my neurons.

All social norms and traditions depend on the default heuristic. But all those trivial choices add up to who you are. Maxwell House or Starbucks? Red meat or vegan? The mountains or the sea? And some of the choices are less trivial than others. Should you continue to vote Republican just because you come from a family of Republicans? Should you reform your church or leave it alone? As that poster from the sixties summarized so graphically: *Not to decide . . . is to decide.*

SELECTED FURTHER READING

Introduction

McCammon, Ian. "Heuristic Traps in Recreational Avalanche Accidents: Evidence and Implications." *Avalanche News* 68 (2004): 1–10.

McCammon, Ian. "Evidence of Heuristic Traps in Recreational Avalanche Accidents." Paper presented at the International Snow Science Workshop, Penticton, British Columbia, September 30–October 4, 2002.

Chapter 1. The VISCERAL Heuristic

Huang, Julie Y., and John A Bargh. "Peak of Desire: Activating the Mating Goal Changes Life-Stage Preferences Across Living Kinds." *Psychological Science* 19 (2008): 573–578.

Williams, Lawrence E., Julie Y. Huang, and John A. Bargh. "The Scaffolded Mind: Higher Mental Processes Are Grounded in Early Experience of the Physical World." *European Journal of Social Psychology* 39 (2009): 1257–1267.

Zhong, Chen-Bo, and Geoffrey Leonardelli. "Cold and Lonely: Does Social Exclusion Literally Feel Cold?" *Psychological Science* 19 (2008): 838–842.

Zhong, Chen-Bo, and Katie Liljenquist. "Washing Away Your Sins: Threatened Morality and Physical Cleansing." *Science* 313 (2006): 1451–1452.

Schnall, Simone, Jennifer Benton, and Sophie Harvey. "With a Clean Conscience: Cleanliness Reduces the Severity of Moral Judgments." *Psychological Science* 19 (2008): 1219–1222.

Chapter 2. The VISIONARY Heuristic

Stefanucci, Jeanine K., and Justin Storbeck. "Don't Look Down: Emotional Arousal Elevates Height Perception." *Journal of Experimental Psychology* 138 (2009): 131–145.

Proffitt, D. R. "Embodied Perception and the Economy of Action." *Perspectives on Psychological Science* 1 (2006): 110–122.

Schnall, Simone, Kent D. Harber, Jeanine K. Stefanucci, and Dennis R. Proffitt. "Social Support and the Perception of Geographical Slant." *Journal of Experimental Psychology* 44 (2008): 1246–1255.

Riskind, John H., Nathan L. Williams, Theodore L. Gessner, Linda D. Chrosniak, and Jose M. Cortina. "The Looming Maladaptive Style: Anxiety, Danger and Schematic Processing." *Journal of Personality and Social Psychology* 79 (2000): 837–852.

Teachman, Bethany A., Jeanine K. Stefanucci, Elise M. Clerkin, Meghan W. Cody, and Dennis R. Proffitt. "A New Mode of Fear Expression: Perceptual Bias in Height Fear." *Emotion* 8 (2008): 296–301.

Chapter 3. The MOMENTUM Heuristic

Roese, Neal J., Florian Fessel, Amy Summerville, Justin Kruger, and Michael A. Dilch. "The Propensity Effect: When Foresight Trumps Hindsight." *Psychological Science* 17 (2006): 305–310.

Markham, Keith D., and Corey L. Guenther. "Psychological Momentum: Intuitive Physics and Naïve Beliefs." *Personality and Social Psychology Bulletin* 33 (2007): 800–812.

Roese, Neal J., and Sameep D. Maniar. "Perceptions of Purple: Counterfactual and Hindsight Judgments at Northwestern Wildcats Football Games." *Personality and Social Psychology Bulletin* 23 (1997): 1245–1253.

Roese, Neal J., and Amy Summerville. "What We Regret Most . . . and Why." *Personality and Social Psychology Bulletin* 31 (2005): 1273–1285.

Roese, Neal J. "Counterfactual Thinking." *Psychological Bulletin* 121 (1997): 133–148.

Roese, Neal J. "Twisted Pair: Counterfactual Thinking and the Hindsight Bias." In *Blackwell Handbook of Judgment and Decision Making,* edited by D. Koehler and N. Harvey, 258–273. Oxford: Blackwell, 2004.

Chapter 4. The FLUENCY Heuristic

Song, Hyunjin, and Norbert Schwarz. "Fluency and the Detection of Misleading Questions: Low Processing Fluency Attenuates the Moses Illusion." *Social Cognition* 26 (2008): 791–799.

Song, Hyunjin, and Norbert Schwarz. "If It's Hard to Read, It's Hard to Do: Processing Fluency Affects Effort Prediction and Motivation." *Psychological Science* 19 (2008): 986–988.

Song, Hyunjin, and Norbert Schwarz. "If It's Difficult to Pronounce, It Must be Risky: Fluency, Familiarity and Risk Perception." *Psychological Science* 20 (2009): 135–138.

Alter, Adam L., and Daniel M. Oppenheimer. "Uniting the Tribes of Fluency to Form a Metacognitive Nation." *Personality and Social Psychology Review* 13 (2009): 219–235.

Alter, Adam L., and Daniel M. Oppenheimer. "Easy on the Mind, Easy on the Wallet: Effects of Fluency on Valuation Judgments." *Psychonomic Bulletin and Review* (in press).

Alter, Adam L., and Daniel M. Oppenheimer. "Effects of Fluency on Psychological Distance and Mental Construal (or Why New York Is a Large City but New York Is a Civilized Jungle)." *Psychological Science* 19 (2008): 161–167.

Alter, Adam L., and Daniel M. Oppenheimer. "Predicting Short-Term Stock Fluctuations by Using Processing Fluency." *Proceedings of the National Academy of Sciences* 103 (2006): 9369–9372.

Chapter 5. The MIMICRY Heuristic

Reed, Kyle, Michael Peshkin, Mitra J. Hartmann, Marcia Grabowecky, James Patton, and Peter M. Vishton. "Haptically Linked Dyads: Are Two Motor-Control Systems Better than One?" *Psychological Science* 17 (2006): 365–366.

Knoblich, Günther, and Natalie Sebanz. "The Social Nature of Perception." *Current Directions in Psychological Science* 15 (2006): 99–104.

Lakin, Jessica L., Tanya L. Chartrand, and Robert M. Arkin. "I Am Too Just Like You: Nonconscious Mimicry as an Automatic Behavioral Response to Social Exclusion." *Psychological Science* 19 (2008): 816–822.

Ackerman, Joshua M., Noah J. Goldstein, Jenessa R. Shapiro, and John A. Bargh. "You Wear Me Out: The Vicarious Depletion of Self-Control." *Psychological Science* 20 (2009): 326–332.

Wiltermuth, Scott S., and Chip Heath. "Synchrony and Cooperation." *Psychological Science* 20 (2009): 1–5.

Gallese, Vittorio. "The Roots of Empathy: The Shared Manifold Hypothesis and the Neural Basis of Intersubjectivity." *Psychopathology* 36 (2003): 171–180.

Chapter 6. The MAPMAKER Heuristic

Williams, Lawrence E., and John A. Bargh. "Keeping One's Distance: The Influence of Spatial Distance Cues on Affect and Evaluation." *Psychological Science* 18 (2008): 302–308.

Fujita, Kentaro, Marlone D. Henderson, Juliana Eng, Yaacov Trope, and Nira Liberman. "Spatial Distance and Mental Construal of Social Events." *Psychological Science* 17 (2006): 278–282.

Fujita, Kentaro, Tal Eyal, Shelly Chaiken, Yaacov Trope, and Nira Liberman. "Influencing Attitudes Toward Near and Distant Objects." *Journal of Experimental Social Psychology* 44 (2008): 562–572.

Henderson, Marlone D., Kentaro Fujita, Yaacov Trope, and Nira Liberman. "Transcending the 'Here': The Effect of Spatial Distance on Social Judgement." *Journal of Personality and Social Psychology* 91 (2006): 845–856.

Fujita, Kentaro, Yaacov Trope, Nira Liberman, and Maya Levin-Sagi. "Construal Levels and Self-Control." *Journal of Personality and Social Psychology* 90 (2006): 351–367.

McCrea, Sean M., Nira Liberman, Yaacov Trope, and Steven J. Sherman. "Construal Level and Procrastination." *Psychological Science* 19 (2008): 1308–1314.

Chapter 7. The ARITHMETIC Heuristic

Peters, Ellen, Daniel Vastfjall, Paul Slovic, C. K. Mertz, Ketti Mazzocco, and Stephen Dickert. "Numeracy and Decision Making." *Psychological Science* 17 (2006): 407–413.

Reyna, Valerie F. "How People Make Decisions That Involve Risk." *Current Directions in Psychological Science* 13 (2004): 60–66.

Pham, Michel Tuan. "The Logic of Feeling." *Journal of Consumer Psychology* 14 (2004): 360–369.

Slovic, P., M. Finucane, E. Peters, and D. MacGregor. "Rational Actors or Rational Fools: Implications of the Affect Heuristic for Behavioral Economics." *Journal of Socio-Economics* 31 (2002): 329–342.

Slovic, Paul. "Why Nations Fail to Act." Paper presented at a seminar on the prevention of genocide hosted by the Auschwitz Institute for Peace and Reconciliation, Auschwitz, Poland, May 18, 2008.

Slovic, Paul. "If I Look at the Mass I Will Never Act: Psychic Numbing and Genocide." *Judgment and Decision Making* 2 (2007): 79–95.

Stephen, Andrew T., and Michel Tuan Pham. "On Feelings as a Heuristic for Making Offers in Ultimatum Negotiations." *Psychological Science* 19 (2008): 1051–1058.

Magen, Eran, Carol S. Dweck, and James J. Gross. "The Hidden-Zero Effect: Representing a Single Choice as an Extended Sequence Reduces Impulsive Choice." *Psychological Science* 19 (2008): 648–649.

Burson, Katherine A., Richard P. Larrick, and John G. Lynch, Jr. "Six of One, Half Dozen of the Other: Expanding and Contracting Numerical Dimensions Produces Preferential Reversals." *Psychological Science* 20 (2009): 1074–1078.

Reyna, Valerie F., Wendy L. Nelson, Paul K. Han, and Nathan F. Dieckmann. "How Numeracy Influences Risk Comprehension and Medical Decision Making." *Psychological Bulletin* 135 (2009): 943–973.

Chapter 8. The SCARCITY Heuristic

Dai, Xianchi, Klaus Wertenbroch, and C. Miguel Brendl. "The Value Heuristic in Judgments of Relative Frequency." *Psychological Science* 19 (2008): 18–19.

Dai, Xianchi, C. Miguel Brendl, and Klaus Wertenbroch. "Value, Scarcity, and Preference Polarization." Unpublished paper.

Jemmott, John B., III, Peter H. Ditto, and Robert T. Croyle. "Judging Health Status: Effects of Perceived Prevalence and Personal Relevance." *Journal of Personality and Social Psychology* 50 (1986): 899–905.

Lynn, Michael. "Scarcity's Enhancement of Desirability: The Role of Naïve Economic Theories." *Basic and Applied Psychology* 13 (1992): 67–78.

Myrseth, Kristian Ove R., Ayelet Fishbach, and Yaacov Trope. "Counteractive Self-Control: When Making Temptation Available Makes Temptation Less Tempting." *Psychological Science* 20 (2009): 159–163.

Chapter 9. The ANCHOR Heuristic

Epley, Nicholas, and Thomas Gilovich. "Putting Adjustment Back in the Anchoring and Adjustment Heuristic: Differential Processing of Self-Generated and Experimenter-Provided Anchors." *Psychological Science* 12 (2001): 391–396.

Epley, Nicholas, and Thomas Gilovich. "The Anchoring-and-Adjustment Heuristic: Why the Adjustments Are Insufficient." *Psychological Science* 17 (2006): 311–318.

Janiszewski, Chris, and Dan Uy. "Anchor Precision Influences the Amount of Adjustment." *Psychological Science* 19 (2009): 121–127.

Klatzky, Roberta L., David M. Messick, and Judith Loftus. "Heuristics for Determining the Optimal Interval Between Checkups." *Psychological Science* 3 (1992): 279–284.

Epley, Nicholas, Boaz Keysar, Leaf Van Boven, and Thomas Gilovich. "Perspective Taking as Egocentric Anchoring and Adjustment." *Journal of Personality and Social Psychology* 87 (2004): 327–339.

Bodenhausen, Galen V., Shira Gabriel, and Megan Lineberger. "Sadness and Susceptibility to Judgmental Bias: The Case of Anchoring." *Psychological Science* 11 (2000): 320–323.

Chapter 10. The CALORIE Heuristic

Briers, Barbara, Mario Pandelaere, Sigfried Dewitte, and Luk Warlop. "Hungry for Money: The Desire for Caloric Resources Increases the Desire for Financial Resources and Vice Versa." *Psychological Science* 17 (2006): 939–943.

Bruner, Jerome S., and Cecile C. Goodman. "Value and Need as Organizing Factors in Perception." *Journal of Abnormal and Social Psychology* 42 (1947): 33–44.

Nelson, Leif, D. , and Evan L. Morrison. "The Symptoms of Resource Scarcity: Judgments of Food and Finances Influence Preferences for Potential Partners." *Psychological Science* 16 (2005): 167–173.

Geier, Andrew B., Paul Rozin, and Gheorghe Doros. "Unit Bias: A New Heuristic That Helps Explain the Effect of Portion Size on Food Intake." *Psychological Science* 17 (2006): 521–525.

Tabibnia, Golnaz, Ajay B. Satpute, and Matthew D. Lieberman. "The Sunny Side of Fairness: Preference for Fairness Activates Reward Circuitry (and Disregarding Unfairness Activates Self-Control Circuitry)." *Psychological Science* 19 (2008): 339–347.

Chapter 11. The DECOY Heuristic

Huber, Joel, and Christopher Puto. "Market Boundaries and Product Choice: Illustrating Attraction and Substitution Effects." *Journal of Consumer Research* 10 (1983): 31–44.

Hedgcock, William, and Akshay R. Rao. "Trade-Off Aversion as an Explanation for the Attraction Effect: A Functional Magnetic Resonance Imaging Study." *Journal of Marketing Research* XLVI (2009): 1–13.

Sedikides, Constantine, Dan Ariely, and Nils Olsen. "Contextual and Procedural Determinants of Partner Selection: Of Asymmetric Dominance and Prominence." *Social Cognition* 17 (1999): 118–139.

Kim, Sunghan, and Lynn Hasher. "The Attraction Effect in Decision Making: Superior Performance by Older Adults." *Journal of Experimental Psychology* 58 (2005): 120–133.

Masicampo, E. J., and Roy F. Baumeister. "Toward a Physiology of Dual-Process Reasoning and Judgment: Lemonade, Willpower and Expensive Rule-Based Analysis." *Psychological Science* 19 (2008): 255–260.

Herbert, Ian. "This Is Your Brain on Politics." *Observer* 21 (2008): 18–22.

Chapter 12. The FUTURISTIC Heuristic

Gilbert, Daniel. *Stumbling on Happiness.* New York: Knopf, 2006, 304.

Caruso, Eugene M., Daniel T. Gilbert, and Timothy D. Wilson. "A Wrinkle in Time: Asymmetric Valuation of Past and Future Events." *Psychological Science* 19 (2008): 796–801.

Wilson, Timothy D., Thalia Wheatley, Jonathan M. Meyers, Daniel T. Gilbert, and Danny Axsom. "Focalism: A Source of Durability Bias in Affective Forecasting." *Journal of Personality and Social Psychology* 78 (2000): 821–836.

Gilbert, Daniel T., Elizabeth C. Pinel, Timothy D. Wilson, Stephen J. Blumberg, and Thalia P. Wheatley. "Immune Neglect: A Source of Durability Bias in Affective Forecasting." *Journal of Personality and Social Psychology* 75 (1998): 617–638.

Koo, Minkyung, Sara B. Algoe, Timothy D. Wilson, and Daniel T. Gilbert. "It's a Wonderful Life: Mentally Subtracting Positive Events Improves People's Affective States, Contrary to Their Affective Forecasts." *Journal of Personality and Social Psychology* 95 (2008): 1217–1224.

Chapter 13. The DESIGN Heuristic

Greif, Marissa L., Deborah G. Kemler Nelson, Frank C. Keil, and Franky Gutierrez. "What Do Children Want to Know About Animals and Artifacts: Domain-Specific Requests for Information." *Psychological Science* 17 (2006): 455–459.

Goldberg, Robert F., and Sharon L. Thompson-Schill. "Developmental

'Roots' in Mature Biological Knowledge." *Psychological Science* 20 (2009): 480–487.

Lombrozo, Tania, Andrew Shtulman, and Michael Weisberg. "The Intelligent Design Controversy: Lessons from Psychology and Education." *Trends in Cognitive Science* 10 (2006): 56–57.

Lombrozo, Tania, Deborah Kelemen, and Deborah Zaitchik. "Inferring Design: Evidence of a Preference for Teleological Explanations in Patients With Alzheimer's Disease." *Psychological Science* 18 (2007): 999–1006.

Lombrozo, Tania. "Simplicity and Probability in Causal Explanation." *Cognitive Psychology* 55 (2007): 232–257.

Loughnan, Stephen, and Nick Haslam. "Animals and Androids: Implicit Associations Between Social Categories and Nonhumans." *Psychological Science* 18 (2007): 116–121.

Jost, John T., Brian A. Nosek, and Samuel D. Gosling. "Ideology: Its Resurgence in Social, Personality, and Political Psychology." *Perspectives on Psychological Science* 3 (2008): 126–136.

Chapter 14. The FORAGING Heuristic

Silvia, Paul J. "Interest—the Curious Emotion." *Current Directions in Psychological Science* 17 (2008): 57–60.

Hills, Thomas T., Peter M. Todd, and Robert L. Goldstone. "Search in External and Internal Spaces: Evidence for Generalized Cognitive Search Processes." *Psychological Science* 19 (2008): 802–808.

Goldstone, Robert L., Michael E. Roberts, and Todd M. Gureckis. "Emergent Processes in Group Behavior." *Current Directions in Psychological Science* 17 (2008): 10–15.

Fredrickson, Barbara. *Positivity.* New York: Crown, 2009.

Chapter 15. The CARICATURE Heuristic

Bodenhausen, Galen V. "The Role of Stereotypes in Decision-Making Processes." *Medical Decision Making* 25 (2005): 112–118.

Bodenhausen, Galen V. "Stereotypes as Judgmental Heuristics: Evidence of Circadian Variations in Discrimination." *Psychological Science* 1 (1990): 319–322.

Macrae, C. Neil, Alan B. Milne, and Galen V. Bodenhausen. "Stereotypes as Energy-Saving Devices: A Peek Inside the Cognitive Toolbox." *Journal of Personality and Social Psychology* 66 (1994): 37–47.

De Neys, Wim, Oshin Vartanian, and Vinod Goel. "Smarter than We Think:

When Our Brains Detect That We Are Biased." *Psychological Science* 19 (2008): 483–489.

Djikic, Maja, Ellen J. Langer, and Sarah Fulton Stapleton. "Reducing Stereotyping Through Mindfulness: Effects on Automatic Stereotype-Activated Behaviors." *Journal of Adult Development* 15 (2008): 106–111.

Levy, Becca R., Alan B. Zonderman, Martin D. Slade, and Luigi Ferruci. "Age Stereotypes Held Earlier in Life Predict Cardiovascular Events in Later Life." *Psychological Science* 20 (2009): 296–298.

Langer, Ellen J. *Counterclockwise: Mindful Health and the Power of Possibility.* New York: Ballantine, 2009.

Chapter 16. The COOTIES Heuristic

Rozin, Paul. "The Meaning of 'Natural': Process More Important than Content." *Psychological Science* 16 (2005): 652–658.

Rozin, Paul, Maureen Markwith, and Clark McCauley. "Sensitivity to Indirect Contacts with Other Persons: AIDS Aversion as a Composite of Aversion to Strangers, Infection, Moral Taint, and Misfortune." *Journal of Abnormal Psychology* 103 (1994): 495–504.

Rozin, Paul, and Sharon Wolf. "Attachment to Land: The Case of the Land of Israel for American and Israeli Jews and the Role of Contagion." *Judgment and Decision Making* 3 (2008): 325–334.

Nemeroff, Carol, and Paul Rozin. "The Contagion Concept in Adult Thinking in the United States: Transmission of Germs and Interpersonal Influence." *Ethos* 22 (1994): 158–186.

Rozin, Paul, and Edward B. Royzman. "Negativity Bias, Negativity Dominance, and Contagion." *Personality and Social Psychology Review* 5 (2001): 296–320.

Chapter 17. The NATURALIST Heuristic

Berman, Marc G., John Jonides, and Stephen Kaplan. "The Cognitive Benefits of Interacting with Nature." *Psychological Science* 19 (2008): 1207–1212.

Kahn, Peter H., Jr., Rachel L. Severson, and Jolina H. Ruckert. "The Human Relation with Nature and Technological Nature." *Current Directions in Psychological Science* 18 (2009): 37–42.

Kahn, Peter H., Jr., Batya Friedman, Deanne R. Perez-Granados, and Nathan G. Freier. "Robotic Pets in the Lives of Preschool Children." *Interaction Studies* 7 (2006): 405–436.

Friedman, Batya, Nathan G. Frier, Peter H. Kahn, Jr., Peyina Lin, and Robin Sodeman. "Office Window of the Future? Field-Based Analyses of a New Use of a Large Display." *International Journal of Human-Computer Studies* 66 (2008): 452–465.

Kahn, Peter H., Jr., Batya Friedman, Brian Gill, Jennifer Hagman, Rachel L. Severson, Nathan G. Frier, Erika N. Feldman, Sybil Carrere, and Anna Stolyar. "A Plasma Display Window? The Shifting Baseline Problem in a Technologically-Mediated Natural World." *Journal of Environmental Psychology* 28 (2008): 192–199.

Greene, Michelle R., and Aude Oliva. "The Briefest of Glances: The Time Course of Natural Scene Understanding." *Psychological Science* 20 (2009): 464–472.

Chapter 18. The WHODUNIT Heuristic

Haidt, Jonathan. "The New Synthesis in Moral Psychology." *Science* 316 (2007): 998–1002.

Cushman, Fiery, Liane Young, and Marc Hauser. "The Role of Conscious Reasoning and Intuition in Moral Judgment: Testing Three Principles of Harm." *Psychological Science* 17 (2006): 1082–1089.

Cushman, Fiery. "Crime and Punishment: Distinguishing the Roles of Causal and Intentional Analyses in Moral Judgment." *Cognition* 108 (2008): 353–380.

Gino, Francesca, Shahar Ayal, and Dan Ariely. "Contagion and Differentiation in Unethical Behavior." *Psychological Science* 20 (2009): 393–398.

Sachdeva, Sonya, Rumen Iliev, and Douglas L. Medin. "Sinning Saints and Saintly Sinners." *Psychological Science* 20 (2009): 523–528.

Sunstein, Cass R. "Moral Heuristics." *Behavioral and Brain Sciences* 28 (2005): 531–542.

Chapter 19. The GRIM REAPER Heuristic

Zhou, Xinyue, Constantine Sedikides, Tim Wildschut, and Ding-Guo Gao. "Counteracting Loneliness: On the Restorative Function of Nostalgia." *Psychological Science* 19 (2008): 1023–1029.

Routledge, Clay, Jamie Arndt, Constantine Sedikides, and Tim Wil. "A Blast From the Past: The Terror Management Function of Nostalgia." *Journal of Experimental Social Psychology* 44 (2008): 132–140.

Arndt, Jamie, Sheldon Solomon, Tim Kasser, and Kennon M. Sheldon. "The Urge to Splurge: A Terror Management Account of Materialism and Consumer Behavior." *Journal of Consumer Psychology* 14 (2004): 198–212.

Isaacowitz, Derek M., Kaitlin Toner, Deborah Goren, and Hugh R. Wilson. "Looking While Unhappy: Mood Congruent Gaze in Young Adults, Positive Gaze in Older Adults." *Psychological Science* 19 (2008): 848–853.

Pyszczynski, Tom, Zachary Rothschild, and Abdolhossein Abdollahi. "Terrorism, Violence, and Hope for Peace: A Terror Management Perspective." *Current Directions in Psychological Science* 17 (2008): 318–322.

Pyszczynski, Tom, J. Greenberg, and S. Solomon. "A Dual Process Model of Defense Against Conscious and Unconscious Death-Related Thought: An Extension of Terror Management Theory." *Psychological Review* 106 (1999): 835–845.

McCoy, S., Tom Pyszczynski, S. Solomon, and J. Greenberg. "Transcending the Self: A Terror Management Perspective on Successful Aging." In *The Problem of Death Among Older Adults,* edited by A. Tomer, 37–61. New York: Taylor and Francis, 2000.

DeWall, C. Nathan, and Roy F. Baumeister. "From Terror to Joy: Automatic Tuning to Positive Affective Information Following Mortality Salience." *Psychological Science* 18 (2007): 984–990.

Hayes, Joseph, Jeff Schimel, and Todd J. Williams. "Fighting Death with Death: The Buffering Effects of Learning That Worldview Violators Have Died." *Psychological Science* 19 (2008): 501–507.

Chapter 20. The DEFAULT Heuristic

McKenzie, Craig R. M., Michael J. Liersch, and Stacey R. Finkelstein. "Recommendations Implicit in Policy Defaults." *Psychological Science* 17 (2006): 414–420.

Johnson, Eric J., and Daniel Goldstein. "Do Defaults Save Lives?" *Science* 302 (2003): 1338–1339.

Baron, Jonathan, Max H. Bazerman, and Katherine Shonk. "Enlarging the Societal Pie Through Wise Legislation: A Psychological Perspective." *Perspectives on Psychological Science* 1 (2006): 123–132.

Frederick, Shane. "Automated Choice Heuristics." In *Heuristics and Biases: The Psychology of Intuitive Judgment,* edited by Thomas Gilovich, Dale Griffin, and Daniel Kahneman, 548–558. New York: Cambridge University Press, 2002.

Thaler, Richard H., and Cass R. Sunstein. *Nudge: Improving Decisions About Health, Wealth, and Happiness.* New Haven: Yale University Press, 2008.

Benartzi, Schlomo, and Richard H. Thaler. "Save More Tomorrow: Using Behavioral Economics to Increase Employee Saving." *Journal of Political Economy* 112 (2004): S164–S187.

Lilienfeld, Scott O., Rachel Ammirati, and Kristen Landfield. "Giving Debiasing Away: Can Psychological Research on Correcting Cognitive Errors Promote Human Welfare?" *Perspectives on Psychological Science* 4 (2009): 390–398.

Bar-Eli, Michael, Ofer H. Azar, Ilana Ritov, Yael Keidar-Levin, and Galit Schein. "Action Bias Among Elite Soccer Goalkeepers: The Case of Penalty Kicks." *Journal of Economic Psychology* 28 (2007): 606–621.

ACKNOWLEDGMENTS

I'S SAID THAT all science writers are dwarfs, standing on the shoulders of giants, and I am certainly no exception. This book would not exist if it were not for the hard and ingenious work of scores of psychological scientists who have devoted their careers to the study of human nature. I thank all who have given generously of their time in helping me to understand the nuances of the heuristic mind. At the risk of omitting someone, I want to mention a few who have been especially encouraging, in the sense that they believe explaining psychological science to the general public is a worthy endeavor. In no particular order: Bobbie Klatzky of Carnegie Mellon, Norbert Schwarz of Michigan, Valerie Reyna of Cornell, Adam Alter of NYU, Morton Gernsbacher of Wisconsin, Walter Mischel of Columbia, Bob Levenson of Berkeley, Roddy Roediger of Washington University in St. Louis, John Cacioppo of Chicago, Laura Freberg of Cal Poly, Scott Lilienfeld of Emory, Barbara Fredrickson of UNC in Chapel Hill, and Ellen Langer of Harvard. Of course, any misinterpretations of the science are mine alone.

I owe a special debt of gratitude to Alan Kraut and Sarah

Brookhart, director and deputy director, respectively, of the Association for Psychological Science. Alan and Sarah have granted me extraordinary freedom to explore and write about psychology in my own way—and to write a lot. This book grew directly out of the research and writing I do for the Association, and I could not have done this project without Alan and Sarah's support and encouragement. I also want to thank Catherine Allen-West, my colleague and deputy, whose conscientious attention to detail freed my time up for reading and thinking. I also thank my editors at *Newsweek,* David Noonan and Susanna Schrobsdorff, for polishing and publishing earlier versions of a few essays as the "Mind Matters" column, and my editors at *Scientific American Mind,* Mariette DiChristina and Karen Schrock, for publishing selected essays in my regular "We're Only Human" column.

A few words about how this book came to be: A few years ago, I received a kind and flattering e-mail out of the blue from Lucinda Bartley, who identified herself as an editor at Crown Publishers. I had been writing short essays on psychology, some published in *Newsweek,* others in *Scientific American Mind,* but mostly in my blog, called "We're Only Human." Lucinda had discovered these essays, and she wondered if I might have a book in me. I was fairly busy at the time and didn't know if there was a book tucked away in my mind, but I passed Lucinda's note on to Gail Ross, my longtime friend and literary agent. Gail had been nudging me to write a book for many years, but she is very picky about proposals she will handle. She didn't much care for my first few ideas, but she introduced me to her colleague Howard Yoon, whose specialty is transforming messy thinking into sharply focused book ideas. Howard and I met and corresponded over the next several months, and from those conversations he very gently extracted the proposal for the book that has become *On Second Thought.* When Gail finally started showing the idea around in summer of 2008, I was delighted to have it land where it belonged—at Crown, and in the hands of Lucinda. The book has continued to evolve under Lucinda's careful stewardship. Many thanks to her for her sharp eye and deft hand, and to Gail and Howard for their early and continuing support. My gratitude, too, to Julian Pavia of Crown for stepping in and putting the manuscript through its final paces, and to Anna Sproul of the Gail Ross Literary Agency for helping bring the book to market.

Several people have given generously of their time to read and critique all or part of the manuscript at different stages. Sara Sklaroff, my former colleague and dear friend, offered helpful editorial suggestions and support, as did my sister, Maggie Goss, and my neighbor, psychologist Learita Scott. I also received invaluable support from Bernie Healy, Marianne Szegedy-Maszak, Joannie Fischer, and Tom Hayden, each in his or her own way.

I also want to express my heartfelt thanks to my immediate family. My sons—Ian, Brendan, and Morgan—have been a continuing source of joy and inspiration to me, and their love has been unconditional even during challenging times. Ian also read and critiqued every page of the book with his keen editor's mind. My stepchildren, Ben Miosi and Megan Miosi, came late to my life, and I have also benefited greatly from their presence.

And I save the most important for last. This book would not have happened without Susie Herbert. She stood by, but stood out of the way, all those dark early mornings and weekends that I stole for this project, never complaining and always encouraging. She has been my first reader, my most incisive critic, my most enthusiastic cheerleader, my helpmate, and my best friend.

INDEX

ABOUT THE AUTHOR

WRAY HERBERT has been a science journalist for more than three decades, specializing in psychology and human behavior. He has been a reporter and editor for *Science News* magazine, editor in chief at *Psychology Today,* and assistant managing editor for health, science, and culture at *U.S. News & World Report.* He has been a regular columnist for *Newsweek, Scientific American Mind,* and *The Huffington Post,* and he currently writes two popular blogs on the quirks of the human mind: "We're Only Human" and "Full Frontal Psychology." He lives with his wife in Washington, D.C.

Herbert, Wray.

On second thought.

DATE			